STRATEGIC NUCLEAR WAR

STRATEGIC NUCLEAR WAR

WHAT THE SUPERPOWERS TARGET AND WHY

WILLIAM C. MARTEL
AND
PAUL L. SAVAGE

AFTERWORD BY MICHAEL CARUSO

CONTRIBUTIONS IN MILITARY STUDIES, NUMBER 43

GREENWOOD PRESS
NEW YORK • WESTPORT, CONNECTICUT • LONDON

Library of Congress Cataloging-in-Publication Data

Martel, William C.
  Strategic nuclear war.

  (Contributions in military studies, ISSN 0883-6884 ;
no. 43)
  Bibliography: p.
  Includes index.
  1. Nuclear warfare. I. Savage, Paul L. II. Title.
III. Series.
U263.M33   1986   355′.0217   85-9869
ISBN 0-313-24192-9 (lib. bdg. : alk. paper)

Library of Congress Catalog Card Number: 85-9869
ISBN: 0-313-24192-9
ISSN: 0883-6884

First published in 1986

Greenwood Press, Inc.
88 Post Road West
Westport, Connecticut 06881

Printed in the United States of America

The paper used in this book complies with the
Permanent Paper Standard issued by the National
Information Standards Organization (Z39.48-1984).

10 9 8 7 6 5 4 3 2 1

To our wives,

Dianne and Jane,

for their support, dedication,
and understanding

Contents

Illustrations

Tables

Preface

This book is the result of two technological revolutions. The first originated in the breakthroughs in quantum mechanics and theoretical physics in the early decades of the twentieth century. The products of this scientific revolution were the fission and thermonuclear weapons. It certainly remains clear that the creation of these weapons of mass destruction not only has altered our historical conceptions of warfare, but it also has demonstrated in stark and unyielding terms that violence, however it might start, quite plausibly could result in the destruction of our civilization. To say that we have hardly begun to understand the dimensions of this technological revolution is an understatement. More profoundly still, we can as observers of military events see that the human predilection for war has an entirely new meaning in the nuclear age.

The second technological revolution centers on the development of the computer, and in particular, the microcomputer toward the end of the twentieth century. What once required acres of space for a computer now can be placed on a desk. While many think almost exclusively in terms of the impact of the microcomputer revolution on the information and financial industries, we prefer instead to imagine how the explosion in cheap, readily-available computer power will alter in fundamental ways how we think about war. More important, this second technological revolution will allow us to ask, and perhaps answer, just some of the questions that once were confined to the select few. The convergence of the nuclear and microcomputer revolutions now permits us to delve into some of the complexities of nuclear war, which is the most difficult, yet critical, issue of the 1980s. More precisely, we propose to ask what can be learned about nuclear war using commercial microcomputers. This, on a number of levels, signifies that the technological revolution has come full circle when we can address issues that even ten years ago could have been answered only by those in the most sensitive areas within the defense and intelligence communities.

In the spring of 1982, we posed the following fundamental question: Is it possible to create on a microcomputer a realistic, accurate as well as *unclassified* model of a strategic nuclear war between the United States and the Soviet Union? Not only must this model provide the results of counterforce (military) and countervalue (city) targeting scenarios, but it must do so with a level of realism and accuracy that precludes either gross over- or underestimation of the consequences of a nuclear war. Moreover, it must be composed of data bases for weapons and targets that are completely *unclassified*, for to do otherwise would limit the dissemination and publication of the results. And to further complicate the picture, the model must compute the results of nuclear attacks on an economical basis, i.e., we did not have the memory of a mainframe computer for the storage of huge data bases and algorithms. Thus, on a comprehensive level, we sought to create a model of nuclear war that is as elegant as it is economical, and as realistic as it is accurate.

After nearly two years, we have completed what is called "Strategic Thermonuclear War." It is a model of nuclear war that contains the deployed strategic nuclear arsenals of the United States and the Soviet Union, and more than 600 cities (by name, population, location, and economic characteristics) representing the majority of the population and economic resources of the two nations. When we began, the dimensions of the project, quite frankly, were largely unknown. It is difficult to imagine the problems and hazards that are associated with the collection of information that has no analogue in the unclassified world. What would easily be found in government archives and computer models of nuclear war, we had to find elsewhere. For both the counterforce (military) and countervalue (civilian) target lists we relied upon government publications, technical and general journals, books, atlases, and a number of academic and general sources. In some cases the creation of the target and weapon lists was a relatively straightforward task, although we should stress that all of the data in the model were subjected to rigorous scrutiny. Yet, in other instances, we must admit that in retrospect purely fortuitous circumstances led to the information required. (A more detailed description of the data and assumptions may be found in the Appendix.)

With this analytic capability, we could begin to ask some of the more fundamental questions about nuclear war. What, for instance, is the meaning of the first-strike attack against either nation? Are there differences in the US and Soviet counterforce capabilities that suggest an advantage for one nation in either broadly or narrowly specified circumstances? What are the consequences of a nuclear war that shifts from military to civilian targeting? How many will die or be wounded in a countervalue nuclear war? How many collateral civilian casualties will result from a purely counterforce exchange?

In a subject as contentious and difficult as that of nuclear war, any work on the consequences of such a war perforce will be found to contain certain errors and biases. While we disclaim the former, with respect to biases we freely admit that our work is premised on the following proposition: That the costs of nuclear war can be calculated in terms of the prompt military, civilian, and (through a certain measure of inference) economic losses. This is not to say that we can predict the long-term ecological or environmental consequences of a nuclear war (such as the possibility of a post-nuclear war winter, which has gained a certain measure of public, but not necessarily scientific, respectability). Clearly, to predict what nuclear conflict will mean for the global ecosystem is to leap far beyond the capabilities of this study. Our claim, therefore, is that within these limits some of the general consequences of a nuclear war can be predicted with this model. In short, we view the *prompt* effects of a nuclear exchange as eminently calculable phenomena using the techniques that are embodied in this research.

Does this mean that we view the results of this model as empirical evidence that a nuclear war is "winnable," that one side has acquired a meaningful military advantage, or that one nuclear strategy is more or less desirable than another? Certainly not. Rather, we prefer to think that this research provides some insights into the general notional boundaries of nuclear war. Yet this approach could hardly be said to engender a consensus among the specialists in the field. For some, there is an inherent predisposition against the possibility of modeling nuclear war on anything smaller than a mainframe computer. How, they would ask, can we begin to understand the nearly infinite permutations and interactions that are involved in an event that is composed of literally millions of complex relationships? Or, would not an analysis of nuclear war on a microcomputer distort the real meaning of the event, and thereby produce false images of the war? We must reply that our task is not to understand, much less explain, the dearth of technical interactions in a nuclear attack, but rather to deduce the broad outlines of the consequences. We accept the argument that many arcane technical issues are best examined with mainframe computers, such as the relationship between height of burst and dynamic overpressure gradients as a function of yield with respect to the structural hardness of the targets in a large-scale nuclear "event." This, however, is not what we sought to do. To be specific, this research has as its primary purpose to provide an outline of the general consequences of a nuclear war. To this end, we believe the results are sound. This, of course, may be a cause of a debate that we most assuredly welcome.

Why, then, did we set out to develop this model and write this book? Perhaps the best answer is that we wanted to know what a nuclear war would look like. To our amazement and chagrin, much of what has passed as an "analysis" of nuclear war has been either too general or too rhetorical to be of scientific or public value. As there are no public sources of which we are aware that provide a detailed, event-level analysis of nuclear war, it seemed worthwhile to write a book with that explicit goal in mind. We wondered how a nuclear war might be fought, what the targets really would be, the sequence of attacking those targets in a nuclear exchange, the consequences of fighting such a war in terms of military and civilian losses, whether one side might have an edge over the other, or if the window of vulnerability was real or imagined. The list of questions can be expanded almost *ad infinitum*. And we suspect that others have wondered about these very same types of questions.

No research, including this study, is ever really conclusive; instead what such a work should do is to examine the general parameters of the problem. The problem as we perceive it is that nuclear war has never been examined on a detailed level beyond that of the semantic proposition that it is a suicidal or an irrational exercise—which it certainly is. Yet, to reach that conclusion, one first must describe what a nuclear war is and how it might be fought, for only then may we properly address the grand philosophical questions of nuclear war. For the present, we seek to examine nuclear war on its own level. As to the ephemeral political and philosophical "meta-questions," we defer those until a later time.

Acknowledgments

As is so often the case, the list of those who, by their counsel and understanding, have contributed to a work is not only quite lengthy but diverse as well, drawing as it inevitably does from individuals whose views are as wide-ranging as their interests. This has been especially true in our case.

First, we owe perhaps the greatest gratitude to Jim Sabin, our publisher, for it was he who saw in these "elegant conjectures" the basis for a work about a war which never has been (or, with any luck, never will be) inflicted on this biosphere. We are indebted as well to Susan Baker, our editor, and Margaret Brezicki for their guidance and assistance on the manuscript. To James Dunnigan and Michael Caruso we want to express special notes of gratitude: Jim, for his uncanny ability to reduce complex and seemingly insurmountable dilemmas to their simplest form, and for his research that made our task simpler in myriad ways; and Michael, whose keen and penetrating journalist's eye brought to light in the Afterword some of the most difficult, yet important, policy issues. We are indebted to Roger Speed, David Saltman, William Hobler, and Kimberly Nolan; and to so many others, whose desire to remain anonymous will be honored, for their thoughts and suggestions. Special notes of thanks are due to David Frelinger and James Mihori for their helpful comments and criticisms of the manuscript.

To the students at Saint Anselm College and Harvard University who, as participants in the Nuclear War Crisis Exercises, displayed a wisdom and an aplomb far beyond their years in their skillful handling of the truly difficult and potentially explosive circumstances in the war games, we are indebted. Far more than any other events, it was they who brought home, in such a compelling and startlingly stark fashion, the human element in nuclear war, one that so often in the past has been buried beneath reams of sterile numbers, "kill" ratios, and scenarios that many, mistakenly, have seen as the reality of nuclear war—which it certainly is not. And to Charles Trueheart who, as Director of the Institute of Politics at Harvard University, brought to fruition the "Exercise," we are grateful to him for his insight and guidance.

To the research staff at the Saint Anselm College Library, we are grateful for their unceasing patience as we again and again sought to expand the limits of "reasonable" scholarship in the search for just one more source. It is no exaggeration to say that their efforts were instrumental in the search for the always elusive targeting information, without which we simply would not have been able to complete this project. Finally, to Annette Butler, who in typing the manuscript translated the oftentimes "untranslatable" with un-flagging skill and patience; and Diane Pulliam, for their assistance in the production of the manuscript, we remain indebted.

Naturally, we alone are responsible for the contents of this book.

Abbreviations

AB	air-burst
ACDA	Arms Control and Disarmament Agency
AFB	Air Force base
ALCM	air-launched cruise missile
ANMCC	Alternate National Military Command Center
ASW	anti-submarine warfare
AWACS	Airborne Early Warning and Control System
BMD	Ballistic Missile Defense
BMEWS	Ballistic Missile Early Warning System
CEP	circular error probable
CF	counterforce
CV	countervalue
CPSU	Communist Party of the Soviet Union
DEW	distant early warning (radar)
EAM	emergency action message
ECM	electronic countermeasures
EMP	electromagnetic pulse
EMT	equivalent megatons
FR	flexible response
GLCM	ground-launched cruise missile
HOB	height of burst
ICBM	intercontinental ballistic missile
IRBM	intermediate-range ballistic missile
JCS	Joint Chiefs of Staff
JSTPS	Joint Strategic Target Planning Staff
KGB	Committee for State Security
KT	kilotons

LCC	launch control center
LOW	launch on warning
LUA	launch under attack
MAD	mutual assured destruction
MIRV	multiple independently targetable reentry vehicle
MR	massive retaliation
MT	megaton
NATO	North Atlantic Treaty Organization
NCA	National Command Authorities
NEACP	National Emergency Airborne Command Post
NMCC	National Military Command Center
OMT	Other Military Targets
OPK	optimum probability of kill
PAL	permissive action link
PD	presidential directive
PK	probability of kill
psi	pounds per square inch
REM	Roentgen equivalent man
RV	reentry vehicle
SAC	Strategic Air Command
SAM	surface-to-air missile
SB	surface-burst
SIOP	Single Integrated Operational Plan
SLBM	submarine-launched ballistic missile
SLCM	Sea-launched cruise missile
SMSA	standard metropolitan statistical area
SPS	Strategic Planning Staff
SRAM	short-range attack missile
SRF	strategic rocket forces
SSBN	strategic submarine, ballistic nuclear
SSPK	single-shot probability of kill
WLS	warhead lethality score
WSI	War Supporting Industry
WTVD	Western Military District (USSR)

STRATEGIC NUCLEAR WAR

1

Evolution of Nuclear Strategy

Perhaps the most logical starting point in a study of the consequences of nuclear war is with the weapons themselves. They are, after all, the principal instruments of such a war, providing both the means and the rationale for the annihilation of our civilization. Yet, we prefer to start at the real beginning of nuclear warfare, which is with strategy. Before we can examine the entire issue of nuclear war, it is necessary first to understand the nuclear strategy that presumably guides the use of nuclear weapons. On the most general level, strategy is a matrix of objectives, ideas, and missions that, taken together, constitute a unified set of assumptions about the use of nuclear weapons in war. And from the perspective of why one might fight such a war, we should find in strategy a coherent framework for policy analysis and a host of political and military actions. In any context, strategy is supposed to be a coherent set of arguments that provides a structure and rationale for the allocation of resources that are aimed at accomplishing specified objectives. So it is with nuclear strategy.

In some senses, we might argue that to use "strategy" in this way is to employ the term in a rather questionable fashion. What passes more accurately as a nuclear policy, which is constructed of an explicit targeting doctrine, is clearly distinct from a nuclear strategy, which expresses the relationship between the threat and use of nuclear weapons and the broader geopolitical framework of national interests. Strictly speaking, the focus here is on the blurred "gray" area between policy and strategy, and how the two drive each other in directions that are framed—but not exclusively so—by political conceptions and technological forces.

Yet nuclear strategy, as both a theoretical and an operational concept, is extraordinarily difficult to elaborate, much less to construct. Bureaucratic, political, ideological, technological, as well as budgetary issues, which we would expect to confront in a modern, pluralistic society, all typically conspire against a coherent expression of purpose. Not surprisingly, resistance to the formulation of strategy is derived, not from a simple rejection of the attempt itself, but because it represents one unified way of thinking and planning for war. Lest we forget the battles that have been fought between the US Air Force and Navy over the issue of control over nuclear weapons, it should be emphasized that creating a strategy implies incremental, yet measurable, victories and defeats for the participants in the process. In view of this fractious process, in the United States one might speak in terms of multiple nuclear strategies if only because the divergent interests of the military and civilian bureaucracies are vying constantly for control over nuclear operations.[1] Similarly, in the Soviet Union there is incessant competition between the Party, the KGB, the Defense Ministry, and the Army, Navy, Air Force, and the Strategic Rocket Forces over the directions that nuclear strategy should follow. For instance, although the CPSU and the Defense Ministry coordinate Soviet nuclear strategy and planning, it is the KGB that reportedly controls the nuclear release codes. In any number of other areas, we find evidence of systemic competition over the framework within which nuclear weapons are to be deployed and used. Today, the military authorities in the Soviet Union apparently are resistant to the notion, as expressed by the political elites, that the USSR will not be the first to use nuclear weapons ("no first use").

On the most theoretical level, therefore, it seems appropriate to think in terms of a semblance of *convergence:* that with time there are signs that the United States and the Soviet Union are moving in increasingly similar directions in the field of nuclear policy and forces.[2] Perhaps the most common expression of this idea is that the two disparate political systems will converge in thought and behavior as the result of analogous bureaucratic and technological forces. If we may think in terms of a convergence in their approaches to nuclear strategy, then it may be on the basis of two forces or imperatives in nuclear forces, such as the tendency toward the deployment of nuclear arsenals that are capable of hard-target kill. The first force is technology. While technology per se does not compel anything, it does seem to provide a common and fundamental framework for thinking. In technology there is the framework for common conceptions about the structure and function of modern nuclear forces. To cite but one example, there is an apparent US-USSR convergence on the utility of hard-target kill capabilities that has matured over the last decade. This is not to say that technology will lead to mirror-image thinking or behavior in the nuclear arena, but rather that we may discern some technological basis for the apparent similarity in several dimensions of American and Soviet thinking on nuclear war.

While it may be practical, indeed illustrative, to think along the lines of a technological convergence in nuclear strategy, the second factor is the complex web of historical and cultural factors that may slow, but certainly not reverse, the convergence process. What we will call "strategic culture" is in fact the multi-factorial (and probably seamless) web of unique political, historical, and cultural events that have shaped the general framework for thinking about strategic nuclear issues. A theory of convergence in nuclear strategy may have enormous explanatory power in the technological realm, yet the essentially divergent strategic cultures of the United States and the Soviet Union will tend to pull in opposite directions. A number of reasons are apparent for this divergence in the strategic cultures of the two superpowers. On a simple level, just the different experiences (or traumas, if you will) of the two nations in the Second World War suggest that they have entirely different conceptions and expectations of the role of force and strategy in warfare. At an even higher level of abstraction, the physicist Freeman Dyson in *Weapons and Hope* sought to explain the fact that the two cultures simply have radically different views on nuclear strategy. In a fundamental way Dyson argues, "Each side sees the other side's [nuclear] doctrine as peculiarly evil. In reality there is nothing peculiarly evil in the Soviet first strike doctrine, just as there is nothing peculiarly evil in our [US] first use doctrine." This occurred, Dyson appropriately suggests, as a result of the "different historical experiences of the two sides." And perhaps worse, "both are firmly rooted and will not be easily changed."[3]

For better or worse, we see the broad outlines of a divergence in nuclear strategy that, despite the apparent technological symmetry in their weapons programs, does not seem to be directly controllable. To deduce the deeper meaning of these approaches to nuclear strategy, this chapter will focus on what could be called "comparative strategy." As we will address, the United States and the Soviet Union have responded to the challenges that are posed by nuclear weapons in dramatically divergent ways. Their respective nuclear strategies, therefore, can be addressed not only with respect to what they are (insofar as that can be discerned), but also in what they are not. We wish to emphasize at the outset that this notional outline for analysis is based on the spectrum of convergence and divergence. Thus, there are adaptive responses to technology that have resulted in similar, if not always identical, approaches to the development of nuclear forces.

US NUCLEAR STRATEGY

At the outset we suggested that the concept of technological convergence highlights one of the driving forces behind nuclear strategy. In a technological society, such as the United States, it is only natural to find an emphasis on—indeed, a singular compulsion for—the products of high technology. In no other society do we find such devotion to the notion that technology, if properly understood and applied, can provide the basis for excellence and competitiveness in the world. While this analogy is quite compelling on the level of industrial and commercial-sector operations, it is substantially less effective if it is applied as the guiding force for war. James Fallows, in *National Defense,* argued that the American predilection for technological solutions is at once a benefit and a hindrance: We benefit when technology supplements a coherent conception of objectives, while conversely, we may suffer if technology becomes the single-minded expression of our strategy. Even the Soviets, as in the words of the Marshal of the Soviet Union Nicholai Ogarkov, admire the United States for its ability to come up consistently with technological "rabbits out of a hat." And it is true as well, as Ogarkov has said, that every major technological breakthrough in military technology since the Second World War has been initiated by the United States. What we see are the barely perceptible outlines of a strategic culture that thrives on technology, to the possibly pernicious extent that we let technology establish not only our weapons, but perhaps our entire method of thinking about war. If this is true—as we more than suspect—then the United States runs the risk of engendering technological superiority and conceptual inferiority. That is to say, there is the possibility that the US ability to create technological miracles may not be matched by an equally impressive strategy for war.

So it is in the realm of nuclear strategy. There are signs that US nuclear strategy since 1945 has been driven less by a coherent sense of what strategy ought to be, and more by the "necessities" of technology. Although technology, in fact, may compel nothing, a technological culture can find itself driven by extraordinary rates of change that are reflected, in one instance, in the evolution of weapons systems. It is no surprise that the United States finds it difficult, to say the very least, to establish a coherent set of expressions that we can call nuclear strategy. As a pluralistic, competitive, and essentially inner-directed society, national coherence is next to impossible to achieve. For nuclear issues, the task is truly herculean. For instance, how would we establish such a framework—on whose authority, by what standards, and with what *weapons?* Here we see the etiology of the problem: were the United States to develop a singular set of rules called a nuclear strategy, then the development and deployment of those weapons would fall to the guardians of that doctrine. Where we now coalesce weapons and general objectives into what some see as a strategy, what is actually produced is an incoherent strategic "philosophy" that has emerged from the infighting and competition among the oligarchic defense bureaucracies. What we have is the illusion of a strategy—not the reality. Many in the nation will find this difficult to accept, not the least of them being the national command authorities.

What, then, is US nuclear strategy? To answer that question, we will start at the beginning, most notably in the post-war 1945 period. To be explicit, we seek less to reconstruct American nuclear thinking than to demonstrate that one of the driving forces has been (and is) technology. As an annotated version of the period, we will stress that the technological ethos and political pluralism have been the overarching forces behind American thinking, and that the US strategic culture is in fact a corollary of the technological-pluralistic imperative. But even if we use technology as the theoretical framework for understanding the evolution of US nuclear policy, then it is only logical to follow the rough historical outlines of American policy. Such a process will dovetail with identifiable policy directives as well as the emergence of increasingly sophisticated techniques of nuclear war.

Phase I: Massive Retaliation

The first general period in the evolution of US nuclear strategy was between 1945 and 1960. What highlights this historical period were the issues concerning the delivery of nuclear weapons and the structure of potential targets in the Soviet Union. Perhaps of primary concern in these years, which coincided with the Truman and Eisenhower administrations, was the means of delivering nuclear weapons and its implications for war. During that time, the bomber was the single delivery vehicle available; nuclear strategy, perforce, could be seen as a slow and responsive annihilating mechanism, for nothing short of a slow, blundering bomber attack was imaginable. For those who were concerned with the formulation of strategic war plans, in particular the Joint Emergency War Plan BROILER, and Joint Chiefs of Staff (JCS) plans FROLIC and HALFMOON, the dominant perspective was the ability to wage an atomic air offensive.[4]

While we remain singularly aghast at the terminology of, much less the concepts behind, these plans, US nuclear strategy was enmeshed in what was known as Massive Retaliation (MR). Absent from the mechanics of MR were the concepts of preemption or first-strike attacks, at least on a convincing scale. Given the length of time that was required for a nuclear war to be launched (measured in days as opposed to hours), US strategic thinking was driven by the notion of retaliatory options. To see that retaliation was indeed the conceptual framework, there are numerous references to concerns by President Truman that the use of nuclear weapons for aggressive or preemptive purposes would be politically unacceptable in the United States. If we step back from the minutiae about the "hows and whys" of nuclear delivery and its effect on strategy, one central issue emerged from this scene: namely, that US nuclear strategy never evolved independently from the pressures of technology. In the case of massive retaliation and the American dependence on strategic bombers for the air offensive, few wondered—or at least asked—what the US goals in nuclear war would be. Air Force General Vandenburg for one, in wondering about the theoretical framework of nuclear strategy, stated his concerns quite bluntly in 1947:

In a war with the USSR, is our purpose to destroy the Russian people, industry, the Communist party, the Communist hierarchy, or a combination of these? . . . Will there be a requirement to occupy, possibly reconstruct, Russia after victory, or can we seal off the country, letting it work out its own salvation?[5]

These are very difficult questions, indeed.

Rather than addressing these Carthaginian alternatives for fighting a nuclear war with the Soviet Union, the conventional American response was to conceptualize in terms of mechanics. That is, how will a war occur? Given that the state of technology in the period was loosely bounded by a policy of massive retaliation, i.e., the bomber force, nuclear war was seen to be a slow-motion event that could evolve over the space of weeks or even months. (In one of the first credible cases for a theory of protracted nuclear war, some estimated that it would take the Soviet Union up to 30 days to deliver its weapons to assigned targets in the United States.) In this climate, a preemptive nuclear attack was hardly an issue of ultimate concern, although it certainly was an issue in many of the procurement and planning debates. The reason for this is clear. Why should we grapple with the potentially intractable issues of nuclear strategy when, by virtue of the technological "solution," there was no politically compelling rationale for doing so? In short, technology, which could be translated as time-to-target, solved the problem of strategy because the evolution of ballistic missiles rendered the slow-motion, protracted view of nuclear war as an obsolete, if not archaic, concept.

The second general issue for massive retaliation was the selection of targets for nuclear attack. In general, we may classify potential nuclear targets as counterforce or countervalue. Typically, a counterforce target is a center that has some military value, such as a missile silo, bomber base, submarine base, command center, or even a conventional military base. Countervalue targets, by contrast, are the population, economic, or political resources of a nation. Outside of the sterile jargon of targeteers and strategic analysts, a countervalue target is a city. To have a countervalue targeting policy, therefore, is to envision the intentional destruction of your adversary's cities and as much of its civilization as possible, in what has often been called a "city-busting" nuclear policy. Accordingly, a fundamental point of order is to decide whether nuclear policy is to be based on the destruction of military or urban targets. This is a problem and an issue, however, that should be analyzed using historical and sociological data to determine the relationship between the outcome of wars and the dominant targets in war. You may have guessed that the United States, in examining this dilemma, did not adopt this approach.

This failure is surprising, particularly when we consider the voluminous data that was collected after the Second World War by the US Strategic Bombing Survey (SBS). Among the illuminating conclusions of the SBS was the finding that allied bombing raids against urban (countervalue) targets in Germany neither reduced wartime production nor crippled the morale of the population. Why the United States never seemed to operationalize these findings in nuclear strategy makes little, if any, sense in retrospect. Perhaps one reason why lies in the difference between the effects of nuclear and conventional weapons. There is a qualitative difference between the two types of weapons due to the greatly increased speed of destruction, shock effects, and collateral damage of a nuclear detonation. This difference is especially pronounced if we consider the consequences of the conventional, area-bombing raids on Germany and Japan toward the end of the Second World War with the nuclear attacks on Hiroshima and Nagasaki, especially in terms of what now appears to be the greater post-attack psychological trauma for the Japanese survivors.

For the student of history, warfare has ordinarily followed the counter-force path. While there have been instances when warfare crossed the threshold to the destruction of countervalue centers, such as the destruction of Carthage by the Roman Empire in the Punic Wars, the Mongol invasion of Europe and the Islamic mideast, or the Allied bombing of Germany and Japan in the Second World War, warfare has more often than not been directed toward the destruction of the enemy's physical means of fighting. In 1832, Carl von Clausewitz, in *On War,* wrote that, "[the enemy] must either be positively disarmed or placed in such a position that he is threatened with it. From this it follows that the disarming or overthrow of the enemy, which-ever we call it, must always be the aim of warfare."[6] In pristine theoretical terms, a counterforce policy is more in consonance with the traditional approach to warfare in history than a countervalue campaign. Whether we think in terms of nuclear or conventional combat, in its most rudimentary and inchoate form, nuclear strategy must provide explicit guidance in the means of, and the results that are derived from, the destruction of counter-force targets. Yet, in US nuclear strategy, a common theme in targeting has been just the opposite: to attack countervalue targets on a scale and with a vengeance that ensures the annihilation of virtually all centers of, in this case, Soviet civilization.

As we looked at US nuclear strategy in the massive retaliation phase, the emphasis on countervalue operations was all too readily apparent. In specific terms, any American nuclear targeting for countervalue effect would have been concentrated on the wanton destruction of Soviet population centers, with only "incidental" interest in industrial targeting.[7] The JCS nuclear war plan BROILER for example, indicated that 24 Soviet cities were to be targeted with 34 weapons, while the HARROW plan called for the targeting of 20 Soviet cities with 50 weapons. Later, the war plan TROJAN would plan to use 133 atomic weapons on 70 Soviet population centers.[8]

Reminiscent of our contemporary interest in the destruction of potential economic choke-points or critical nodes in an economic system that, if de-stroyed, could seriously hinder recovery, some in the late 1940s selected the Soviet petroleum industry as the most vulnerable part of the Soviet Union's economic system. Whether, in fact, this concept of targeting economic choke-points with nuclear weapons is a valid approach remains to be seen, insofar as there is no consensus, even today, on what is defined as a critical node or choke-point in the US or Soviet economic systems.

By 1950, the JCS moved to establish the foundation for limited counter-force capability when it called for "the destruction of known targets affecting the Soviet capability to deliver atomic bombs." Codenamed DELTA (as part of the triad with BRAVO and ROMEO), this was the first formal indication that the US, in its' nuclear strategy, had contemplated the destruction of counterforce targets in the USSR.

The object of the DELTA plan was the physical destruction of Soviet bomber bases and those facilities that were responsible for the production of fission weapons. To be fair, one must acknowledge that at this stage MR was not a purely countervalue concept, for it contained several elements of a counterforce policy. Yet, we would be remiss not to note that there were those who, discontented with the apparent evolution of US targeting plans, urged that there should be a careful analysis of the consequences of a coun-tervalue campaign. The eminent strategist, Bernard Brodie, for instance, indicated a discontent with countervalue policies when he signaled that we should study "city-avoidance strategies to enhance deterrence."[9] The in-ference is that, independent of the actual magnitude of countervalue actions in US targeting plans, once a nuclear war starts, it will inevitably disinte-grate into an unrestrained city-busting exchange. The paradox is that today there is the widespread impression that a countervalue policy—even in its most limited form—is anathema in nuclear war, and that countervalue oper-ations never have or will constitute the mainstay of US war plans. Even so, there are numerous instances in which nuclear strategists, civilians, and military officials have expressed a conviction that a downward spiral into the maelstrom of urban-industrial destruction is an inevitable consequence of a nuclear war.

At any rate, during the formative years of US nuclear strategy there was clear evidence that the US did not come to grips with the fundamental *raison d'être* of strategy. Rather than relying upon conceptual instruments for the formulation of strategic concepts, the US instead unintentionally deferred solving some of the basic issues of nuclear strategy (namely, what ought nuclear strategy to do, beyond the avoidance of war) and concentrated instead on the "solutions" that were made available by the technology of nuclear war. Although nothing really changes in the subsequent phases of nuclear strategy until the 1970s, let us proceed to phase two.

Phase II: Flexible Response: 1960–1973

At the outset of the decade, roughly coincident with the waning years of the Eisenhower Administration and the first years of the Kennedy Administration, there were signs of a slowly emerging shift in US nuclear strategy. While this shift was not directly the result of evolutionary patterns in strategic thinking, it is clear that US doctrine had begun to respond to the impact of technological modernization in both the United States and the Soviet Union. From the relatively primitive bomber forces of the 1940s and 1950s, with their generally soft countervalue and counterforce capabilities, the distinct shape of a new technology was emerging. Starting in the 1960s, the nuclear strategy of Flexible Response (FR) meant to restore a measure of credibility to the US deterrent in the face of a Soviet capability to inflict unacceptable damage on the US homeland in response to any American attack (whether massive or limited) on Soviet urban-industrial centers. On a general, theoretical level we can attribute this partially to the velocity of the delivery vehicles: ICBM and SLBM technologies reduced the time-to-target by roughly one and a half orders of magnitude so that strategic decisions were compressed from days or weeks to minutes or hours. In other words, what nuclear strategy confronted was a significant and radical reduction in the time available for the nation to respond to a nuclear attack, and second, that this resulted in an expansion of the potential target classes that could be "acquired" in a preemptive or retaliatory attack. To be sure, it is not altogether clear that US nuclear strategy after this period adjusted correctly to the challenges mandated by technology. We could argue, moreover, that the response—toward the assured destruction of the US and Soviet populations—was indicative of the inability to link technological and conceptual modernization.

Perhaps the dominant issue as we look back on the FR phase was the effect of a significant reduction in the time between the detection of the launch and the impact of the warheads. From the first receipt of unambiguous signs that an enemy attack was in progress to the first warhead detonations, the National Command Authorities (NCA) might have as little as 25–30 minutes. Indeed, in the days before the Defense Satellite Program network of geosynchronous and low-altitude infrared and ionization-detecting satellites, the time available for a response might be as little as 10–15 minutes—coinciding roughly with the detection range of the Ballistic Missile Early Warning System (BMEWS) radar network in Canada, Greenland, and England. The cumulative effect of this reduction in warning time is threefold.

First, nuclear strategy must now anticipate, or at least consider, the possibility of a preemptive nuclear attack. Independent of the specific details of the Soviet ICBM or bomber "threat," in theoretical terms nuclear strategy began to shift to a preemptive, anticipatory stage. In part, the dimensions of this revolution could be seen in the transition to assured destruction, i.e., what, at a minimum, could the United States do in a retaliatory attack if the enemy succeeded in thwarting our warning system and launching a preemptive attack. Broadly defined, nuclear strategy no longer was dominated by the slow and unwieldy pace of retaliation by a bomber force. Instead, the central issue in nuclear strategy became the ability of the US to retain a nuclear reserve force that would be sufficient for decisive retaliation after any conceivable Soviet strike. More often than not, this was expressed in terms of the *number* of survivable ICBMs and bombers, or deliverable warheads, after the best conceivable Soviet preemptive attack.

The second effect was to create enormous incentives for the United States to enhance its' system of warning sensors in order to reduce the probability of a truly effective Soviet surprise strike. This, for instance, was one reason why the US moved to replace its sensing system of horizon radars and U-2 overflights of the Soviet Union with sophisticated deep-space satellite warning system and near-earth reconnaissance satellites. For US nuclear strategy to be resilient in the face of all *plausible* threats of preemption, it must be able to pose a credible retaliatory threat in all conceivable scenarios. This, then, was the rudimentary form of nuclear deterrence in this era.

This brings us to the third effect: preemption. To address this issue, it is necessary first to examine the fundamental options in nuclear war that were available to the United States. As the technology of warhead delivery moved to a level where first-strike attacks were conceivable, nuclear strategy must move in the direction of a preemptive posture. And this is the crux of the problem: in the US, an explicit rule of nuclear strategy—at least vis-à-vis western democratic traditions—has been to reject nuclear preemption on political, ethical, and moral grounds. This being the case, the only logical alternative was to choose a policy that was based on the threat of retaliation. Although the exact dimensions of retaliation would be left to targeting policy, we would argue that the US, which was forced to think principally in terms of retaliation, was compelled to limit the range of optimal nuclear options. Eisenhower, for instance, stipulated that "the United States and its allies must reject the concept of preventive war or acts intended to provoke war."[10] And while Eisenhower conceded that "the only possible way of reducing losses would be for us [United States] to take the initiative sometime during the assumed month in which we had the warning of an attack and launch a surprise attack against the Soviets," he appeared to accept that such a course of action would run counter to the American abhorrence of preemptive attacks. In effect, Eisenhower believed that it "would appear impossible" for the United States to do "any such thing."[11]

The question is whether nuclear strategy can retain a sense of coherence if, on the one hand, the technology presents the possibility of preemption, while on the other hand, there are extraordinary political constraints forbidding serious planning for preemption. Where does one "go," so to speak, with respect to nuclear strategy? The only plausible response would be to move in the direction of retaliation. Yet, the nature of retaliation is such that we must consider the classes of targets that are potentially available in a nuclear attack. To this we turn next.

In massive retaliation, US nuclear strategy centered on large-scale responses against Soviet cities and military targets, contingent only on the magnitude of the Soviet attack. This constraint, however, is only of limited value because the strategy was not particularly selective or discriminatory. From the perspective of targeting, as well as technology, massive retaliation focused on two large classes of targets—some counterforce, but principally countervalue targets. The paradox is that FR, in the age of preemption, shifted to countervalue targeting because the hardness and transience of counterforce targets made the effects of retaliation highly uncertain and therefore problematic for the nuclear planner. That is, retaliation against counterforce targets always ran the considerable risk of hitting empty targets, while conversely, retaliation against countervalue targets minimized the risk of inefficient targeting because, as a stationary target, the planner always was certain of destroying the city. In an age of ICBMs and SLBMS, it is more than a remote plausibility that the attacker will find his forces attacking empty targets in the enemy homeland. Thus, we see a reinforcement of the already perceptible emphasis in US nuclear strategy on countervalue retaliation because it guaranteed an effective response at some level. Forced by the speed and technology of delivery systems—nuclear war will now be a very fast event—US nuclear strategy now entered a period that was characterized by an increased commitment to targeting countervalue centers in the Soviet Union. We do not argue that counterforce targeting was entirely absent from US targeting plans, for it clearly was not. Rather, the central issue is that the essential dimensions of US targeting in retaliation for a Soviet provocation was countervalue annihilation principally because the US was unable to sustain a credible preemptive CF policy. In any event, in the jargon of the nuclear theologians, this was the era of assured destruction, later to become known as mutual assured destruction or its acronym "MAD." For instance, David Rosenberg writes that, if the US was to concentrate on retaliation, then "the most appropriate retaliatory targeting system would be *political* and military command and control centers, and critical *industries*."[12] (Emphasis added.) For those who were concerned that the United States might adopt a purely countervalue policy for retaliation, Herbert Goldhammer and Andrew Marshall suggested that "the *exclusive* threat by the United States of pure population attacks may be interpreted, not unjustly, as a confession of weakness."[13]

In its simplest state, MAD was the ability to *retaliate* after any conceivable Soviet nuclear attack against both counterforce and countervalue targets, but ironically as the technology of nuclear war grew more complex and reduced the time-to-target, counterforce as a targeting policy gained increasing credibility. Now, for instance, we could think in terms of attacks—albeit in a short time—against the full panoply of Soviet military resources: ICBM silos, bomber bases, submarine bases, general purpose forces, and other military targets (OMT) in Eastern Europe and the Western Military District (WTVD) of the Soviet Union. Yet, in view of, or despite this growing capability against counterforce assets, US nuclear strategy, particularly on the declaratory level, was fixated on the assured destruction of Soviet counter-value targets. We see this fixation as a function of two factors. First, as the ability to destroy targets quickly in nuclear war increased, there were the concomitant pressures to adopt the first-strike option as at least one generic set of options, which for obvious reasons, could never be an accepted declar-atory policy. Second, with this inhibition on targeting, counterforce options were reduced to an illusion: What could one do against Soviet counterforce targets in retaliation if they already had been launched by the enemy? By definition, whatever Soviet counterforce resources remained after the pre-emptive Soviet attack would be of secondary importance. Although one can conceive in theory of retaliatory strikes against Soviet counterforce targets, such attacks have perhaps only marginal utility, certainly in comparison with the damage that is expected in a preemptive counterforce operation.

While there was a clear emphasis on counterforce preemption in US nuclear policy, in a phase that is known as damage limitation, it must be stressed that the preemptive counterforce option did not remain un-challenged. It lost support in the defense establishment because the United States could not possibly deploy enough nuclear weapons to ensure the destruction of the (then rapidly expanding) Soviet nuclear arsenal. Nor could US intelligence and reconnaissance capabilities provide precise knowledge of the location of all Soviet counterforce targets, especially the remote air-fields to which Soviet bombers would disperse in the event of a crisis. Since few believed in a premeditated preemptive attack that was not preceded by some period of pre-war hostilities during which the two sides would alert and disperse their forces, a preemptive attack against an alerted Soviet nuclear force could not destroy all of the force. The magnitude of the force that would survive any realistic US preemptive attack, combined with the impossibility of defending against Soviet retaliatory attacks with surviving nuclear forces against American urban-industrial centers, led to a damage limitation policy that lost credibility in the minds of defense planners.

Under the apparent influence of retaliatory planning, US nuclear strategy shifted ever more perceptibly to an increasingly dominant retaliatory policy against Soviet countervalue targets. It is not hard to explain this evolution of thinking, especially if we consider that there is higher confidence in counter-value retaliatory strikes (irrespective of civil defense) than there is in retalia-tion against counterforce targets, which may be empty by the time the warheads arrive. For the nuclear planner, a credible ability to retaliate against cities is an attractive option because it intertwines both deterrence and retaliation into one neat concept. Eisenhower, for instance, argued that "central question is whether or not we have the ability to destroy anyone who attacks us, because the biggest thing today is to provide a deterrent to war."[14] From a theoretical viewpoint, however, it is quite risky to mix the conceptual paradigm of deterrence with the necessities of fighting a war.

How, we ask, does US nuclear strategy differentiate between the avoidance of war and fighting a nuclear war with a strategy of MAD? We submit that the overarching principle of MAD—countervalue retaliation as opposed to counterforce preemption or retaliation—became enshrined in US declaratory policy, because the political climate all but precluded a serious consideration of preemption. Therefore, whatever large-scale utility a counterforce policy really might offer would in reality be very low. Furthermore, the technology of war that was developed by the United States was not sufficiently advanced to include effective counterforce attacks.

At the technological level, we see the deployment of an early generation of ICBMs and SLBMs that were relatively inaccurate. Unable to hit hard point targets, ballistic missile technology in the 1960s was best suited to countervalue operations. One need hardly dispute the fact that cities are the ideal—not to mention, only—target that can be attacked with a grossly inaccurate weapon. If the highest priority targets, such as Soviet silos in the late 1960s and early 1970s, could not be destroyed, it was only logical to select the hundreds of countervalue targets in the Soviet Union as the object of retaliation. We have thus come full circle in US nuclear strategy. From the vantage point of US strategy, it appears that the US was not capable of a preemptive counterforce policy and only marginally capable of an effective retaliatory attack against Soviet counterforce targets.

How do we address the "rationality" of the US nuclear strategy of MAD? To say that the destruction of "x" percentage of Soviet population and industry is hardly an admirable state of affairs will incur the wrath of those who claim—rightly—that MAD has worked very well indeed for decades. The point, whether US nuclear strategy was coherent or rational, now somehow seems irrelevant if deterrence prevailed. We cannot in substance refute this proposition. What we can do, however, is to illustrate that the origins of the strategy were not the product of coherent analysis, but rather the product of a series of technological and political accommodations to the realities of the time. Of more concern, however, is the effect of this strategic thinking on the present, when we find that the US has leveraged itself into an undesirable position with respect to growing Soviet counterforce capabilities. Indeed, we wonder about the relationship between US and Soviet thinking when there are indications that the USSR never really accepted the reasoning behind a MAD (countervalue) policy. The suspicion is that one consequence will be a measurable, and not insignificant, US inferiority in the ability to attack Soviet counterforce targets. In Chapters 3 and 4, we begin to explore some of the implications of this condition.

Phase III: Counterforce and War-fighting (1974–1985)

While it is difficult to specify the exact dynamics and pace of the transition to a counterforce and war-fighting nuclear policy, it remains clear that in the early 1970s the US nuclear strategy was transformed—albeit in theory only—into an entirely new targeting policy. While countervalue targeting (MAD) still remained an important element in US planning, we can discern an increasing emphasis on the destruction of Soviet counterforce targets during some stage of a war. For the purpose of clarity, some have called this period the transition to a nuclear war-fighting strategy, which meant that US nuclear strategy began to be conceived of (at least, more so publicly) in terms of the execution of a nuclear war, with particular emphasis on the retention of control over one's nuclear forces for as long as the war might last. Survivability, for instance, was enshrined as one of the new strategic concepts, as the survival of command and control systems and the retention of a secure nuclear reserve force became the central tenets of a US nuclear policy that threatened to destroy Soviet leadership targets and ICBM silos.

Ever so slowly many prescient analysts in the nuclear community argued that the development of MIRVs and highly accurate guidance systems would pose a fundamental, and quite probably, an irreversible challenge to nuclear strategy as we had understood it in the past. If the CEP (circular error probable, i.e., accuracy) of ballistic reentry vehicles (RVs) could be reduced to 250–400 meters or less, then the destruction of even the hardest silos and command posts would become a practical targeting alternative. Suddenly, the SIOP (Single Integrated Operations Plan, or US plan for nuclear war) could contain an additional component of high-priority, time-urgent counterforce targets. First, there would be the roughly 1,400 Soviet ICBM silos, as well as a number of command and control centers and warhead storage facilities. Second, the targeting policy would require the destruction of the nearly 700 underground shelters that have been designated for the Soviet political and military leadership. If these targets were incorporated into the (SIOP) as high-value, priority targets, then the target plan might represent a credible counterforce capability. The assumption, of course, is that the US would have the requisite nuclear forces for the destruction of these targets.

Thus, as the result of technological progress, there was a detectable shift to a large-scale counterforce policy that focused on the targeting of Soviet central strategic forces, which was in sharp contrast to the substantially less comprehensive counterforce options of the past. Again, it is essential to stress that we do not attribute this evolution in US nuclear strategy to a conceptual revolution. More precisely, the US was driven in this direction by technology.

Even today, the recent doctrinal shift has been opposed for numerous reasons, ranging from the theoretical difficulties of executing countersilo strikes, to the general principle that a counterforce policy is much more provocative and destabilizing. We agree insofar as everyone probably felt more secure with the MAD policy of the past, but that is irrelevant.

An issue of special interest in discussions about the structure of current US nuclear strategy is the influence of the Presidential Directives. The most commonly cited, PD-59, was concerned with nuclear targeting priorities. The first category was political targeting, with emphasis on leadership targets at all levels, from top Party leadership through both Party and governmental structures down to the local level. In general, PD-59 was seen as the driving force behind the targeting of leadership, strategic forces, and the issue of maintaining a secure reserve force for countervalue targeting in the waning years of the Carter Administration. A second critical document, PD-58, was concerned with the preservation of the US government, and all the essential functions thereof (war direction, negotiation, and economic and social reconstruction). And finally PD-53 was concerned with the preservation of the US communication system in a nuclear war, including the continuity of government through nuclear conflict. Although it is tempting to view US nuclear strategy as an embodiment of PDs, we instead take the view that these PDs provide at best a conceptual, as opposed to an actual, operational statement of the preferred American strategy.

SOVIET NUCLEAR STRATEGY

At the most general level of abstraction, we have isolated some of the dominant factors that have determined the evolution and the shape of US nuclear strategy. Using the technological and strategic-cultural "factors," we hypothesized that strategy, that is any military framework, can be understood if we apply these factors. In the case of the US, it is relatively easy to discern the general trends in the evolution of nuclear thinking and planning, principally because of the US penchant for the public dissemination of information. Yet, in the case of the Soviet Union, this task is not nearly as facile, for the Soviet Union historically has been concerned with the preservation of sensitive information, including that which appears to border on the purely trivial. For a society with a pronounced affinity for guarding its military information, including the debates within the military hierarchy against the prying eyes of the West, it is naturally difficult for western analysts to understand what the Soviets think about nuclear strategy. Even if we inject a healthy sense of skepticism into our interpretation of published Soviet works, it nevertheless is still difficult to argue about what Soviet nuclear strategy is or is not.

Phase I: Understanding the Dilemma

Nuclear weapons pose a fundamental dilemma for the military strategist: They are incredibly destructive instruments that appear to have only limited military and political utility. For the discerning thinker, what nuclear weapons can do is to exert enormous political leverage. Thus, what we cannot achieve in an operational sense, such as "winning" a nuclear war, we clearly can do in a political sense: to deter the adversary from undertaking certain courses of action that are considered inimical to the national interest. Of more importance, it is essential to see that the only way of integrating nuclear weapons into a coherent military framework is to ask precisely how such weapons might be used in concert with the global interests of the United States or the Soviet Union. For a western state, asking these generic questions can become a very messy political problem, while in the Soviet Union questions of this sort can be examined on a level that precludes public consent and involvement. In this pristine environment in the Soviet Union, one theoretically could ask questions singularly in terms of the projected effect on the military utility of nuclear strategy. This means that nuclear strategy, in the sense of public understanding, has little or no basis in the Soviet political system. Where in the Soviet Union nuclear strategy can be formulated within the insulated grounds of a secretive political, bureaucratic, and budgetary environment, the United States must operate with far less ease and considerably greater constraints, such as that which is demanded by public opinion and the formation of a political consensus. It is hard to avoid the thought that for US planners the central dilemma of nuclear strategy is how to think about it in purely military terms, all the while avoiding the political consequences if the implications of such thinking were exposed to public scrutiny and the resultant outrage.

Once we understand that the evolution of Soviet nuclear strategy did not occur in a system that is guided by public consensus, and further, that the Soviets were far more free to develop a "rational" nuclear strategy (whatever that might be), we begin to see the crucial distinction between the Soviet and the American variants of nuclear strategy. Notions such as limited nuclear war, preemption, victory, and first-strike attacks could be examined (and dismissed, as well) purely on the basis of their military plausibility and utility. In this atmosphere of detachment from the forces of political consensus in the western sense of the word, Soviet nuclear strategy was free to evolve in directions that only recently have found expression in the United States.

The first issue of Soviet nuclear strategy is the milieu within which it evolved. The essence of Soviet thinking appears to be a single-minded concern with the military rationale behind nuclear strategy. For the Soviet Union, the use of nuclear weapons is an event that will occur only in the most catastrophic of struggles, i.e. in the well-worn phraseology of the final clash between socialism and capitalism—not forgetting that the clash will kill between one and two billion people. Bereft of a meaningful empirical foundation, this concept means that nuclear war is the last step, representing the actions of states that are literally fighting to the death. In the writings of V. D. Sokolovskiy, Marshal of the Soviet Union, it is apparent that, in the Soviet view, war, including nuclear war, will be fought as suddenly and violently as possible with the central objective of destroying the forces of the enemy. And any military confrontation is likely, in the Soviet mind, to escalate rather quickly to the widespread and uncontrollable use of nuclear weapons. Marshal Nicholai Ogarkov, formerly Chief of Staff of Soviet Armed Forces, argues that "nuclear war has never been tested. But by logic to keep such a war limited will not be possible . . . . Inevitably such a war will extend to allout war."[15] One interpretation of this view is that immediately after the initiation of hostilities, the Soviets will attack with all they have, suddenly and with enormous ferocity, with nuclear weapons a logical, if not annihilatory extension of their strategy. From this evidence, it seems to us that the Soviet military planning staff (Stavka) and political (CPSU, KGB) elites have enunciated a theory of war in which the use of nuclear weapons will be an immediate option if it is clear that a major conflict is in the offing.

If we contrast this thinking with that of the United States, it is immediately obvious that the Soviets have a primitive—if not crude—version of nuclear strategy. Namely, nuclear weapons will not be used in the selective, often confusing scenarios that people have conjured up in the West. Rather, nuclear weapons will be used solely in order to destroy enemy nuclear and conventional forces. If we examine the early Soviet technologies of nuclear war, it seems clear that their primitive bomber force was hardly capable of much beyond limited nuclear strikes against Europe or the United States. The USSR's limited stockpile of nuclear weapons probably meant as well that potential targets would be either large countervalue centers or theater-level logistical targets. Even as we proceed into the early stages of the Soviet ballistic missile program, the Soviets clearly lacked the ability to destroy more than a handful of sprawling targets. Applying the technological yardstick, the first 15 or 20 years of Soviet nuclear thinking most likely hinged on the ability to destroy a limited number of large targets, US cities being the target of choice given the capabilities of their primitive ICBMs. Indeed, it is evident that the Soviet inability to design accurate ballistic missile guidance systems in the early years was compensated for by the deployment of very large warheads. Throughout this period of Soviet nuclear strategy, the severe technological limitations on the range of targets that could be attacked was translated into a rather confusing mixture of counterforce and countervalue schemes. It was only later—after the deployment of modern ICBMs—that Soviet nuclear strategy began to take on a character all its own.

If we accept the proposition that the first two decades of Soviet nuclear strategy suffered from technological shortcomings, as opposed to the influence in the US of technological prowess and strategic-cultural shortcomings, then it becomes clear that the effect of Soviet thinking grew in importance after the 1960s. As the Soviet nuclear arsenal grew in scope and capabilities, we see the outlines of a concentration on counterforce options. When the Soviets deployed their early generation of ICBMs, the enormous throw-weight of the boosters enabled the Soviets to field very large warheads. The ability later to fractionate (multiply) the payload into a number of individual warheads (later MIRVs) brought with it a simultaneous effect: the theoretical ability to destroy more targets than missiles launched. While the US concentrated on the assured destruction mission and a limited effort to expand the hard-target kill capabilities of its ICBM force, throughout the early to mid-1970s (circa 1974), the Soviets proceeded to deploy weapons that had an increasing ability to destroy counterforce targets on a large-scale basis. Although we do not posit that the USSR anticipated this trend in targeting, it most certainly recognized the utility of counterforce missions at an early stage when the feasibility of attacking such targets appeared.

The Soviets seem to have prepared for the possibility of incorporating counterforce targeting as the framework of their nuclear strategy. Henry Trofimenko, for instance, argued that "[w]e in the Soviet Union do not naturally think that a situation of mutual deterrence through the threat of *assured destruction* is the highest theoretical achievement."[16] (Emphasis added.) This is a clear affirmation that the Soviets do not think of nuclear strategy as a contemplatable exercise in civilian (or urban) annihilation. What remains by exclusion is a counterforce policy. Yet, it is interesting to note that the Soviets may see counterforce as a codename for the ability to launch a preventive nuclear war, whether by the Americans or the Soviets. In the vein of considering a US preemptive attack, Sokolovskiy writes that, "the threat of unleashing [a] preventive war by American imperialists . . . is [a] quite real possibility." It is for this reason that a counterforce policy has such a strong meaning for the Soviets, who (probably rightly) see preemption and counterforce as essentially synonymous concepts in US policy.[17] Thus, whether one agrees with the intimation that the United States is driven by a predilection for nuclear preemption, there is evidence that the Soviets have linked the concepts of counterforce and preemption as the *sine qua non* of nuclear strategy. We infer from this that the Soviets believe that preparations must be made for a world war that might erupt suddenly, merging into nuclear violence at both the strategic and tactical levels. Sokolovskiy continued to say that "possibilities exist not to allow a surprise attack by an aggressor" by delivering "nuclear strikes to him at the right time."[18]

In a reading of Soviet military thinking, one senses a certain measure of Soviet contempt for the lack of constancy in US nuclear strategy, as if to suggest that nuclear strategy has but one variant: counterforce preemption. Trofimenko, in one instance, expressed concern over the "periodic fluctuations in Washington's officially declared strategies—transitions from the counterforce strategy to that of the countervalue retaliatory strike and back again."[19] His explanation for this conceptual *impermanence* is technology: "the moment some new technical idea is glimpsed at the Defense Department's Office of Defense Research and Engineering, the 'whiz kids' instantly elevate it to a doctrine or a strategy."[20]

While the Soviets go to great lengths to argue that they do not accept a counterforce strategy or a first-strike concept, they do admit that "Soviet strategic forces also have components capable of precision strikes against hardened points targets," which "is the inevitable result of qualitative improvements in strategic armaments."[21] Quite correct. This, however, is not to say that the superpowers should (or in fact have) chosen an exclusively counterforce strategy. Contrary to Soviet statements, however, it seems that the Soviet Union does in fact have the capability for counterforce operations, quite irrespective of what it says it intends to do.

This thinking can take on the character of a diatribe if our thoughts are not clear. Thus, what we see is a Soviet nuclear strategy that inadvertently tripped over the counterforce concept—after the deployment of the large ICBM boosters that later could support the fractionation of the missile payload with large numbers of accurate hard-target-kill MIRVs. Faced by this possibility, and sustained by nearly two decades of strategic thought that focused on the destruction of enemy military forces, the Soviet Union took advantage of a unique historical opportunity to merge doctrine and capability. Rather than being the subject of derision and contempt, we think that the Soviet Union adapted quite well to a series of unanticipated technological capabilities. To drive Soviet activities further in this field, there is also the Soviet belief that American technological superiority will not go unchallenged. Trofimenko writes, of the "deep-rooted (although oft-disproven) U.S. conviction of its marked and irreversible superiority in military . . . technology."[22]

Let us retrace our steps in this section to the initial propositions about technology and strategic culture. With respect to the former, we find that Soviet nuclear strategy evolved in an atmosphere of technological semicompetence. This is not to say that the Soviets are technically inferior, but rather that it has been the United States, and most definitely not the Soviets, who have led the technological race. It is natural to infer that, bounded by greater limits on their technology, the Soviets examined nuclear strategy on its own terms. Pursuing the fundamental notions of nuclear war and strategy, the USSR appears not to have fostered a dependence on technology for the formulation of its strategy. This means that Soviet thinking, unencumbered by the disparate forces and eddies of democratic political pluralism, as in the US, was driven at the highest levels by a single-minded determination to equate nuclear strategy with national interests. Nuclear war, accordingly, is an instrument of the state only in the most extreme circumstances, but then the war is to be pursued with all available means. Hardly rhetorical in form or substance, we interpret this expression to mean that concepts, which are anathema in the West (preemption, counterforce) became the foundation of strategy, paradoxically, long before the USSR had the means for implementing this strategy.

At the present, we find evidence that counterforce remains the guiding light of Soviet thinking, particularly as we became further entrenched in the age of "hard-target kill." Thus, writes Trofimenko "the Soviet Union will not change its long-range defense programs and measures directed at *neutralizing* all possible threats presented by the American . . . armaments and armed forces."[23] This is instructive insofar as the writer did not say "deterring," which would imply a more conventional (to wit, American) interpretation of nuclear strategy. In any event, there are indications that the USSR accepts the rationale behind counterforce, and indirectly preemption, given the caveat that this logic applies only in the most serious (and therefore, unlikely) of circumstances.

On a more general level, we may examine Soviet nuclear strategy as a product of this unique historical and cultural atmosphere. Relatively unbounded by political constraints, we see Soviet thinking as the outcome of near fatal encounters in the past, particularly World War II, and the enormous human losses that were sustained by the Soviets. No longer willing to risk their survival on the ability to absorb the enemy offensive, only to counter-attack until the enemy is exhausted and eventually driven away, the Soviets probably are more likely to launch a preemptive nuclear attack than they are to ride out a US preemptive attack. Thus, indicative of its more unified and centralized political and military decision-making hierarchy, Soviet nuclear strategy reminds us of that which might be called a "political" strategy for war, which is a complex matrix of intentions and capabilities, circumscribed by the exigencies of the moment. Still, we detect a fundamental convergence in US and USSR nuclear strategy only insofar as the United States now appears to more gradually mirror Soviet thinking on the utility of a counterforce/preemptive policy. Does this mean that the Soviets have a more sophisticated approach to nuclear war? Probably not. But what it does mean is that the Soviets were the first to recognize that nuclear strategy ought to be guided by counterforce operations and preemption. It also was the first to move authoritatively in the direction of deploying a large-scale operational capability for destroying American hard-target complexes, such as ICBM silos, with the side-effect of destabilizing US strategy. We think that some of the implications of this mode of strategic thinking—not to mention actual deployments—will be clear in the forthcoming chapters on counterforce and countervalue nuclear wars.

2

American and Soviet Strategic Nuclear Forces

From a theoretical perspective, a nation's nuclear strategy provides the framework for understanding how it might fight a nuclear war and the nuclear forces that will be used fighting such a war. It is presumed that, with a coherent nuclear strategy, many of the mechanical issues of nuclear war, such as how, why, and when one would fight, will be clear and unambiguous to the policymaker and the adversary as well. All too often, nuclear strategy can become a conceptual "trash heap," littered with the remnants of policies that come and go at an alarming rate in a democracy, such as the United States, and perhaps less often in a totalitarian system, such as the Soviet Union. Yet, it should never be forgotten that nuclear strategy is no more than a conceptual matrix of objectives and options for guiding the nuclear forces that are available to a nation. This means that, in a somewhat tautological fashion, it is the capabilities of the nuclear arsenal that ultimately determine what a nuclear strategy will be. Indeed, we could go so far as to say that there is, more often than not, a great disparity between a nation's declaratory nuclear policy on the one hand, and the exact operational capabilities of the force on the other, precisely because the capabilities of the force are never as variable as declaratory policy, which seems to change roughly every four or so years. In the United States, at least, alterations in nuclear policy seem as commonplace as political change—except that the capabilities of US strategic offensive forces remain essentially static on a year-to-year basis. Thus, given what is known about the difficulties of formulating a nuclear strategy in a democratic—or even totalitarian—political system, it is no small wonder that the deployment of nuclear forces often seems ill-defined and confused with respect to what national policy is thought to be at any given time. Indeed, this entire subject is fraught with a

number of inherent tensions, not the least of which is the difficulty of recon-
ciling a coherent policy for the threatened use of nuclear weapons with the
fact that such use will signal the end of a political and ecological era.

We can search at length for an explanation for the turbulence that charac-
terizes American nuclear strategy. On a more pedestrian level, the bureaucratic, political, and service rivalries that typically resist the deployment
preferences of each other quite often result in deployment "strategies" that
are ill-aligned with respect to national nuclear strategy. It is unfortunate, but
nonetheless true, that the deployment of a particular array of nuclear forces
signals that one interest group has attained dominance over the others, and
that it reinforces the prevailing strategies that a given nuclear force theoretically represents. For instance, the decision to deploy the Poseidon
SLBM force in the 1960s signaled not only the growing ascendancy of the
American Navy in nuclear targeting, but more important, that the US would
have a large-scale operational commitment to assured destruction, which
would persist well beyond the time that such a policy might be beneficial.
Since the Poseidon SLBM does not have a hard-target counterforce capability, the US is limited to a largely countervalue or very soft counterforce
capability even after the ascendancy of hard-target kill as a quite plausible,
and certainly more humane, option in a nuclear war. From this example
alone, we can understand most US (as well as USSR) deployment decisions
insofar as they provide evidence of the ascendancy of a particular nuclear
strategy.

Clearly, the argument that weapon deployments are an indicator of a
nation's general strategic preferences is neither a novel nor illuminating
concept. Yet, this concept is a critical determinant of the assessment of the
nuclear capabilities of the United States and the Soviet Union that will
emerge in the following chapters. To begin with, by looking at the dominant
nuclear strategies (as we did in Chapter 1), we will provide a conceptual (and
perhaps normative) framework for what a nation might seek to do in nuclear war. It is at this level that we find the more grandiose assertions about
the relationship between thinking and doing, planning and executing. Indeed, we expect to find numerous instances when a superpower's strategic
expectations typically are far in excess of what it can realistically do with
existing operational capabilities. In general, what is believed to be "true" or
evident in nuclear strategy often is assumed to be the case in terms of a
nation's actual ability to attack certain classes of targets, and achieve the
desired results, without in fact there being any direct, much less necessary,
relationship between the two. It is even more startling to realize that there is
evidence that many of the dominant assumptions about the structure of
nuclear policy do not in fact reflect nuclear realities. It often seems that
there are those who actually believe that declaratory (or actual) policy will
change what we can really do with deployed nuclear forces, or that we can
change policies as facilely as we change presidential administrations.[1]

For every illusion, there is a reality. In nuclear matters, a time comes when nuclear strategy and nuclear capabilities will be assessed on a detailed level. This, in fact, is exactly what we propose to do here. By examining the nuclear capabilities of the US and USSR, we intend to examine the general capabilities of the respective strategic nuclear arsenals. In looking at the separate elements or "legs" of the triad of nuclear forces, we will employ static measures of comparison in order to understand the *attributes* of the forces (numbers, yields, CEPs, potential for hard-target kill, reliability, and so forth). From this attribute level, we can address the general *capabilities* of the nuclear forces of the United States and the Soviet Union, and thereby understand how such forces might be used. Finally, the *vulnerabilities* of the nuclear forces will be analyzed, including assessments of the pre-launch and post-launch survivability of the legs of the triad in the nuclear arsenals of the superpowers.

In essence, this chapter is devoted to static comparisons of the American and Soviet strategic nuclear arsenals. It is recognized that this level of analysis can be misleading insofar as nuclear war is, by any standard, an extraordinarily complex and *dynamic* event. Thus, in chapters 3, 4, 5, and 6 we consider some of the dynamic and interactive dimensions of nuclear war, while for the present, we first seek to know about the dimensions and characteristics of the US and USSR's nuclear triads of ICBMs, SLBMs, and bombers.

A word about the data is in order. Using a large number of sources, we have compiled what we think is a relatively accurate picture of US and USSR nuclear capabilities. It is to be stressed that all of this information was derived in its entirety from *unclassified* sources; for references, the reader should refer to the Appendix, Tables, and the Bibliography.

US NUCLEAR FORCES

The central theme here will be to provide a detailed assessment of the current elements of the US nuclear triad. This is not intended to be an examination of the historical issues, or the genesis if you will, of the process that determined the structure and composition of the existing arsenal.

On another level, much of what is addressed in this chapter will, by necessity, use the jargon of strategic analysis. Insofar as jargon typically leads to confusion and an obfuscation of the fundamental issues, and does so with the implicit assurance that the writer "really" understands the issues at hand, we have kept jargon to an absolute minimum. In those instances when jargon is the only language that we have, we urge the reader to examine the appendix and the list of acronyms for the meaning of the terminology used.

ICBM Force

For a number of reasons, the ICBM often is viewed as the ultimate delivery system for nuclear warheads. In general terms, the ICBM is the

Table 1
US Nuclear Forces

Name	No.	MIRVs	Yield	CEP	WLS*	SB**	AB***	Launch	Detonate
MMIIIA	300	3	335KT	220m	.91	32	88	.9	.85
MMIIIB	250	3	170KT	315m	.81	25	69	.9	.85
MMII	450	1	1MT	630m	.81	85	227	.9	.8
TITAN	52	1	9MT	1482m	.82	380	962	.75	.75
POSEIDON	256	10	40KT	463m	.74	10	25	.6	.8
TRIDENT	256	10	100KT	250m	.81	17	45	.6	.8
B52A	84	12	200KT	100m	1.02	30	72	.8	.3
B52B	160	6	1MT	100m	1.14	85	227	.8	.3
B52C	59	2	24MT	100m	1.37	860	2301	.8	.3
B52D	16	12	200KT	100m	1.02	30	72	.8	.5
FB111A	30	4	200KT	100m	1.02	30	72	.8	.3
FB111B	30	4	1MT	100m	1.14	85	227	.8	.3

* Warhead Lethality Score
** Surface-burst area of damage
***Air-burst area of damage

most responsive, reliable, and controllable leg of the triad, and for this reason, policymakers and analysts alike have focused on the ICBM as perhaps the most essential portion of the US nuclear arsenal. Indeed, it was the theoretical vulnerability of the American ICBM fields that surfaced in the late 1970s that caused much of the current concern about the survivability of American nuclear forces.[2] We would argue that part of the reason for the clamor over ICBM vulnerability was related precisely to the critical importance of the ICBM in American nuclear "culture." In any event, in this chapter we will examine the disparate elements of the US contingent of ICBMs: Minuteman IIIA and IIIB, Minuteman II, and Titan II (see Table 1). By applying the same analytical framework to each of the missiles, it will be possible to construct a composite sketch of their probable function in the US nuclear triad. (The reader who is conversant with the details of the nuclear arsenals may wish to skip to the Appendix and then directly to Chapter 3.)

Minuteman IIIA As the result of a modernization program in the 1970s, the Minuteman III arsenal of 550 ICBMs was divided into 300 Minuteman IIIA (MMIIIA) and 250 Minuteman IIIB (MMIIIB) ICBMs. The primary reason for this modification was the desire to enhance the hard-target-kill capability of the MMIII force and to do so until such time as the MX ICBM was deployed in the 1980s to fill the gap in US hard-target kill capabilities. Accordingly, the MMIIIA today is the most capable hard-target counterforce weapon in the US nuclear arsenal. Deployed in two wings of 150 silos at Grand Forks Air Force Base (AFB) and Minot AFB in North Dakota, the MMIIIA missiles comprise roughly 30 percent of the US land-based nuclear force. As shown in Table 1, the MMIIIA is configured with three multiple, independently targetable reentry vehicles (MIRVs), with each warhead having a yield of 335 kilotons (KT) and a circular error probable (CEP or accuracy) of 220 meters (m). Following the methodology outlined in the Appendix, we have calculated that a single MMIIIA warhead has a single-shot probability of kill (SSPK) of .73. If, however, two MMIIIA RVs are targeted against each hard target, then the optimum probability of kill (OPK) is .93. To calculate the optimum warhead allocation for each hard target, we refer to the warhead lethality score (WLS). Using the method specified in the Appendix, we find that the WLS of .91 for the MMIIIA implies that two MMIIIA RVs must be allocated against each silo (hard target) in order to achieve the highest probability of kill, but to do so in the most economical fashion, i.e., to expend the least number of warheads.

It should be noted that if one assumes an optimum height of burst (HOB), then the 335 KT warhead has areas of damage for air-burst and surface-burst detonations of 88 and 32 square miles, respectively. (For those who prefer to think in terms of lethal radii, the areas of damage correspond to radii of 5.3 and 3.2 miles, respectively.) Again, as noted in the Appendix, these calculations are based on the 2 pounds per square inch (psi) ring of overpressure.

Finally, it is necessary to think about the reliability of the launchers and the weapons in the arsenal. Two values are important here. First, there is the *launch reliability* of the delivery system. Briefly, this is the probability (or attrition rate in this model) that the ICBM will be launched successfully from the silo. Second, there is the *detonation reliability* for the RVs; this second value includes the full range of possible failures *after* launch, from malfunctions of the MIRV "bus" to failures of the warheads to explode once they reach the assigned targets. By taking the product of the launch and detonation reliability rates, we obtain an approximate measure of the operational reliability of the system.[3] In the case of the MMIIIA, the values for the launch and detonation reliability rates are .9 and .85, respectively. Thus, on a cumulative level, we find that the MMIIIA leg of the ICBM arsenal has 900 RVs with an overall reliability rate of .76. Given the projected lethality of the RVs on the MMIIIA, it can function as a relatively effective countersilo weapon. In reality, the greatest limitation on the counterforce capability of the MMIIIA is the total number available RVs which is substantially less than is required for any effective attack against 1,400 Soviet ICBM silos.[4]

Minuteman IIIB The remaining fraction of the original Minuteman III ICBM force has been designated as the MMIIIB. The MMIIIB has the same general operational attributes as the MMIIIA for the missile is the same as the MMIIIA, with the exception of the different yield and CEP values of the warhead. The 250 MMIIIB ICBMs currently are deployed at Malmstrom AFB in Montana and Warren AFB in Wyoming. Each missile carries three MIRVed RVs, each of which has a yield of 170 KT and a CEP of 315 m. By virtue of its larger CEP and smaller yield warhead, the MMIIIB RV has a SSPK of .63; using the WLS for warhead allocation, the attack will generate an OPK of .95 if three RVs are targeted against each hard target. As a direct consequence of the smaller yield of the warhead, the areas of damage for air-burst and surface-burst detonations are 69 and 25 square miles, respectively, which corresponds to lethal radii of 4.7 and 2.8 miles. The launch and detonation reliability rates of the MMIIIB are .9 and .85, which are equivalent to those of the MMIIIA.

Perhaps the most obvious consequence of the greater yield and lessened CEP of the MMIIIB RV is that it effectively degrades its hard-target kill capability. To be specific, once it becomes necessary to exceed a "two-on-one" RV allocation scheme (two warheads against each hard target) in a countersilo attack, the difficulties imposed by fratricide greatly increase the uncertainties of planning and successfully executing such an attack. While this is not to say that the MMIIIB could not be used in countersilo operations, for in fact, we did so in some of our computer "runs," it certainly reduces our confidence in the outcome of the attack. To this extent, even under ideal conditions, we would prefer not to use the MMIIIB in a counter-silo attack against the Soviet Union. In reality, however, it is clear that the United States simply would have no choice but to do so.

Minuteman II There are 450 Minuteman II (MMII) ICBMs in the US arsenal, which are deployed at Ellsworth AFB in South Dakota, Malmstrom AFB in Montana, and Whiteman AFB in Missouri, in three wings of 150 MMII missiles each. Each missile has a one megaton (MT) RV with a CEP of 630 m (i.e., one-third of a nautical mile). This gives the MMII RV an SSPK of .62; using an allocation scheme of three RVs per hard target theoretically would result in an OPK of .95. The reliability of the MMII is only slightly less than that of either the MMIIIA or MMIIIB, as it has launch and detonation reliability rates of .9 and .8, respectively. While the MMII is not an appropriate weapon for an optimal countersilo strike, the one MT warhead—with areas of damage for AB and SB of 227 and 850 square miles, respectively—would be very useful in countervalue operations. The reason is that a large, sprawling urban-industrial center is the ideal type of target for a high-yield, yet inaccurate, RV. However, as shown in Chapter 3, we were forced to use the MMII in one wave of a countersilo attack on the Soviet Union in large part because of a shortage of hard-target kill RVs in the American ICBM arsenal.

Titan II The Titan II ICBM is the oldest component of the US ICBM arsenal. The age and generally low reliability of this liquid-fueled missile have led to the decision to dismantle the force by 1987. At the time of the writing (June, 1984), the Titan II is still deployed as part of the active ICBM arsenal. Stationed in two wings of 17 missiles and one wing of 18 missiles, the Titan II is deployed at Davis-Monthan AFB in Arizona, Little Rock AFB in Arkansas, and McConnell AFB in Kansas. Each ICBM can deliver a 9 MT RV with a CEP of 1482 m (nearly one nautical mile). The RV has a SSPK of .60, and OPK of .94 if *three* RVs are targeted against each target silo. As a function of its age and the comparatively primitive technology that was available when the Titan II was built, it has launch and detonation reliability rates of .75 and .75, respectively. The area of damage for the 9 MT warhead for AB and SB detonations are 962 and 380 square miles, respectively, which corresponds to lethal radii of 17.5 and 11 miles. Thus, there can be little question about the logical mission for the Titan II. Clearly, the Titan II is most appropriate for an attack on large, sprawling countervalue targets in the USSR, on the assumption that countervalue operations are desirable. In summary, the US ICBM arsenal, which has 1,052 missiles with 2,152 RVs, has the ability to attack a limited number of hard counterforce targets, and a comprehensive array of soft counterforce or countervalue targets.

ICBM Vulnerability

It is hardly a surprise to those analysts who have followed the evolution of strategic issues to say that we have entered the age of ICBM vulnerability. This is perhaps the most contentious issue of the 1980s, for reasons that include not only the effect of vulnerability (whether real or perceived) on the

strategic balance, but also the enormous political consequences of vulnerability, such as the decision to modernize the US nuclear arsenal. On the
broadest level, therefore, we must reformulate our thinking about nuclear
deterrence in terms of the effect of ICBM vulnerability on strategic stability
and the US-Soviet nuclear balance.

The first level of concern focuses on the *pre-launch* survivability (here we
will use "vulnerability" and "survivability" interchangeably). It is known
that American ICBMs are maintained on a very high alert rate, even in
peacetime; most reliable reports estimate that the ICBM force is at a 90
percent readiness rate on a day-to-day (non-generated) basis. Yet, in a series
of missile tests in the 1970s at Vandenburg AFB in California in which a
group (seven, actually) of Minuteman ICBMs were selected at random from
missile wings, 100 percent failed to launch (i.e., seven failures in seven
attempted launches). In the trans-attack and post-attack phases of a nuclear
war, however, there is enormous uncertainty about the ability of the NCA to
establish and maintain communication with the ICBM force, much less the
SSBNs at sea. In effect, the entire American C3 system that binds the
nuclear forces to the NCA is an extremely complex system whose survivability in the face of a sustained Soviet attack is subject to severe doubt,
immediately after the first few nuclear explosions. What this suggests is that
the ability to launch ICBMs always is constrained by some level of uncertainty. In any event, one of the positive features of the US ICBM force that
contributes to its survivability is the allegedly high state of readiness of the
force.

A related issue is the responsiveness of the ICBM force. By all accounts,
the US command, control, and communication system between the launch
control centers (LCC) and the silos and the National Command Authorities
(NCA) is quite robust, at least in the peace-time and pre-attack environ-
ments.[5] However, it is clear that both the readiness rate and level of responsiveness are affected proportionately by the threat of disruption from the
physical destruction of the C3 system and the electromagnetic pulse (EMP)
of nuclear detonations. In effect, EMP potentials could degrade the entire
C3 system that transmits the emergency action message (EAM) from the
National Command Authority, i.e., the President or the designated suc-
cessor, to the ICBM launch control centers.[6] If we think in terms of the
aggregate pre-launch survivability of the US ICBM force, it is difficult to
avoid the conclusion (or at least the suspicion) that, quite independent of the
possibility of an effective countersilo attack, some parts of the ICBM force
also may be degraded by nuclear explosions that occur in space over the
United States. While it is foreseeable that the US will continue to armor the
C3 system in order to maintain (theoretically) tight control over the ICBMs,
for the present, however, we are concerned that the entire ICBM force
could be incapacitated by less than a large-scale Soviet nuclear attack that
used a limited number of high-altitude nuclear explosions.

One of the more critical factors in an assessment of the vulnerabilities of the US ICBM force is the hardness of the silos. According to published reports, US Minuteman silos are hardened to withstand approximately 2,000 psi of dynamic overpressure.[7] This structural feature of the silos was employed in order to lessen the vulnerability of the silos to anything but a direct nuclear hit. Today, however, the yield and CEP of recent Soviet RVs makes the issue of silo hardness seem increasingly irrelevant. When Soviet RVs are reportedly able to land within several hundred meters of a silo, the hardness of the silo seems to make less and less difference in the survival of the silos in an attack. Nevertheless, the hardness of the silo is an important determinant of the aggregate vulnerabilities of the US ICBM force. As noted in Appendix, while this work does not consider silo hardness directly, it uses the relationship between yield (to wit, the cratering potential of the warhead) and the CEP to project a warheads lethality against hard targets.

One issue that will figure prominently in an assessment of the outcome of a counterforce nuclear war will be the relative concentration of US ICBM silos in the central sector of the nation. As will be seen in Chapter 4, this deployment pattern will have severe consequences for the American civilian population in terms of the expected damage to collateral civilian populations after a Soviet countersilo strike. The indirect effects (fallout, and so forth) from an attack of this magnitude will be enormous. Indeed, one could go so far as to say that the location of US ICBM silos could not be worse—even if one sought, for some unimaginably perverse reason, to maximize civilian casualties. Finally, there is the matter of post-launch survivability, which is the ability of the ICBM to penetrate enemy space to the target. With the exception of the USSR's *very* limited deployment of the *Galosh* anti-ballistic missile system that is situated near Moscow, there is relatively little uncertainty about the ability of the United States to reach Soviet targets in a nuclear attack. While this issue is of substantially more concern in the case of the American bomber force, in terms of the ICBM force there is no question about its ability to hit Soviet targets once the ICBMs are launched. It is not altogether unlikely at some time in the not-too-distant future that the post-launch survivability of US ICBMs will be in doubt *if* the Soviet Union moves in the direction of ballistic missile defense. But in the calculations that follow, we have assumed that there are no active or passive Soviet defense measures that could interfere with the penetration American ICBMs in any phase of an attack. In other words, once launched it is assumed that US ICBMs will have a "free ride" to their assigned targets.

In summary, we can state the boundaries of the ICBM vulnerability in the following terms: while the ICBM is vulnerable in the pre-launch phase (to either disruption or destruction), it is for the time being invulnerable after it is launched. It will be interesting to compare this assessment with the bomber force, for instance, which is highly vulnerable during virtually all phases of a nuclear war.

SLBM Force

The second most important component of the US strategic nuclear arsenal is the fleet of strategic submarines, ballistic nuclear (SSBNs) that carry submarine-launched ballistic missiles (SLBMs). In an age that is characterized by doubts about the survivability of the US ICBM force, and perhaps the bomber leg of the triad, it is the *relative* "invulnerability" of the US SSBNs that reinforces the essential dictum of deterrence: the irrevocable ability of a nation to launch a nuclear attack in retaliation against the aggressor. On continuous patrol in the North Atlantic and Pacific Oceans, it is generally acknowledged that US submarines could survive virtually any Soviet attempt to locate and destroy them.[8] As up to 60 percent of the 31 boats in the US SSBN force are on patrol at any time, the survival of, say, 12 SSBNs out of the 16 normally on patrol, still provides the US with quite substantial retaliatory capabilities—as long as we emphasize that such retaliation will be confined primarily against soft counterforce and countervalue targets. In any event, there are two types of SLBMs in the US force: the Poseidon and Trident SLBMs.

Poseidon After the recent retirement of ten American SSBNs and the Polaris SLBM, the Poseidon SLBM became the oldest member of the US SLBM arsenal. First deployed in the 1960s, the Poseidon represents missile technology from the late 1950s and early 1960s. For this reason, the Poseidon is not capable of effectively attacking anything but soft-targets. The Poseidon force provided the bulk of the warheads for the assured destruction mission throughout the 1960s and 1970s, as well as additional warheads for soft-counterforce attacks.

At present, there are 256 Poseidon SLBMs deployed on roughly sixteen of the *Lafayette*-class and *Ethan-Allen*-class submarines, each of which carries 16 Poseidon missiles. A Poseidon SLBM has 10 MIRVed 40 KT RVs with a CEP of 463 m, and has an SSPK of .55, and a theoretical OPK of .98 if four RVs are targeted against each hard target; the WLS value of .68 signifies that an optimal warhead allocation scheme against hard targets would be four RVs per hard target. The 40 KT warhead has areas of damage for AB and SB detonations of 25 and 10 square miles, respectively; or lethal radii of 2.8 and 1.8 miles. In general, the Poseidon is best described as a low-yield, comparatively inaccurate RV, which has launch and detonation reliability rates of .6 and .8, respectively. The value of .6 signifies that roughly 60 percent of the SSBNs are on patrol at any given time, whereas the remainder of the SSBNs (40 percent, or 13) are in port for routine maintenance and repairs. Once launched, the Poseidon SLBM is approximately as reliable as the ICBMs, as can be seen by its detonation reliability value of .8. A word of historical caution is in order. While we infer that the Poseidon may be a reliable weapon today, it was discovered in the late 1960s that possibly 75 percent of the Poseidon SLBM warheads suffered from a mechanical defect that could have precluded detonation.[9] We *presume* this is not the case today.

Trident The second, and increasingly more important, leg of the SLBM force is the Trident C-4 SLBM. Many of the older SSBNs—as well as the new *Ohio*-class SSBNs—are equipped with the Trident SLBM. Currently, it is deployed on *James Madison*-class, *Benjamin Franklin*-class, and *Ohio*-class SSBNs. Two *Ohio*-class boats have 24 SLBMs each, and 13 *Madison*- and *Franklin*-class boats have 16 SLBMs each, for a total of 256 Trident SLBMs. At the time of this writing the Trident SLBM is deployed on fifteen submarines.[10]

The Trident SLBM has 10 MIRVed, 100 KT RVs with a CEP of 250 m.[11] The SSPK for the Trident is .64, while the OPK is .95 if it is assumed that three Trident RVs will be targeted against each hard target, which was derived from the allocation scheme that is implied by the WLS of .81. The areas of damage for the 100 KT RV for AB and SB detonations (assuming optimum HOB) are 45 and 17 square miles, respectively; this corresponds to lethal radii of 3.8 and 2.3 miles. And, like the Poseidon, because it is assumed that 60 percent of the Trident force is at sea, the launch reliability rate is .60. Likewise, the detonation reliability rate for the Trident is .8.

While it is clear that the Trident has an enhanced hard-counterforce capability—at least in comparison with that of the Poseidon—it nonetheless remains the case that the Trident C-4 has limited hard-target kill capabilities. The deployment of the Trident II (D-5) SLBM toward the end of this decade will create a significant hard-target kill capability in the US SLBM force. (Even this point is still uncertain in view of the technical debate about the projected SSPK and OPK for the Trident II. It seems that recent calculations on the effect of the greater-than-expected increases in the hardness of Soviet silos and command centers in terms of the hard-target kill capabilities of the Trident II suggests that the yield of Trident II RV may have to be increased from 335 KT to 475 KT.)

Overall, the US SLBM force of 512 missiles and 5,120 RVs poses a limited threat to hard counterforce targets in the Soviet Union, as we well as a significant threat to countervalue targets the USSR. Just how this force theoretically might be used will be the subject of the analysis in the forthcoming chapters.

SLBM Vulnerability

The issue of SLBM/SSBN vulnerability must be approached on two levels. The first level is that of the SSBNs in their bases, which by any definition are soft counterforce targets. SSBNs at their bases, therefore, are especially vulnerable to an attack, say, by Soviet SLBMs from their normal coastal patrol routes. And, like the bomber bases, it is doubtful that US submarine bases would receive sufficient warning of an attack, and even if they were to receive some warning, there would be little that could be done. Short of launching one's SLBMs (which would be useless for the United States, because its SLBMs cannot reach Soviet targets from their bases), the SSBNs in port would have few options once warning of a Soviet attack was received. Of the 31 SSBNs in the US fleet, roughly 40 percent (13) of the boats are in port at any given time. This means that, on a day-to-day alert level, the United States should expect to lose that same number of its SSBN force in a Soviet preemptive attack. But what of the remaining SSBNs on patrol?

While an SSBN is on patrol in the Atlantic or Pacific Oceans, the conventional wisdom is that it is relatively immune to destruction. Generally, analysts agree that most of the boats will survive for weeks or months—long enough for them to launch their missiles over a protracted time. The fundamental reason for this overall survivability is the difficulty of locating SSBNs while they are on patrol in view of the number of acoustic and non-acoustic (electromagnetic) measures have been taken to protect US submarines against Soviet anti-submarine warfare (ASW) efforts.

Despite this general line of thought, there are those who are less sanguine about the survival of US SSBNs, particularly as we proceed into the future. For instance, in the most noteworthy case, Under Secretary of Defense for Research and Engineering, Dr. William Perry, argued in the late 1970s that US submarines might be vulnerable to a "barrage" attack by Soviet ICBMs by the 1980s. If the USSR could locate US SSBNs within a 50 kilometer grid, then the sub-surface detonation of between 10 and 20 high-yield warheads could well result in the destruction of a submarine and its 200 + warheads. If this ability to localize submarines extended to the bulk of the SSBN force (perhaps only 15 boats), the effectiveness of the sea leg itself would be called into question. In concert with the imminent threat to the American ICBM force, the consequences of the deterioration of a second leg of the triad would have disastrous implications for the United States. Needless to say, the reaction of the Navy to this assertion was so strong that Perry subsequently withdrew his statement. Still, we wonder whether this barrage attack might not be plausible in a nuclear war. On the positive side, it is unknown how rapidly the Soviet Union could retarget its missile warheads for an attack against a force of rapidly moving SSBNs.

In this study, we have assumed that US SSBNs *at sea* can be targeted by Soviet delivery systems, and equally that the United States can target Soviet SSBNs. If the attack is composed of at least ten, high-yield, sub-surface detonations, then we have estimated that there is a .5 probability that the submarine will be destroyed. On a conceptual level, we think that this option in our model provides a realistic, as well as a relatively fair, indication of the nuances of targeting in nuclear war. Indeed, as an authoritative naval source has argued, while it is probably not realistic to assume that such a "barrage" attack might destroy large numbers of SSBNs, it is safe to assume that "several" US SSBNs could well be lost with this tactic.[12] In any event, we have pursued this line of argument in our analysis principally in order to emphasize that there are a host of uncertainties surrounding any large-scale nuclear operations. Thus, while we do not challenge the *basic* assumption of SSBN survivability, the possibility that SSBNs may suffer some losses through attrition should at least be considered in this study. Accordingly, in this study the SSBN is considered both as a launching platform and as a counterforce target.

Bomber Force

The remaining leg of the US nuclear triad is composed of strategic bombers, which are deployed at some 25 bases throughout the continental United States. As the US struggles to maintain a triad of nuclear forces, bombers— as well as ICBMs—have come under increasing criticism as inherently vulnerable elements of the triad. Yet, the diversity of the US bomber force continues to present certain difficulties for the Soviets. Not surprisingly, the US itself faces a period during which it must come to grips with the future of the bomber force. Here, our task is limited to an assessment of the two types of bombers in the American arsenal—the B-52 and FB-111—in terms of their attributes, capabilities and vulnerabilities in the context of alternate types of nuclear wars.

B-52 First deployed in the 1950s, the B-52 is the mainstay of the US bomber force. With roughly 319 B-52s deployed at 25 bomber bases in the continental US (see Table 1), the B-52 force can be broken down into four operational subgroups, for which we have used a rather simple taxonomy for the classification of the B-52s. This scheme is defined on the basis of the type of payload or weapon that is carried on the aircraft. These designations are to be used for purely analytic purposes, and should not be confused with those designations employed by the US Air Force.

The B-52A, of which there are 84, are deployed with SRAMs (short-range attack missile). The function of the SRAM, among other things, is the destruction, or at least the suppression, of Soviet air defenses. Each SRAM has a yield of 200 KT and a nominal CEP of 100 m. We say "nominal" because, while we have no reliable data on its CEP, the prevailing view is that the SRAM is a relatively accurate weapon. Given the high WLS value of the weapon, it is clear that the SRAM would have high utility against hard targets—assuming, of course, that the bomber can penetrate far enough into Soviet airspace to launch the weapon against hardened ICBM silos or command centers in the heart of the Soviet Union. For the 200 KT warhead, the areas of damage for AB and SB detonations, respectively, are 72 and 30 square miles. In the case of the reliability of the SRAM, we must make a distinction that has no analogue for ballistic missiles: post-launch interception. The launch reliability rate for the B-52A is .8; the detonation reliability rate, however, is .3, which means that after the penetration of Soviet airspace, losses to the attacking bomber force may approach seventy percent.

As one can see in Table 1, the bombers, which are designated as B-52B,

B-52C, and B-52D, are variations on the data for the B-52A.[13] The primary difference is the yield of the warhead on the B-52B and B-52C. For reference, the B-52B and B-52C carry gravity bombs, whereas the B-52A—as noted—carries SRAM missiles and the B-52D carries air-launched cruise missiles (ALCM). A further distinction is that the detonation (penetration) rate of the ALCM, which we have estimated is .5, is slightly higher than the penetration rate for the SRAM. The assumption is that the ALCM will have a higher penetration rate, particularly if the ALCM launch points are well outside Soviet airspace. Once launched, however, it is believed that the ALCM will be a difficult target for Soviet air defenses to intercept and destroy.

FB-111 The second bomber in the US arsenal is the FB-111, of which there are 60 deployed at six bases in the continental United States. See Table 1 for information on the bombers and basing. In many senses, the FB-111 is analogous to the operational features of the B-52. For instance, the FB-111A is deployed with SRAMs just as the B-52A; the FB-111B, on the other hand, carries 1 MT gravity bombs, much like the payload of the B-52B. In general terms, the FB-111 may be viewed as a counterpart to the B-52, both in the sense that its payload of weapons and general mission characteristics are roughly the same as are those of the B-52 force.

Bomber Vulnerability

In order to think about the vulnerability of the US bomber force, it is essential to examine the bomber force during the pre-launch and post-launch phases. During the pre-launch phase, there is considerable circumstantial evidence to at least raise the possibility that much of the US bomber force is vulnerable to a preemptive Soviet attack from SSBNs that are on patrol along the eastern and western coasts of the United States.[14] In view of the short flight time of Soviet SLBMs from their normal patrol locations to the US bomber bases along the coasts and well inland, the warning time available to the bombers could be as little as six to eight minutes, assuming of course that the Pave Paw radars on the Atlantic and Pacific coasts are able to detect the launch of the attack and subsequently track the incoming SLBM RVs. It is not surprising to find that a substantial fraction (at least 60–70 percent) of the American bomber force could be caught by surprise in such an attack. While the remaining bombers on alert, roughly 30 percent or some 90–100 aircraft, might be able to escape destruction in such a preemptive attack there is considerable uncertainty about the survival of the alert bomber force principally because the bomber is a very soft target. Anticipating that an SLBM attack against bomber bases will aim to distribute warheads evenly over the bases, as well as in the most likely bomber escape routes, even fairly optimistic assessments indicate that the US bomber force faces a significant level of vulnerability.[15]

In the post-launch phase of war, the US bomber force could face not only a barrage attack by Soviet SLBM RVs as they exit their bases, but also the quite extensive Soviet air defense system if they survive a preemptive attack. Not surprisingly, assessments about the quality of the Soviet air defense system range from the robust to the not-so-robust. In this study, we have assumed that the Soviet air defense system will intercept roughly 70 percent of whatever US bombers enter Soviet airspace, being aware that this 70 percent attrition rate applies only to those bombers that actually have been launched from their bases. Thus, if 100 bombers escape from their base, it is projected that 30 will reach the assigned targets.

The issue of foremost concern here is not the quality of the Soviet air defense network. Rather, the overriding issue is to address the general consequences of US bomber attacks using what we see as realistic (or perhaps, moderate) assessments of the ability of US bombers to penetrate Soviet airspace. While the actual level of penetration for the bomber force might in reality be somewhat higher or lower than we have projected here, fluctuations in the response do not seem to alter drastically the magnitude of the US bomber threat.

Synergism and Vulnerability: Multiplying Uncertainties

In these sections, the aim is to address on a case-by-case basis the general vulnerabilities of the ICBM, submarine, and bomber legs of the US nuclear triad. On the simplest level, it is easy to isolate the sometimes severe vulnerabilities of the individual legs of the triad, for in theory all systems have certain flaws and weaknesses that can be exploited by a dedicated adversary. An ICBM in a fixed silo will be vulnerable once the adversary achieves the requisite accuracy (and, of course, yield) on its RVs—leaving aside the possibility of superhardened silos which, as recent studies suggest, might be able to survive a proximate nuclear explosion to remain standing in the middle of a crater. Yet, even if we can agree that the vulnerability of individual classes of delivery systems can be threatened with destruction, what of the synergism of three legs of the triad, which while vulnerable by themselves, can be relatively secure when taken together?

Conventional strategic wisdom posits that the vulnerability of one, or even two legs, of a nuclear triad is not wholly catastrophic so long as one, but preferably two, legs remain secure. In a nuclear attack against US ICBM silos, for instance, the Soviets would be likely to launch ICBMs, but that launch would leave time to flush the alert portion of the bomber force. Alternatively, an attack on US bomber bases with SLBMs would leave time to alert and launch the ICBM force. And in both cases, the SSBN force at sea would be available for retaliation even if the two other legs of the triad were destroyed in a surprise attack. This means that the asymmetric vulnerabilities of the three legs of the triad (excluding for the moment the SSBN force) combine synergistically to decrease the overall vulnerability of the force. Thus, this discussion of the vulnerabilities of discrete elements of the American nuclear triad is not meant to imply by exclusion that the entire arsenal is vulnerable. Yet, the question remains: To what limits can we stretch the vulnerability of individual legs of the triad without creating some corresponding deterioration in the stability of deterrence?

USSR NUCLEAR FORCES

In this section we will address the array of weapons in the Soviet Union's triad of nuclear forces. In each of the forthcoming sections the attributes, capabilities, and vulnerabilities of the USSR's ICBM, SLBM, and bomber forces are examined. Since the data are summarized in Table 2, the reader may wish to refer to it during the discussion. Again, we urge the reader to examine the Appendix for an analysis of the methodological and technological issues that are embedded in this study.

ICBM Force

Beginning in the 1970s, the US has been increasingly concerned about the threat posed by the Soviet ICBM force, particularly insofar as its hard-target-kill capabilities are concerned. This, to be sure, is the dominant (though hardly unanimous) western perspective on the USSR's ICBM arsenal. We think that, from the Soviet vantage point, its ICBM arsenal represents the culmination of two decades of successful development and deployment. By any imaginable standard, the USSR has deployed an ICBM arsenal of the highest quality that, second to none, has become *the* standard for comparison in analyses and projections of modern, hard-target kill capable weapons. In just one respect, for instance, the magnitude of the capabilities of the Soviet Union's ICBM force is evident: the nearly 6,000 RVs on the ICBM force represent not only roughly 70 percent of total Soviet strategic nuclear warheads, but also it appears to be sufficient firepower for the execution of a massive counterforce attack on the United States. Indeed, as will be shown, a relatively small fraction of the USSR's ICBM force has more than enough RVs for the destruction of the US ICBM force.

It is of interest to note that the Soviets have placed the same (if not more) degree of emphasis on ICBMs as the Americans. Our perception is that the USSR has invested substantial resources in its ICBMs, not because of its symbolic meaning as the ultimate measure of nuclear power, but rather because of the ICBMs' inherent power, controllability, and flexibility. It is difficult to avoid the suspicion that, because the Soviets are *relatively* unconcerned with the possibility of a US preemptive attack, the USSR prefers a force of ICBMs to SLBMs and bombers as a result of the ICBMs more centralized and secure command and control systems.[16] Again, if the reader

Table 2
Soviet Nuclear Forces

Name	No.	MIRVs	Yield	CEP	WLS*	SB**	AB***	Launch	Detonate
SS19M1	280	6	550KT	400m	.84	56	155	.75	.75
SS19M2	100	1	10MT	250m	1.09	394	1029	.85	.85
SS18M2	107	8	900KT	400m	.87	78	211	.75	.75
SS18M3	26	1	20MT	350m	1.06	632	1691	.85	.85
SS18M4	175	10	500KT	250m	.91	53	145	.75	.75
SS17M1	160	4	750KT	400m	.86	66	181	.75	.75
SS17M2	20	1	6MT	400m	.98	283	707	.80	.85
SS13	60	1	600KT	1900m	.67	58	165	.80	.85
SS11M3	470	1	950KT	1400m	.72	81	215	.75	.80
BearA	30	2	1MT	100m	1.14	85	227	.80	.30
BearB	75	1	1MT	100m	1.14	85	227	.80	.30
Bison	49	1	1MT	100m	1.14	85	227	.80	.30
Backfire	65	1	1MT	100m	1.14	85	227	.80	.30
SSN5	57	1	1MT	2800m	.66	85	227	.35	.60
SSN6	468	1	1MT	1300m	.73	85	227	.35	.65
SSN8	289	1	750KT	1500m	.72	66	181	.65	.65
SSN17	12	1	500KT	1400m	.69	53	145	.35	.70
SSN18	160	3	1MT	1400m	.72	85	227	.65	.75

* Warhead Lethality Score
** Surface-burst area of damage
*** Air-burst area of damage

is familiar with the details of the Soviet Union's nuclear forces, then it may be appropriate to proceed immediately to the next chapter.

SS-19M1 The SS-19M1 belongs in the class of modern Soviet ICBMs. At present, there are 280 SS-19M1 ICBMs deployed in two wings at the Kozelsk SRF (strategic rocket forces base) and Pervomaysk SRF. For geographic reference, the nearest major collateral cities to these bases are Tula and Kirovograd. Each SS-19M1 carries six 550 KT MIRVed warheads, with a CEP of 400 m. Based on this yield and CEP, the RVs have a SSPK of .65, and an OPK of .96 if three RVs are allocated against each hard target. The WLS of .84 means that optimal kill probabilities will be achieved by targeting three RVs against each hard target. In terms of area destruction, the 550 KTRV will cover 155 and 56 square miles for air-burst and surface-burst detonations, respectively, which translates into lethal radii of 7 and 4.2 miles. The launch and detonation reliability rates are .75, a value that will be found to be similar to the reliability rates of the other Soviet ICBMs. In view of the large number of RVs on the SS19M1s, which is 1,680, one of its primary missions would appear to be counterforce targeting. Indeed, in any large-scale countersilo operation, the SS-19M1 will be a dominant force in the attack. As shown in Chapter 4, the SS-19M1 ICBM will—in conjunction with the SS-18M4—be perhaps one of the more critical Soviet resources in a counterforce attack against the United States.

SS19M2 In the SS19M ICBM force there are roughly 100 missiles deployed at the Tatischevo SRF. Designated as the SS19M2, each ICBM carries a 10 megaton warhead with a CEP of 250 meters. What is unique about the SS19M2 is the yield and CEP ratio. As denoted by the WLS of 1.09, the delivery of one SS19M1 RV is sufficient for the destruction of one hard target. The SSPK for this RV is .95, which is extremely high for a single RV; moreover, the OPK of .99 indicates that the allocation of multiple SS19M2 RVs will have only a marginal effect on the probability of destruction and, therefore, on the outcome of the attack. The 10 MT warhead has areas of destruction for air-burst and surface-burst detonations of 1,029 and 394 square miles, respectively, assuming an optimum height-of-burst. And in comparison with the SS19M1, the SS19M2 ICBM has slightly higher launch and detonation reliability rates (.85). In sum, the SS19M2 ICBM carries a highly accurate, high-yield warhead that is best suited for the destruction of hardened targets. Yet, given the relatively small number of RVs deployed, it is unlikely that the SS19M2 would participate in large-scale countersilo operations. By exclusion, the more obvious function of the SS19M2 is to attack hardened command centers in the United States, such as Cheyenne Mountain in Colorado or Mount Weather in Virginia.

If we consider that the primary US C3 centers are relatively hard targets, then the utility of the SS-19M2 lies in the low CEP and high yield of the warhead. What warheads would be better suited for destroying hardened command posts than a 10 megaton warhead with a low CEP (other than an earth-penetration warhead)? Thus, as we will show in the forthcoming chapters, the SS-19M2 probably will participate in nuclear strikes that are designed to decapitate the US command system. Parenthetically, we should note that the SS-18M3 ICBM is also an appropriate weapon system for nuclear decapitation attacks.

SS-18M2 One of the more critical countersilo weapons in the USSR's ICBM force is the SS-18M2. At present, there are 107 deployed at the Kartaly SRF, which is located near the Soviet city of Kustanay. The SS-18M2 carries 8 MIRVed 900 KT warheads that have a CEP of 400 meters. Based on the WLS of .87, in an optimum attack against hard targets, three SS-18M2 RVs should be allocated against each hard target. In terms of hard-target kill, the RV has an SSPK of .66, and an OPK of .96. The 900 KT warhead has an area of destruction of 211 square miles for air-burst detonations, and 78 square miles for surface-bursts, which corresponds to lethal radii of 8.2 and 5 miles respectively. Like the SS-19M1, the SS-18M2 has launch and detonation reliability rates of .75. The mission for the SS-18M2 appears to be countersilo operations. Given the PK of the RVs and relatively high number of MIRVs on the ICBM, it is logical to use the SS-18M2 against US ICBM silos. The force of 107 SS-18M2 missiles carries 856 RVs, a number that is sufficient to cover roughly 25 percent of the US Minuteman force, assuming that the allocation schemes and attrition rates are factored into the analysis. In any event, the SS-18M2 can be included in the class of Soviet ICBMs that seem to be designated for large-scale, coordinated countersilo attacks.

SS-18M3 The SS-18M3 ICBM is analogous in many respects to the SS-19M2: It carries a single warhead with a yield of 20 megatons and a CEP of 350 m, and each RV has an SSPK of .93. The 20 MT warhead has an area of destruction of 1,691 square miles for air-burst detonations and 632 square miles for surface-burst detonations, and like the SS-19M2, the SS-18M3 has launch and detonation reliability rates of .85. There are 26 SS-18M3 ICBMs, all of which are deployed at the Aleysk missile field that is located near the Soviet city of Barnaul. By all accounts, the SS-18M3 belongs in the class of decapitation missiles, based on the extraordinarily high yield and correspondingly low CEP of the RV. Accordingly, it is likely that the SS-18M3 will be targeted against primary US command and control centers.

SS-18M4 For those who are concerned about the vulnerability (or incipient vulnerability) of land-based forces, perhaps the most worrisome Soviet weapon is the SS-18M4 ICBM. There are 175 SS-18M4 ICBMs deployed at the Dombarovskiy SRF, which means that the primary collateral target for that missile field is the city of Orsk, which has a population of 247,000. The SS-18M4 is a MIRVed missile that carries ten 550 KT warheads with a CEP of 250 meters. The WLS of .91 indicates that, in an optimal attack, two RVs should be allocated against each hard target. The SSPK for one RV is .72 and an OPK of .92 for two-on-one attacks. The 500 KT warhead has an area of destruction of 145 square miles for an air-burst detonation, and 53 square

miles for a surface-burst detonation. The SS-18M4 has launch and detonation reliability rates of .75. In sum, the SS-18M4 ICBM force of 1,750 warheads constitutes the foundation for a Soviet counterforce attack against US
ICBM silos. If we assume that the 1,750 warheads will be targeted in a two-
on-one pattern, then—excluding attrition rates—roughly 825 US silos could
be destroyed. By all accounts, the SS-18M4—as we will show in later chapters—presents the greatest cumulative threat of any Soviet ICBM to US
silos. Indeed, the SS-18M4 is the closest analogue in the Soviet arsenal to
the MX ICBM, which is a salient comparison because it reinforces the view
that the MX has a significant countersilo potential just like the SS-18M4.

SS-17M1 The SS-17M1 also belongs in the class of counterforce-capable
Soviet ICBMs. There are 160 SS-17M1 ICBMs deployed at the Kostroma
SRF, which is near the Soviet city of Gorky. The SS-17M1 is a MIRVed
missile that carries four 750 KT warheads, and has a CEP of 400 meters. This
RV configuration produces an SSPK of .65, and OPK of .96—assuming that
it is a three-on-one attack, i.e., three such RVS per target. The 750 KT
warhead has an area of destruction of 181 square miles for air-burst detonations and 66 square miles for surface-burst detonations. The SS-17M1 has
launch and detonation reliability rates of .75, a value which approaches the
mean reliability rate for Soviet ICBMs.

From this, we can infer that the primary mission for the SS-17M1 also is
likely to be countersilo attacks against the United States. The 640 RVs on the
SS-17M1 force will add to the already large size of the SS-18M4 and
SS-19M1 ICBMs that are available for countersilo operations. Like the afore-
mentioned ICBMs, the SS-17M1 is a typical, although slightly less potent,
Soviet weapon for use in an attack on US ICBM silos.

SS-17M2 Patterns often emerge from an analysis of nuclear forces.
Whether it is yield/CEP relationships, or the reliability rates, certain trends
in the deployment of strategic offensive forces can be detected. So it is with
Soviet ICBMs. A classic example is the SS-17M2, an ICBM that quite closely mirrors the capabilities of the SS-19M2 and SS-18M3. Thus, it is easy to
infer that the SS-17M2 ICBM seems to be well-suited for decapitation nuclear strikes against command centers.

The 20 SS-17M2 ICBMs are deployed near Vologda at the Yedrovo SRF
base. Each missile carries a 6 megaton warhead with a CEP of 400 meters.
The 6 MT warhead has an area of damage of 707 square miles for air-bursts
and 283 square miles for surface-bursts, which corresponds to lethal radii of
15 and 9 nautical miles. It has launch and detonation reliability rates of .8
and .85, respectively. Against hard targets, the SS-17M2 RV has an SSPK
of .79 and an OPK of .96 for two-on-one attacks. In view of the high yield of
the warhead, as well as its relatively low CEP—as reflected in the WLS and
PK values—we surmise that the SS-17M2 also will be targeted against US
command posts. If the warheads in the "decapitation" group (SS-17M2,
SS-18M3 and SS-19M2 ICBMs) are totaled, then there are 146 prompt hard-
target kill RVs that are available for an attack against US C3 centers. The

dimensions of this threat will be examined in more detail in the decapitation attacks in Chapter 4.

SS-13 The SS-13 belongs in the category of less capable Soviet ICBMs. As such, it is likely to be used against soft, sprawling countervalue centers in the United States. The 60 SS-13 ICBMs are deployed near the Soviet city of Kazan (population: 1,040,000) at the Yoshkar Ola SRF base. Each ICBM carries one 600 kiloton warhead with a CEP of 1900 meters; it has an SSPK of .53 against hard targets, and an OPK of .97—if we assume, albeit theoretically, that it is used in a five-on-one attack. But this is clearly a preposterous tactic because the effects of fratricide imply that greater than three-on-one attacks on one target will raise the probability of warhead interference, and therefore will require a prohibitively large number of warheads. Thus, by exclusion it is easy to infer that the SS-13 is useful only in attacks on non-hardened targets. The 600 kiloton warhead has an area of damage of 165 square miles for an air-burst and 58 square miles for a surface-burst, which is equivalent to lethal radii of 7.2 and 4.3 nautical miles, respectively. The SS-13 has a launch reliability rate of .80, and a detonation reliability rate of .85.

Even a cursory examination of the SS-13 ICBM leads inexorably to the conclusion that is likely to be used in attacks against urban-industrial centers in the US—despite the fact that the Soviet Union has never explicitly endorsed the rationale behind an assured destruction policy. Nevertheless, as a remnant of the early days of inaccurate, city-busting ICBMs, the SS-13 remains one of the weapons that quite plausibly could be used in an attack on some of the large urban centers in the United States.

SS-11M3 The final missile in the USSR's ICBM arsenal is the SS-11M3. The 460 SS-11M3 ICBMs are deployed in six missile fields: Teykovo SRF, Perm SRF, Derazhyna SRF, Svobodnyy SRF, Drovyanaya SRF, and Zhangiz Tobe SRF. The SS-11M3 is a single warhead missile with an RV yield of 950 kilotons and a CEP of 1400 meters. It has an SSPK of .55 and an OPK of .96—if it is assumed that it will be used in a four-on-one attack against hard targets. The 950 kiloton warhead has an area of damage of 215 and 81 square miles for air-burst and surface-burst detonations, respectively, which is equivalent to lethal radii of 8.3 and 5.0 nautical miles. Finally, the SS-11M3 ICBM has launch and detonation reliability rates of .75 and .80, respectively. As we noted for the SS-13 ICBM, the SS-11M3 appears to be designed for urban-industrial targeting. As shown in Chapter 6, the SS-11M3 is well suited indeed for countervalue targeting operations.

ICBM Vulnerability

While it may seem somewhat iconoclastic in the 1980s to think about the vulnerability of Soviet ICBMs, especially in view of the frequent (and often, rhetorical) exhortations about the threat posed by Soviet ICBMs, to be fair we must say that the United States poses a significant threat to the Soviet

ICBM force. While the magnitude of the vulnerability of Soviet ICBMs admittedly is less than the vulnerability of US ICBMs, it is true that US forces theoretically could destroy a large fraction of the Soviet ICBM force. Indeed, if the United States were virtually to disarm itself, it is conceivable that it might be able to destroy Soviet land-based missile forces in a preemptive attack. Thus, while we argue that US ICBMs, and other legs of the triad, certainly appear to be vulnerable to a Soviet attack, there are indications that Soviet ICBMs are in substance vulnerable to a US preemptive attack, although somewhat less vulnerable than American forces.

Like any land-based force, Soviet ICBMs face the same generic problems as US ICBMs, except that the United States has not marshaled the forces necessary for the elimination of Soviet ICBMs on a level that is less than self-disarming. In fixed silos, the Soviets would have the usual difficulties in maintaining communications with its nuclear forces in the face of an American attack. Moreover, the concentration of Soviet forces in their ICBMs means, in effect, that the Soviet Union eventually will find that the largest fraction of its nuclear forces (in terms of number of RVs, EMT, or throw-weight) are at risk. For instance, the deployment of the MX ICBM in far greater numbers than now envisioned, as well as the Trident D-5, would give the US a substantial hard-target kill capacity. In the foreseeable future, however, we would argue that the vulnerability of Soviet ICBMs is only of theoretical concern, principally because the US does not have sufficient numbers of RVs to pose a credible threat to the Soviet ICBM force. Thus, while Soviet ICBMs will be at risk at sometime in the future, in substance today they are not in immediate danger.

Paradoxically, the Soviet Union apparently has initiated a new silo modernization hardness program that is designed to increase the blast resistance of the silos to between 5,000 and 7,000 psi. Even while the magnitude of the American hard-target kill program continues to grow slowly, the Soviet Union has proceeded to reinforce its silos on the grounds that this enhancement will increase the survivability of its ICBMs. From the available evidence, it is clear that this increase in hardness will have an effect on Soviet ICBM survivability—especially in light of the yield and CEP of projected US forces. In any event, the asymmetrical vulnerability of US ICBMs (in comparison with the lesser vulnerability of Soviet ICBMs) probably will be revised in the next decade as the United States enhances its counterforce capabilities. As for the present, a detailed assessment of US counterforce capabilities against Soviet ICBMs, as well as submarines and bombers, will be presented in Chapter 3.

SLBM Force

In comparison with Soviet ICBMs, the USSR's SLBM force is of no more than secondary importance. Yet, the USSR's SSBN program has a number of attributes that lend both strength and adaptability to Soviet capabilities, particularly in an environment that is marked by constantly changing strategic threats. For instance, in response to the NATO deployment of the Pershing II intermediate-range ballistic missile (IRBM) and the ground-launched cruise missile (GLCM), the Soviet Union increased the number of *Yankee*-class SSBNs that are on patrol along the US coasts. While this is without doubt neither a particularly provocative nor threatening action, it certainly does signify that the preemptive potential of Soviet SSBNs against US bomber and submarine bases has increased. From this vantage point, most bomber and submarine bases, as well as command posts, are within short reach of the SLBMs on the Soviet ballistic-missile submarines. Thus, while there is a near unanimous consensus that the USSR's SLBM force is decidedly inferior to that of the US SLBM force in terms of, say, CEP or undetectability, and clearly inferior in comparison with the USSR's own ICBM force, it is safe to say that the Soviet SLBM force has identifiable strengths. We will explore some of these as well in later chapters.

At the time of this writing, the USSR has 84 SSBNs: 15 *GOLF*-class, 7 *HOTEL*-class, 30 *YANKEE*-class, and 32 *DELTA*-class. There are four primary SSBN bases in the USSR, located at Kamchatshiiy, Polyarnyy, Severodvinsk, and Murmansk (we have excluded the SSBN base on the Black Sea). Although the exact figures are unknown, most western sources estimate that approximately 10 percent of the Soviet SSBN force is on patrol in the Atlantic and Pacific Oceans at any time, with the remainder (90 percent) in port. (This is in sharp contrast to the United States, which maintains roughly 60 percent of its SSBNs on patrol.) This means that approximately eight Soviet SSBNs are on patrol at any given time if we assume non-crisis, day-to-day alert conditions. We assume that the remaining 74 SSBNs are distributed equally at the four submarine bases. Now, we will examine each of the five types of SLBMs that are deployed on Soviet SSBNs.

SSN-5 One of the earliest, and perhaps most primitive, of the SLBMs is the SSN-5. The 57 SSN-5s are deployed in clusters of three on 19 SSBNs, primarily on the *GOLF* II- and *HOTEL* II-class boats. Each of the SSN-5 SLBMs carries a single one megaton nuclear warhead with a CEP of 2800 meters. With an SSPK of .53 and a WLS of .68 (indicating on a notional basis that five RVs are required for the destruction of each hard target), the SSN-5 obviously is not designed for counterforce missions. The one megaton warhead has an area of damage of 227 square miles for air-bursts and 85 square miles for surface-bursts; this corresponds to lethal radii of 8.5 and 5.2 nautical miles, respectively. It has launch and detonation reliability rates of .35 and .6, respectively. By all standards, the SSN-5 SLBM is designed for countervalue targeting options, i.e., the destruction of the large American urban centers wherein gross RV inaccuracy—indeed, a low overall level of reliability—will not have appreciably negative consequences on the outcome of the attack.

SSN-6 Although the SSN-6 represents only a marginal improvement over the SSN-5 in terms of aggregate capabilities, it constitutes one of the essential foundations of the USSR's SLBM force. The 468 SSN-6s are deployed on 30 submarines, specifically on the *GOLF* IV- and *YANKEE* I-class SSBNs. The SSN-6 SLBM carries a single one megaton warhead with a CEP of 1,300 meters, and it has an SSPK of .56 and a WLS of .73. Having the same areas (radii) of damage as the SSN-5, the SSN-6 has launch and detonation reliability rates of .35 and .65, respectively. In most respects, the SSN-6 is analogous to the SSN-5, particularly insofar as its most likely targeting missions are concerned. Thus, the SSN-6 probably would be assigned to US urban-industrial centers, soft counterforce targets, such as bomber and submarine bases, as well as general purpose forces targets in the continental United States and Western Europe.

SSN-8 The SSN-8 SLBM is deployed on 24 Soviet SSBNs, specifically on *GOLF* III-, *DELTA* I-, DELTA II-, and *HOTEL* III-class boats. The 289 SSN-8s in the USSR's SLBM arsenal each carry one 750 kiloton warhead with a CEP of 1500 meters. Against hard targets, the SSN-8 has an SSPK of .50; moreover, it has launch and detonation reliability rates of .65. The 750 kiloton RV has areas of damage of 181 and 66 square miles for air-bursts and surface-burst, respectively. Again, as an average SLBM in the USSR arsenal, the SSN-8 may be said to be capable of effective targeting against countervalue centers. Thus, like the SSN-5 and SSN-6, the SSN-8 is an appropriate weapon for use in soft urban targeting.

SSN-17 There are only 12 SSN-17 SLBMs deployed in the USSR's arsenal, all on one *YANKEE* II-class SSBN. It carries one 500 kiloton warhead with a CEP of 1,400 meters, and has an SSPK of .54. The 500 kiloton warhead has an area of damage of 145 square miles for air-bursts, and 53 square miles for surface-bursts. In terms of lethal radii, this is equivalent to 6.8 and 4.1 nautical miles for air-bursts and surface-bursts, respectively. And, the SSN-17 has launch and detonation reliability rates of .35 and .7, respectively. Similarly, the SSN-17 would appear to be most appropriate for targeting against soft countervalue centers.

SSN-18 The most modern SLBM in the USSR's arsenal is the SSN-18. There are 160 SSN-18 SLBMs, which are deployed on 11 SSBNs on the *YANKEE* II-, *DELTA* II- and *DELTA* III-class submarines. Each SSN-18, SLBM carries three MIRVed one megaton warheads with a CEP of 1,400 meters, and it has an SSPK of .55. The one megaton warhead has areas of damage for air-bursts and surface-bursts of 227 and 85 square miles, and launch and detonation reliability rates of .65 and .75, respectively. Although the SSN-18 is the most capable in the USSR's force of SLBMs, it clearly does not have the ability to destroy hardened targets—unless, of course, one were to attempt saturation bombing attacks against each such target. One of the logical classes of targets for which the SSN-18 would be suited is soft counterforce targets, including bomber and submarine bases. It also could be a dominant part of a decapitation strike that was targeted against Washington, D.C., and other soft command centers in the United States.

SLBM Vulnerability

In many senses, the vulnerability of Soviet SSBNs, and hence, SLBMs, is roughly analogous to that of the US force, at least in the generic sense. Yet, we can discern several issues that provide critical frameworks for an understanding of the vulnerability of the USSR's submarine fleet.

Perhaps the single greatest dimension of vulnerability is the concentration of SSBNs in port during peacetime, which leaves almost all Soviet SSBNs vulnerable to destruction in an attack against its submarine bases. Using either SLBMs or bombers, the US theoretically could destroy virtually all of the USSR's SSBNs with a relatively insignificant number of warheads. If we assume that 74 SSBNs (i.e., 90 percent) are located in *four* bases, then an equal number of nuclear detonations (four) probably would be sufficient to disable or destroy the Soviet SSBN force. There are a number of reasons that account for the high concentration of SSBNs in Soviet ports. The first is that the USSR's SSBNs are not as sophisticated as their US counterparts, meaning that they are unable to sustain high readiness rates due to reliability problems with their SSBNs and the associated SLBMs. Perhaps a second reason is political: SSBNs on patrol are less controllable than ICBMs or bombers, and hence the Soviets may want to avoid the diffusion of authority over nuclear weapons that SSBNs on patrol imply. Thus, the relative concentration of SSBNs in USSR ports suggests that, if we assume day-to-day alert rates, roughly 90 percent of the SSBN fleet could be put out of commission in a surprise US attack.

If it is difficult to assess the C3 system that links the US NCA and SSBNs on patrol, it is even more difficult to predict the relationship (i.e., the degree of control) that is exercised by the National Defense Council over the Soviet Union's fleet of submarines. However, on a general level we can say that the Soviet command and control system is likely to be less capable. This assertion seems reasonable in view of the technological fragility of the SSBN communication system, and it is but one factor in the apparent decision by the military and political authorities of the USSR to keep a limited number of boats on patrol.

A related issue is the *detectability* of USSR SSBNs. The standard for submarine "invisibility" belongs to the US fleet, which has long been cited as the most quiet and undetectable of SSBNs. Since the vulnerability of SSBNs is principally a function of its ability to remain extremely quiet while on extended patrol, Soviet boats are more vulnerable to US ASW efforts because they are, by and large, far noisier, and thus easier to locate and destroy than their American counterparts. One factor that might mitigate the detectability of Soviet SSBNs would be the theoretical ability either to launch SLBMs quickly once it was clear that the SSBN was being followed or the ability to launch while on the move. For example, if we hypothesize that USSR SSBNs could launch their SLBMs in a shorter period of time than, say, US SSBNs, then the detectability of the SSBNs might decrease by some small, but measurable, amount.[17] This, however, is purely conjectural. The point remains that the SSBN maximizes its vulnerability once it begins to launch SLBMs; once the missiles are launched, the US will have an easier time locating the submarines. Although such an effort at that time would be pointless, unless the SSBN were to launch one missile, move on, and launch another at a much later time.

In any event, it appears that the vulnerability of Soviet SSBNs is a function of their low alert rate, the tenuous connection with the USSR's NCA, and the relative noisiness of the boats. This leads to the conclusion that some of the USSR's SSBNs on patrol may be destroyed by US forces, a possibility that we will explore in the next chapter.

Bomber Force

The final leg of the USSR's triad of nuclear forces is the bomber. In comparison with its ICBMs, the Soviet bomber force is composed primarily of inferior, technically obsolete aircraft—with the exception of the more modern BACKFIRE bomber. Based on the bomber technology of the 1950s and 1960s, the USSR's bombers are both propeller- and jet-driven aircraft. This means that they are relatively slow, and ill suited to the low altitude missions required to penetrate modern defenses. However, since the US lacks an effective air defense system, they pose some threat by virtue of their high-yield weapons. Yet, despite the asymmetry between the capabilities of the Soviet Union's ICBM and bomber forces, the USSR retains the bomber as an active element of its nuclear triad. Accordingly, we will examine each of the bombers (BEAR, BISON, and BACKFIRE) in terms of its attributes, capabilities, and vulnerabilities in order to provide an outline of the general structure of the force. We should note at the outset that, while the information pertaining to the basing of the USSR's bomber force is highly uncertain, we are in general reasonably confident about our estimates of the general capabilities of the bombers. Still there are inadequate references in the public domain as to the location of the bomber bases in the Soviet Union. For further data and an analysis of our assumptions in this model, the reader should refer to the Appendix.

BEAR Bomber Perhaps the oldest and least capable of the Soviet bombers is the BEAR. Of the 105 BEAR bombers in the Soviet force, we have projected that they are deployed at roughly ten bases. Moreover, the BEAR bomber force has been divided into two subgroups: 30 BEAR-A and 75 BEAR-B. The only real difference between the two is that the BEAR-A carries two warheads as opposed to the one warhead on the BEAR-B; for reference, each carries a one megaton warhead that has areas of damage of 227 and 85 square miles for air-bursts and surface-bursts, respectively. It also is estimated that the CEP of the warhead will be extremely low, on the order of 100 meters, which suggests that the warheads on the BEAR-A and BEAR-B bombers have a significant hard-target kill capability. Both the SSPK and OPK for the BEAR bomber are extremely close to 1.00, principally as a result of the ability of a bomber to deliver its warheads very close to the assigned targets. This translates into a clear counterforce capability, as long as we recognize that the bomber is not really able to destroy hard targets on a time-urgent basis.

There is the matter of the launch and detonation reliability of the BEAR bomber force. Admittedly, the US has no significant, much less effective, air defense system—even if we include the handful of fighter-interceptors and peripheral radars that are scattered throughout the continental United States. Thus, while the USSR's bomber force would encounter only minimal interference from US defenses, we chose to assign reliability rates of .8 for launch and .3 for detonation to the BEAR (as well as BISON and BACK-FIRE) bombers. As a result of the decision to select these values for the performance of the bomber, which admittedly is an arbitrary procedure, the aggregate effect of the Soviet bomber force—particularly the BEAR—is reduced to a level that precludes large-scale, effective strikes. One conclusion is that the BEAR bomber would pose only a minimal threat to the US especially in comparison with the capabilities of the Soviet ICBM and SLBM forces.

BISON Bomber The second bomber in the Soviet arsenal is the BISON. Like the BEAR, the BISON carries a one megaton warhead with a CEP of 100 meters. In virtually all respects, the BISON is an analogue of the BEAR—regardless of which attributes one seeks to highlight. We have somewhat arbitrarily assigned the 49 BISON bombers to ten bases in the USSR, thus keeping the bomber force within range of probable US weapons. (See Table 2 for a listing of these bomber bases.) Again, the BISON seems to be configured for the destruction of either counterforce or countervalue targets, as long as the target is not time-urgent. Perhaps the most likely mission for the BISON—and BEAR—is the targeting of urban-industrial centers well into the war—specifically, when the USSR's reserves of ICBMs and SLBMs are almost gone.

BACKFIRE Bomber The last bomber in the USSR's arsenal is the BACK-FIRE, which is the most modern and sophisticated aircraft in the USSR's bomber force. We have assigned the BACKFIRE to a total of six bases in the USSR, using the same assumptions that were outlined above. Many see the BACKFIRE employed principally in the theater roles of anti-naval attacks against US and NATO naval forces. Be this as it may, we suspect that the BACKFIRE could as well be used in strategic nuclear strikes, assuming that the BACKFIRE was supported by aerial refueling. In this mode it is capable of one-way missions to the US with recovery in, say, Cuba. From an operational point of view, the BACKFIRE carries a one megaton warhead with a projected CEP of 100 meters. This yield and CEP ratio would generate very high SSPK and OPK values, and thus present an unambiguous counterforce capability in either a delayed or protracted nuclear war. However, the slow speed of the aircraft suggests that American counterforce targets, such as silos, will be empty before the bombers arrive. Accordingly, the BACK-FIRE probably would be assigned to attack countervalue targets during the later stages of the war.

Bomber Vulnerability

As a soft target, the bomber—whether in flight or at base—is extremely vulnerable to the effects of nearby nuclear detonations. For this reason, the most obvious vulnerability of a bomber is from an attack by SLBMs or cruise missiles that are launched from SSBNs near the coasts. In this case, the Soviet bomber force is vulnerable to US attacks, if we assume that the attack will be composed of SLBMs fired from US submarines on coastal patrol routes. While US SSBNs cannot reduce their flight times to levels that are as low as those of Soviet SSBNs, by virtue of the greater distance from probable launch points to the targets, it is plausible that US ALCMs, which are launched from B-52Ds, could destroy Soviet bombers. To make this scenario realistic, the problem is that we must assume nearly total surprise, an assumption that is difficult to maintain given the magnitude of the Soviet air defense system and the large-scale network of radar warning stations around the perimeter of the Soviet Union.

The other obvious vulnerability of a bomber is its susceptibility to interdiction from air defenses. In the case of Soviet bombers, the most realistic assessment finds that Soviet bombers would face only marginal resistance from US interceptors. The US decision to dismantle its air defenses during the 1960s now means that Soviet bombers, which pose at best only a minor threat to the United States, will not suffer high attrition rates in a penetration attack. Accordingly, it seems that the degree of Soviet bomber vulnerability is significantly less than the vulnerability of the US bomber force. And if we consider that the Soviet bomber force poses such an insignificant threat to the United States, at least in comparison with the threat posed by the USSR's ICBM and SLBM forces, then the dismantlement of the American air defense system probably made good sense.

3

US Counterforce Attack

Nuclear war is perhaps the single most pressing issue in modern times, outranking by a considerable margin concerns about domestic and other international problems. This is entirely proper, for nuclear war threatens to destroy the fabric of modern civilization without regard for the millions who will die a horrible, if not quick, death. Because nuclear war is such a common theme in contemporary thinking, many specialists and non-specialists alike, have speculated about the origins of a nuclear war: who might start it, how it might be started, and most important, why it might begin in the first place. To these and other questions, analysts have posed a variety of answers, most of which we have found to be based on scenarios and assumptions that, in plain language, are just too simplistic or are based on an improbable set of circumstances to provide satisfactory solutions to the question of how such a war might begin. We can never know unambiguously how a nuclear war will start. After all, if we could imagine realistically how a nuclear war might begin, then it is only logical to assume that, armed with such knowledge, a nuclear holocaust could be averted from the start. In this sense, so many of the popular scenarios of nuclear war offer the public, and clearly decision-makers, the fleeting (and false) illusion of thinking that, armed with this "knowledge" of the future, they can avert armageddon. This is a dangerous illusion that should be dispelled, for the "causes" (if you will) of a nuclear war will be a series of nearly transcendent political, military, and psychological factors that are so elusive and fleeting, or perhaps based on such essentially accidental or unexpected events that any planning will be essentially irrelevant. Indeed, there is the prospect that, if the superpowers ever move to the brink of nuclear war, they will do so probably thinking that, by their very actions, they will be able to avoid such a suicidal conflict. War, in this sense, might be upon the superpowers quite literally before they know what has happened. The event, quite possibly, may present itself *de novo* despite our best intellectual and emotional efforts to understand, not to mention sidestep, the maelstrom without being pulled by cataclysmic political and military currents into the war.

On first reaction, this would appear to be based on an entirely pessimistic view of international relations and the human inability to control events. Indeed, it is not hard to discern a Spenglerian twist to the notion that nuclear war—if it is part of our global "destiny," a possibility about which there are no clear or compelling answers—will unfold as part of a complex matrix of events for which there will be no relevant human experience or historical analogue upon which to base our understanding.[1] In a sense, nuclear war might be a historical "naked singularity" in the same way that a black hole is an astrophysical singularity. Indeed, if we were to hold to a true Spenglerian theory of nuclear war, it would imply that, should the unthinkable happen, it will be because it is part of the destiny of mankind. This view is not as simpleminded as crude pessimists or "realists" might aver. Instead, the idea of inexorable and regular violence in international relations has found common expression from the dualistic Augustinian synthesis of the 5th century, wherein mankind was torn between the ethos of the state (which is "evil") and God (which is "good"); to the "fortuna" of Machiavelli, on the proper balance between virtue and power; and the "war of all against all" in the 17th century classic *Leviathan* by the English political theorist Thomas Hobbes. Each thinker, in his own theoretical terms, established the evident relationship between human behavior and the regularity of violence, and did so without explicit reference to the sociological theories of Lorenz, Ardrey, and Tiger and Fox, who argued that violence or aggression is an endemic trait (whether inherited or learned) in man.[2] Thus, when we speak—as we most certainly will—about how a nuclear war might happen and how the superpowers might fight such a war, it is not out of some perverse sense of pessimism. But rather it is with the view that there are ample historical precedents for the occurrence of a nuclear war. This is only to say that there is an appearance of regularity in the incidence of warfare in history. Moreover, if warfare in some way is a regular process, it also is apparent that the scope, range, and destructive power of the event has become asymptotic over time. Stated otherwise, the curve of violence on an historical line rises to infinity, wherein "Doomsday" emerges as a statistical possibility. The Harvard study group on nuclear weapons several years ago asserted that the probability of a nuclear weapon or weapons being employed in a war by 1990–1995 was relatively moderate. Indeed, much the same conclusion was reached by Carl Sagan in *Cosmos*, when he updated Lewis Frye Richardson's *Statistics of Deadly Quarrels*, concluding that a world destroying war could occur sometime around the year 2010, with the usual margin of plus or minus ten years. Still, the only analytic proposition to which we feel bound in this study is that a nuclear war can happen, independent of any general consensus that it ought not to happen.

By definition, once a nuclear war is initiated, the conflict can assume an arbitrarily large number of forms. Whether it is a limited exchange or an all-out nuclear war, in reality we can never know in advance with any reasonable degree of precision what it will be like. It is nonetheless possible to give in general terms a quantified expression of the initial effects of such a war provided, however, that we specify the type of attack and the targets involved. Given the data base available, the characteristics of nuclear weapons, as well as the nature of the targets upon which this study is based, it is possible to provide a rough measure of the prompt effects of a nuclear war. What we will do here is to examine in general form how a counterforce nuclear war might be fought in which US nuclear forces are used against Soviet counterforce (military) targets. In this chapter, we will examine such a war in terms of five discrete targeting phases: ICBM silos, bomber bases, submarine bases, submarines on patrol, and command posts. Clearly, the reality is that a nuclear war against counterforce targets could involve attacks against any or all of these target classes, in a virtually infinite number of patterns or sequences. Since this study is not about the exact shape of nuclear war, we contend that the results of this study will reveal the general consequences of a counterforce attack against the USSR in a level of detail that is sufficient for a general understanding of such a conflict. It really does not matter whether such a war follows the path we outline here; it is essential only that the analysis be robust enough to support the conclusion that this would be the basic result of such a war. Whatever the sequence of events in a nuclear war, from a limited number of nuclear countersilo strikes, to an attack that involves all conceivable counterforce targets, we think that this study will provide an outline for a comprehensive understanding of what may happen. To be specific, it is not the sequence of the targeting in a war but the results that ultimately are important for those who think about the consequences of a counterforce nuclear war. This, then, is an analysis of the results of our model of nuclear counterforce attacks that are explicitly independent of specific scenarios. We believe that this will contribute to an understanding of a nuclear war that is equally neutral and dispassionate and that does not become enmeshed in a debate about the fine details of a particular scenario that provokes a nuclear conflict. In effect, once such a war begins, we could argue that the cause will be reduced to the level of a mere historical triviality.

There are to be sure a number of ways by which a nuclear war might begin. A few are:

—The Soviets might become pressured by the "scissors curve effect." That is, they now possess a strategic edge in counterforce capabilities with some chance to destroy most if not all US ICBMs in a preemptive attack. This is to say that their counterforce capabilities have exceeded ours and that they perceive a strategic advantage or superiority. Countervailing their momentary edge is the potential represented by the US MX program and the Strategic Defense Initiative which, if successful, in a few years will neutralize their expensively achieved superiority. Here "use it or lose it" may take over and repeat "The Guns of August" syndrome.

—War could begin at sea from a reenactment of the "Bedford Incident" syndrome where a nuclear-armed ASROC (torpedo) is launched accidentally against a Soviet submarine. Also, since SSBNs have independent launch authority, circumstances might permit or even dictate an SLBM launch if the submarine commander believes he is in imminent danger of attack and destruction.

—A terrorist-activated nuclear detonation in either a large US or Soviet city could be so camouflaged as to make it appear that one of the two major antagonists was the perpetrator.

—Increasing proliferation of nuclear weapons among lesser powers makes general control nearly impossible, with the Mideast as the likely place for next use.

There are of course other possibilities. But such a range of hypotheticalities cannot detain us here, since from the available evidence we can discern no clear way of predicting how a nuclear war might begin, expand, or be controlled. What we can do is propose workable damage-limiting steps that are designed to limit the costs of any strategic nuclear exchange between the United States and the Soviet Union. These will be considered in Chapter 7.

At the distant edges of our imagination, the first evidence of a nuclear war will come to us as a series of intense bursts of light from either space-based bursts over the United States that are to disrupt the US C3 system with EMP, or from nuclear explosions on the horizon against the nearest nuclear target, which is the SAC bomber base at Pease AFB in Portsmouth, NH. The war probably will not begin with attacks against American cities, nor do we imagine that the war will be close to us—how common it is for humans to think that the worst will happen far away from them. We imagine that the war will begin at night—which is daytime in the USSR—probably for the simple ethnocentric reason that it is more conceivable that the Soviets, rather than the United States, would start such a war in the first place. Hardly rigorous or penetrating in its analytic scope or depth, this nevertheless is what we and others imagine when and if we think about the "unthinkable." Nuclear war, in all its horror and destruction, will come to many of us as a series of distant, iridescent bursts of incredibly bright white light—launched in all likelihood by Soviet submarines off the coast. (For those immediately under the fireball, obliteration will be instantaneous.) And if this vision is correct, then in an incredibly short time, both the power and havoc of a nuclear war will be upon us with all its fury, as we, the helpless and hapless observers of armageddon watch the beginnings of the end. It is no less fitting, therefore, that we should attempt to examine this vision of the end of civilization for, from a theoretical perspective, what we say here will in reality be more detailed than what will be known after the war. The cruel paradox is that some of those who will know for certain just what happened will be among the first to die.

For this reason, the task before us is audacious, for we seek to know a future that few will see or be able to recount with any degree of accuracy. Perhaps some among us us might find solace in the thought that to step imaginatively into the void of the unknown carries few risks. Who, for instance, can challenge our description of a nuclear war that has never been fought? How can we be challenged as optimists or pessimists—or simply publicists—for looking into a future catastrophe when few among us have seen even one nuclear explosion, much less thousands of nuclear "events"? (One of the authors, Savage, was a witness to the detonation of a 60 kiloton nuclear warhead in 1953 in the West. He was in a trench 3000 meters from ground zero.) Thus, while a few have seen test detonations of nuclear weapons, nothing in these isolated experiences possibly can compare with what will unfold here. Thus, we make no pretense about the fact that we may be entirely wrong in our judgments as to how a nuclear war will be fought.[3] All we seek to do is present an account of what in general we think may happen in a nuclear war. Right or wrong, it seems likely that few will be able to contest our sketch of the end. Even if we are ultimately wrong by several orders of magnitude in this projection of the shape of the war (such as off by half in the number of impacting warheads) the naked reality of thermonuclear war will exceed anything presented here. Despite this element of uncertainty in our analysis, the awful reality of a thermonuclear war will be so great that it will be incomprehensible to those who happen to survive.

With these thoughts as an introduction, let us proceed into an analysis of a large-scale American counterforce nuclear attack against the USSR. And in the next chapter, we will examine in detail the effects of a Soviet counterforce strike against the United States.

Sequence of Events

Before we proceed into an analysis of the structure of a US counterforce attack against the Soviet Union, some thought must be given to the sequence of events. While many prefer to think—albeit superficially—that an understanding of an actual nuclear war will emerge as the product of thousands of crescively interacting factors within a relatively short time, there is the risk that considerable detail can be lost in the "fog" of events. In order to avoid this type of distortion, nuclear war, in this case, a counterforce nuclear war, will be examined in terms of the results of five discrete types of targeting activity concerning the mechanics of hitting different types of targets.[4] In this model, we have defined the nuclear forces of the Soviet Union into five operational (and, therefore, targetable) categories: command, control and communication (C3) targets; ICBM fields; submarine bases; bomber bases;

and submarines on patrol in the Atlantic and Pacific Oceans. Not by coinci-
dence, this list provides the basic order of events in the American attack
against Soviet counterforce targets, and parenthetically, in the Soviet attack
against US counterforce targets in Chapter 4.

There is a considerable risk in using this sort of typology because it suggests implicitly that these are the only targets in a counterforce nuclear war,
or worse that we can distinguish a counterforce from a countervalue war.
This is hardly the case. Although it is recognized that a nuclear war against
even "pure" counterforce targets probably will involve the destruction of
general purpose forces targets (such as conventional army, navy, and air
force bases in the Soviet Union or the Warsaw Pact nations) as well as
numerous collateral civilian areas, in this study we have concentrated explicitly on strategic nuclear counterforce targets. In a theoretical sense, this
approach admittedly simplifies the analysis of a nuclear war inasmuch as we
did not have to deal in the model with the complexities of targeting hundreds of conventional forces bases.[5] But it is to be emphasized that the point
here is to examine the heart of the matter, which is the destruction of the
primary, strategic nuclear forces that are deployed in a crescent-shaped
swath throughout the eight million square miles of the Soviet Union.

Some would direct the criticism that the cardinal error in this model is the
assumption that it is "reality," or that this model of nuclear war compels us
to think strictly in terms of its own internal structure and logic, such that the
model creates a compelling (or necessary) view of reality.[6] Still others would
argue that a nuclear war is in reality a series of events, which by their very
nature are so complex that it is not possible to anticipate what a nuclear war
will be like. There is substantial truth in both of these positions, for each
urges that studies of nuclear war be viewed with a heightened sense of
caution. Each suggests that, at best, a study of this nature ought to be
conservative in its estimates, both as to the sequence of events and the
effects of nuclear targeting. To be frank, we have tried to maintain a position
of strict neutrality. We do not assume that this is what a US counterforce
attack against the Soviet Union will be like, for in reality the US might strike
any combination of Soviet targets in an order that is quite different from that
which is proposed in this study. While in this particular analysis, strikes
against Soviet C3 targets are followed by strikes against ICBM fields, a US
attack might concentrate only on bomber bases or submarine bases. This
certainly is an unlikely possibility, yet the power of this model is derived
from the fact that the reader can mix scenarios against these five target
classes in any order desired. The effect is *roughly* the same, for it produces
the same general consequences of a counterforce nuclear war that we will
outline here. Neither do we advance this analysis, model, or vision of the
future, if such a future occurs, as a recommendation for the strategy of
nuclear "war-fighting," nor do we suggest any particular nuclear strategy.[7]
Since strategy is a "rational" use of influence, power (in many dimensions

other than military), and naked military force in pursuit of national interests, the use of thermonuclear weapons even at limited thresholds never will fit the sensible definition of political rationality. This, of course, in no way limits the fact that they may be used as we have observed. To this end, we think this study is eminently useful.

Nor, on the other hand, do we assume that the results of this study are necessarily correct, that the effect of a US strike against, say, Soviet ICBM fields will be as predicted here. What this model provides is a notional *outline* of the broad consequences of scenarios of a counterforce nuclear war. Any number of variables, such as the failure of extraordinarily complex weapons, could increase or decrease significantly the number of warheads that ultimately detonate, all of which could alter the outcome of the war. Thus, any number of variables could cause this assessment of US counterforce capabilities to shift in numerous and unexpected directions. Accepting this as much more than a remote theoretical possibility, in this study we have proceeded to look in detail at a future that few (ourselves included) seek to know.

SOVIET COMMAND, CONTROL, AND COMMUNICATIONS TARGETS

As this is an unclassified study of nuclear war, we are not reticent to admit from the outset that very little is known about the structure or organization of the Soviet Union's command and control systems for nuclear—much less its conventional—forces. The highly sensitive nature of the Soviet Union's C3 network means that a study of this type will not be able to address many of the more fundamental questions about scenarios for the destruction of the Soviet command system.

In nuclear jargon, decapitation is a term that, surfacing in the late 1970s, came to signify the destruction of the "head" of the command and control system that directs nuclear forces in a war.[8] Given the apparent popularity and topicality of the option, it is quite easy to say that, for a number of reasons, decapitation has become an important policy option for the United States in a counterforce exchange. First, the destruction of Soviet C3 targets suggests that, after the initial onslaught, the very nature and structure of nuclear retaliation will be altered in fundamental, yet largely unknown, ways. After the elimination of Soviet C3 centers, it is at least conceivable that Soviet retaliation would be less effective—and thereby less threatening to the United States—than it otherwise would be in comparison with the retaliation that could occur with a fully functional and intact C3 system. The second possibility that is inherent in nuclear decapitation, however, presents a picture of a future that is somewhat less than appealing. It is that decapitation may mean the uncontrolled release of Soviet nuclear forces over an indeterminate length of time against some mix of counterforce and countervalue targets in the United States. Thus, a weakening of the Soviet Union's ability to control its retaliation effectively may cause a nuclear war to shift uncontrollably and decisively to the civilian slaughter that a counterforce attack sought to avoid in the first place. Whether it is prudent to attack Soviet C3 targets, therefore, is a question that properly should plague American policymakers, if only because the possible benefits of decapitation are as appealing as the costs are horrifying.[9] A tangentially related question that ought to be raised here, which poses a troubling prospect, is whether Soviet subordinate missile "wing" commanders or discrete missile field complexes have independent launch authority, if, say, communications are suddenly severed with the Soviet Strategic Rocket Force staff or the National Defense Council in Moscow. We mention this possibility only because there have been frequent references in the defense literature to the fact that American and Soviet SLBM commanders have independent launch authority on a collegial basis, if and only if it was unambiguously apparent that communications with the command centers had been severed for some predetermined length of time. In this circumstance the presumption would be that these command centers had been obliterated by a US nuclear attack.

Seeing that the destruction of Soviet C3 targets is more than an ephemeral or casual American targeting alternative for the 1980s and beyond, then logically we ought to consider the mechanics of this problem in our study. Yet, the data on the Soviet C3 system are woefully imcomplete. Still, based on a small number of sources on Soviet command and control, we can infer that the Soviet Union has roughly 200–700 command centers in locations ranging from Moscow to deep underground complexes in the Ural Mountains, not to mention probable dummy installations. Some sources, for instance, place upwards of 80 such targets in the Moscow region alone, which signifies that there is a high probability that Moscow will be destroyed in a nuclear war even if the war is limited strictly to counterforce targets. And, to further complicate the matter of targeting command centers, it is easy to infer that each command center by itself is expendable due to the redundancy of the command network: that no one command center or communication complex constitutes a critical node in the system. In this way, the destruction of any given target, or theoretical combination thereof, is not likely to have a significantly debilitating effect on the ability of the Soviet Union to execute a retaliatory strike. In a word, what we have is a situation in which the secrecy and complexity of the topic, by necessity, means that unclassified studies can shed little, if any, light on the subject.

From the perspective of this study, our dilemma is that we cannot ignore the possibility of decapitation; nor, can we make any claims about the verisimilitude or reliability of our data. With these not so insignificant caveats in mind, it still seems useful to attempt to establish the general boundaries of the problem. Accordingly, in this computer model of nuclear war, the critical assumption is that there are hundreds of second-order command centers in the Soviet Union, in which the loss of any particular command center will not materially affect the execution of a nuclear war. These are the "survival" centers for the Soviet Union's political (party), industrial, technical, and managerial elites; there are estimates that as many as 100,000 people can be accommodated—as opposed to *protected*—in these shelters. This network of secondary Soviet command centers did not affect the computational basis of the model, as we attributed this subset of the C3 target base to theoretical indeterminancy on the grounds that there is no available evidence to suggest otherwise.

This model, however, does contain provisions for the possibility that the US might seek to target what we call *primary* C3 targets: command centers that clearly will affect the shape and outcome of a nuclear exchange in significant—if not clearly understood—ways. From an intellectual perspective, the assumption is that there are command centers in the Soviet Union whose destruction will alter the ability of the USSR to retain control over its nuclear forces. Although in reality the precise location or number of these command centers is unknown, we have assumed that there might be five (the number five was chosen for purely arbitrary reasons, for there might be 1, 10 or 100) primary command centers in the Soviet Union. These were designated as the Military Command, Political Command, Recovery Command, Soviet Defense Council, and Air Defense Command, as shown in Table 3. To be explicit, the precise function of these targets in the model is to provide *notional* examples of the structure of the Soviet command and control system. While we more than suspect that these examples are not sufficient by themselves to provide an understanding of the USSR's command system, it is possible to give a reasonably accurate portrayal of the possible consequences of decapitation.

In terms of the effect on the model of the destruction of these C3 centers, we simply could not postulate their level of connectivity with Soviet nuclear forces. Moreover, while it is safe to assume that these are relatively hard targets, there are no data on their hardness. To compensate for this sketchy information, the destruction of these targets was predicated on at least ten surface-burst detonations. The assumption is that even the hardest of targets would not survive an attack that involved several proximate, surface-burst nuclear explosions.

In this analysis, the assumption is that this set of Soviet C3 centers was attacked by a squadron of B-52s, armed with ALCMs (air-launched cruise missiles). As shown in Tables 1 and 3, the ALCM has a 200 KT warhead and a CEP on the order of 100 meters. It is hypothesized that this yield/CEP combination would be sufficient for the destruction of these Soviet command centers, particularly in view of the fact that in this computer "run," roughly twelve warheads detonated sequentially on the targets. The discerning analyst might note that the B-52 is a curious delivery system for the destruction of such time-urgent, critical counterforce targets given the relatively slow

Table 3
US Attack on Soviet Command Centers

Target	US Weapon	No.	Total	Detonations	Yield	City	Casualties
Sovad Command	B52D	3	36	12	200KT	Chelyabinsk	1,205,000
Pres. Command	B52D	3	36	12	200KT	Moscow	8,400,000
Mil. Command	B52D	3	36	12	200KT	Volograd	1,210,000
Attack Command	B52D	3	36	12	200KT	Vologda	----------
Pol. Command	B52D	3	36	12	200KT	Irkutsk	550,000
Total		15	180	60			11,365,000

speed of the bomber and its ALCMs. Since, however, these C3 targets would be attacked in close conjunction with the attack on the Soviet Union's ICBM fields, and given the shortage of hard-target kill warheads in the US arsenal, we allocated the available resources to the more critical strikes against the USSR's ICBM silos. One rather crude reason for this allocation decision was that a C3 target literally won't shoot back if it is not destroyed, while an ICBM silo most certainly will. In any event, others may select different options in this phase of the counterforce campaign for reasons of speed and time-to-target. Yet, in deliberately identifying this action as an overt instance when an undesirable option may have negative consequences (e.g., the Soviets may be able to order a more effective retaliatory strike before the ALCMs reach the command centers), this will serve to highlight the generic class of decisions in nuclear war that hardly may be described as optimal. And as an exemplar of a sub-optimal targeting decision, we hope to illustrate one instance of the inflexibility of the US arsenal in the limited case of counterforce operations.

Once the concept of surface-bursts on C3 targets is introduced as an important element of these nuclear attacks, the nature of the war shifts quite radically toward large-scale civilian destruction, as will be shown. While the entire underground and hardened complex at any C3 target may not be obliterated completely, the resultant deep craters almost certainly will disrupt Soviet communications, including the destruction of the armored underground communication cables that the Soviets may have installed. In terms of targeting optimality, this tactic makes perfect—if only limited— sense. But the immediate post-attack consequences of using surface-bursts is that it will generate prodigious amounts of radioactive fallout, in amounts that are roughly proportional to the yield of the warhead (and therefore the volume of the crater at the point of detonation). It is this fallout that, if we are to judge from available historical data, is the most injurious to those populations who are not exposed to the prompt effects of the nuclear blast. The fallout will contaminate large areas downwind of the explosion, including urban and agricultural areas.

How we calculate the collateral casualties that will result from an attack against Soviet C3 centers bears some explanation. Since we assumed that these C3 targets would be located near or (in some instances) within large Soviet cities—an assumption that, again, is purely arbitrary—the obvious effect is to create large civilian casualties. The population of Moscow alone, which is in excess of eight million, is calculated as a direct loss in the attack against the command centers in Moscow. Some will observe that this assumption has the obvious effect of increasing Soviet casualties beyond what might in reality be the case. To this extent, these estimates of the total Soviet casualties that would result from an American attack against Soviet C3 centers may be of the worst-case variant. In this series of calculations, total Soviet losses were in excess of 11 million, a figure which, not coincidentally and somewhat tautologically, equals the total population of the five Soviet cities (Moscow, Chelyabinsk, Volgograd, Vologda, and Irkutsk) that were selected for the location of the C3 centers. This estimate, therefore, may be an order of magnitude larger than the actual Soviet collateral losses that would be sustained in an American strike against C3 targets; or conversely, the actual casualties may be far greater if—as seems reasonable—the US attacks the Soviet C3 centers that are scattered in a large number of cities throughout the nation. For example, if we were to assume that the SIOP lists more than 700 elite centers in the USSR, then the physical destruction of these centers would create far higher losses over time than we have projected here due to the prolonged effects of radiation, not to mention the prompt blast-induced casualties that are projected here.

From the perspective of this study, we have deliberately sought to avoid the pernicious effect of minimizing or maximizing the losses that would result from an attack on Soviet C3 centers. Using this model as only a rough approximation of the consequences of "C3-busting" nuclear attack, the evidence suggests that these calculations are probably quite realistic—especially since an actual attack might generate roughly 10–15 million or more casualties if the hundreds of C3 centers that are dispersed throughout the USSR were attacked. For now, we are content to rest with these figures until such time as there are more conclusive (and unclassified) data for the use in the model. In that case it would be interesting to restructure this scenario using ICBMs or SLBMs, or perhaps the NATO Pershing II IRBMs (intermediate-range ballistic missiles), for clearly, there are a number of alternative targeting options that might be examined.

In summary, the United States used a total of 15 B-52 bombers with 180 ALCMs (although, due to the attrition by Soviet air defenses, only 60 reached their targets) to destroy the five designated primary C3 centers in the Soviet Union. At this point in the war, prompt (i.e., less than 30 days after the attack) casualties in the Soviet Union are in the vicinity of 15 million. If the war were to stop at this stage of hostilities, the Soviet Union would have sustained a level of casualties that approaches 5 percent of its population. Yet so much more remains to be done in a large-scale counterforce nuclear war.

SOVIET ICBM FIELDS: COUNTERSILO STRIKES

By most contemporary standards, the ICBM is the ultimate strategic weapon in the American and Soviet nuclear arsenals. As a measure of the importance of the ICBM, one need only consider the public debate that surfaced in the late 1970s and early 1980s regarding the deleterious effects of ICBM vulnerability on political and strategic stability. From the domain of presidential politics to the esoterica of debates by the nuclear experts, the ICBM always has been the central *leitmotif* of the concepts of survivability, war-fighting, first-strike attacks, and so forth. In many real and imagined senses, a relatively telling and powerful history of the nuclear age could be constructed by focusing on the status of the ICBM in both American and Soviet strategic thought. It should be no real surprise that recent Soviet advances in ICBM warhead guidance technologies and the MIRVing of the missile payload would cause a sensation in the United States over the theoretical vulnerability of US ICBMs in a Soviet first-strike attack. If this still theoretical Soviet capability were to become a fundamental and inexorable element of nuclear deterrence, there would be catastrophic consequences for the United States, as well as a degradation in the stability of nuclear deterrence and the geopolitical balance of power. All that had been accomplished in the past decades to lend a measure of crisis stability to the nuclear balance would vanish in a blur of technological progress. And worse yet, perceptions of the global balance of power, the durability of nuclear politics, and fundamental rules of the nuclear stalemate which had provided the basis for international stability for more than 40 years and during numerous crises, would be transformed forever. At the risk of sounding cavalier, let us say that things would go terribly astray in the nuclear arena.

Yet, during all the agitation that surrounded this debate over the vulnerability of US nuclear forces—recognizing that some dismissed the ability of the Soviet Union to execute a successful large-scale, countersilo strike for a number of technical reasons—the truly fundamental question never really had been asked: What could the United States achieve in a hypothetical first-strike attack against the ICBM fields in the Soviet Union? Perhaps one of the basic reasons for the failure to address this basic question was the all-consuming nature of the US ICBM vulnerability debate, whose advocates, in their fascination with countering the arguments of the opposition, somehow forgot to think about the countersilo capabilities of the United States. We, however, will not let this issue go unanswered. Here we will examine the structure of an American attack against the USSR's ICBM silos in order to determine, as precisely as possible, the dimensions of Soviet ICBM vulnerability. And even more important, this will provide an assessment of the second phase of a counterforce nuclear war that is launched by the United States.

Perhaps the most intriguing aspect about the question of US countersilo capabilities is the exact utilization of US nuclear forces in a countersilo attack. Unlike the USSR, which theoretically could attack American ICBM silos with a relatively small fraction of its ICBM force (see Chapter 4 for more details), the finding in this study is that the US must use not only all of its 1,000 land-based ICBMs, but a large percentage of its 684 SLBMs and 365 bombers as well. The significance of this finding is that a credible, high-confidence US countersilo strike would require the use of a significant fraction of the entire US strategic nuclear arsenal—remembering that these calculations are based partially on the presumption that the force would be subjected to relatively high attrition rates. In any event, in this model of counterforce operations, we have allocated US ICBMs, SLBMs, and bombers against Soviet missile fields. Therefore, this section is divided into three phases that correspond to the type of launch vehicle that is used. In reality, however, an operation of this type would be closely coordinated for, in reality, the three phases would occur as part of a more or less simultaneous wave of RVs. In other words, while we have divided a countersilo operation into three phases in this analysis, this is not to blur the fact that the actual campaign would occur in a salvo that might extend over perhaps several hours.

Phase I: ICBM Strikes

In the first phase of this hypothetical counterforce attack on the USSR's ICBM fields, the US ICBM force of 1,000 missiles (we have excluded the 52 Titan II ICBMs from this phase because of its extremely low probability of kill against hard silos) was allocated against seven missile fields in the USSR. As shown in Table 4, US ICBMs will strike roughly 629 Soviet ICBM silos at the Dombarovskiy, Tatischevo, Aleysk, Yedrovo, Kartaly, Kostroma, and Pervomaysk missile fields. For reference, the data in Table 4 are arrayed in descending order of the target's potential lethality: the first field (Dombarovskiy) contains the SS-18M4 ICBM, which poses the greatest countersilo threat to the United States.[10] To be consistent, in Phase I the US ICBM force was allocated so that the most lethal American missiles would be assigned to hit the most threatening Soviet target silos. For instance, in this analysis we assigned the Minuteman IIIA ICBM to attack the USSR's SS-18M4 ICBM silos. A salvo of 155 MMIIIA missiles with a total of 465 RVs was assigned to strike this force of 175 SS-18M4 ICBMs. Of the 465 MMIIIA RVs, 351 actually detonated at the targets, which translates into an allocation scheme of "two-on-one" (two RVs for each target silo in the USSR). Further, the first group of 150 MMIIIAs had an attrition rate of 24.3 percent, i.e., 75.7 percent of the 450 RVs theoretically detonated at the silos. In the second group of 5 MMIIIA missiles, 66.6 percent of the RVs (10) actually detonated at the silos. Since we are concerned with an approximate picture of the collateral casualties that would result from this hypothetical attack, it is important to note that the primary collateral city in this attack is Orsk, which has a population of 247,000 (1980 population). Given that the RVs in the attack against the Dombarovskiy missile field were programmed to detonate as surface-bursts, it is assumed that the resultant cloud of radioactive fallout would contaminate the city of Orsk.[11] If, at the time of the attack, there are winds of average speed and direction, then the population of Orsk will be counted as immediate collateral casualties. Some 50 percent of the 247,000 people most probably will be fatalities, and the remainder will be casualties. Thus, what we have in this limited example of a US countersilo

Table 4
US Attack on Soviet ICBM Fields

Target	ICBM	No.	US Weapon	No.	Total	Detonations	Yield	City	Casualties
Dombarovskiy	SS18M4	175	MMIIIA	155	465	351	335KT	Orsk	247,000
Tatischevo	SS19M2	100	MMIIIA	88	264	201	335KT	Saratov	1,075,000
Aleysk	SS18M3	26	MMIIIA	24	72	53	335KT	Barnaul	600,000
Yedrovo	SS17M2	20	MMIIIA	19	57	43	335KT	Vologda	237,000
Kartaly	SS18M2	15	MMIIIA	14	42	30	335KT	Kustanay	164,000
	SS18M2	92	MMIIIB	122	366	275	170KT		
Kostroma	SS17M1	97	MMIIIB	128	384	293	170KT	Gorkiy	1,875,000
	SS17M1	63	MMII	272	272	193	1MT		
Pervomaysk	SS19M1	41	MMII	178	178	127	1MT	Kirovograd	237,000
	SS19M1	99			660	297	100KT		
Kozelsk	SS19M1	140	TRIDENT	94	940	424	100KT	Tula	610,000
Teykovo	SS11M3	55	TRIDENT	38	380	176	100KT	Ivanovo	465,000
Perm	SS11M3	82	TRIDENT	54	540	248	100KT	Perm	1,075,000
	SS11M3	3	POSEIDON	5	50	24	40KT		
Derazhyna	SS11M3	55	POSEIDON	65	650	288	40KT	N/A	
Svobodnyy	SS11M3	55	POSEIDON	65	650	288	40KT	Blagoveshensk	172,000
Drovyanaya	SS11M3	110	POSEIDON	127	1270	576	40KT	Chita	302,000
Zhangiz Tobe	SS11M3	79	POSEIDON	91	910	408	40KT	U.Kemenogorsk	274,000
	SS11M3	5	POLARIS	80	80	30	600KT		
	SS11M3	26	B52A	16	192	43	200KT		
Yoshkar Ola	SS13	60	B52A	23	276	61	200KT	Kazan	1,040,000
Total		1398		1724	8688	4429			8,374,000

attack against one important, yet relatively small, field of 175 Soviet ICBMs
is a composite picture of the allocation of US weapons against Soviet silos, as
well as the attrition rates, the number of Soviet missiles destroyed, and the
projected level of Soviet collateral civilian losses. From this example alone,
one begins to gain an appreciation of the wealth of data that can be derived
from an austere model of a counterforce nuclear war.

But what of the rest of the results in Phase I? As shown in Table 4,
Minuteman IIIA ICBMs were assigned to strike 100 SS-19M2 ICBMs at the
Tatischevo base, 26 SS-18M3 ICBMs at the Aleysk base, 20 SS-17M2
ICBMs at the Yedrovo field, and 15 of the 107 SS-18M2 ICBMs at the
Kartaly missile field. In all of these strikes, it was assumed that the RVs
would be detonated as surface-bursts, and that there would be extensive
collateral civilian casualties at the primary cities, also as indicated in Table 4.
Next, 250 MMIIIB ICBMs were assigned to attack 92 SS-18M2 ICBMs at
the Kartaly field, and 97 of the 160 SS-17M1 ICBMs at the Kostroma missile
base. Finally, 450 MMII ICBMs (from the Davis-Monthan, Little Rock, and
McConnell Air Force Bases in the United States) were assigned to strike 63
of the 160 SS17M1 ICBMs at the Kostroma field, and 41 of the 140 SS-19M1
ICBMs at the Pervomaysk field in the USSR.

As an overview of Phase I, we found that 629 Soviet ICBMs (45 percent of
the 1,398 ICBMs in the Soviet arsenal) were destroyed. In this attack the
United States launched a force of 1,000 ICBMs in which 1,566 RVs detonated out of a total attacking force of 2,100 RVs, which means that approximately 75 percent of US ICBM RVs actually detonated at the target silos in
allocation schemes of two-on-one and three-on-one. In this attack the USSR
lost 45 percent (629) of its ICBMs and 4,435,000 collateral civilian casualties,
of which roughly 50 percent will be counted as fatalities as a result of the
deposition of post-attack radioactive fallout on Soviet cities. The following
Soviet cities were projected to be affected directly in this American attack:
Orsk, Saratov, Barnaul, Vologda, Kustanay, Gorkiiy, and Kirovograd. In
effect, this countersilo attack translates into the loss of 1.6 percent of its
population and a higher proportion of the USSR's economic potential from
the first phase of a countersilo attack by the US, and does not include many
of the smaller cities and towns that inevitably would be contaminated by the
fallout. These Soviet civilian losses will increase shortly as will be seen when
we examine the results of Phase II.

Phase II: SLBM Strikes

The most distinguishing feature of Phase II in the American countersilo
attack against the USSR that otherwise would be quite similar to the first
phase, is that it was executed by US SLBMs. For some, this is a paradoxical,
not to mention strange, turn of events given that the SLBM typically has
been thought of as a countervalue ("city-busting") weapon. It was the Ger-

man statesman, Helmut von Moltke (the elder) who argued that no plan lasts even for the first few hours of battle. Indeed, this observation is appropriate for, the present scenario notwithstanding, few strategists would expect the United States to use SLBMs against hard targets, such as ICBM silos, in a large-scale counterforce attack. Perhaps this approach would not have been necessary if we had used lower attrition rates in the ICBM phase of the countersilo attack. Even if the attrition rates were significantly lower, the present US ICBM force still would not be numerically sufficient for targeting the nearly 1,400 silos in the USSR. Under the best of circumstances, a perfect two-on-one countersilo attack against the 1,400 Soviet silos theoretically would require 2,800 RVs, which is 700 more than the 2,100 RVs on the US Minuteman force. So, once we assume that there will be a reasonable level of failure when these operationally untested mechanisms are launched, then it becomes increasingly apparent that the SLBMs will have to be used against Soviet silos. More important, despite the fact that it is obviously undesirable to use SLBMs in attacks against hard targets, it may be difficult for the United States to avoid this tactic if it expects to destroy the entire Soviet ICBM force. Perhaps it is the uncertainty of using the SLBMs in this mode that forms the basis for the systemic pessimism that surrounds estimates about the ability of the United States to destroy the critical counterforce targets in the USSR. But more of this later.

If we recall that the first phase of the countersilo operations concluded with the theoretical destruction of 629 Soviet ICBMs, in Phase II we will be concerned with targeting 683 Soviet ICBMs using a mix of Trident, Poseidon, and Polaris SLBMs. The American SLBM attack will be launched against varying numbers of SS-19M1 and SS-11M3 ICBMs that are arrayed in eight missile fields in the USSR. While, in reality, the attacks in the SLBM phase would be waged simultaneously with Poseidon, Trident, and Polaris SLBM, we will examine the results of this targeting scheme in a sequential fashion, beginning with the Trident phase of the attack.

One illustrative example, as is shown in Table 4, is the SLBM attack on 140 SS-19M1 ICBMs in the Kozelsk field. Approximately 94 Trident C-4 SLBMs, each of which carries ten 100 kiloton RVs, were launched against this field. Given the expected launch and detonation attrition rates of the Trident, 424 of the 940 RVs actually would detonate at the targets, i.e., roughly 45 percent of the Trident RVs would operate as we might expect. In view of the probability of kill and WLS of the Trident RVs, this attack would involve a three-on-one allocation scheme (three RVs per ICBM silo), that clearly would pose a number of difficulties for the planner. It seems, for instance, that the timing interval would have to be arranged carefully in order to allow three RVs to hit one silo without encountering the effects of warhead fratricide. Thus, it is assumed that the RVs would be targeted in a south-to-north pattern in a sequential fashion, so that each RV lands north of the preceding one to minimize fratricidal effects. In any event, we anticipate that some will raise the argument that three-on-one allocation schemes would be difficult, if not impossible, to execute successfully in a nuclear war. The counter argument, however, is that three-on-one attacks are not neces- sarily impractical as long as it is realized that this will increase the amount of time required for the execution of the attack because the attacker must increase the time (or the spacing) between the incoming RVs.

In the Pervomaysk and Kozelsk missile fields, the target silos contain SS-19M1 ICBMs, and in the Teykovo and Perm ICBM fields there are SS-11M3 ICBMs. In a comprehensive Trident SLBM attack, approximately 252 Trident SLBMs would be launched, translating into an attack by nearly 2,500 RVs. If one looks at the attrition rate in the overall strike with the Trident, the overall rate of loss approaches 55 percent. This relatively high attrition rate can be attributed primarily to the lower level of readiness of the SSBN force, and the generally lower reliability of the SLBMs that, on the whole, are not considered to be either as reliable or dependable as the land-based ICBM leg of the triad. In operational terms, the consequences are stark: the necessity of using SLBMs results in a very high level of attrition for US nuclear forces.

In summary, the Trident phase of the SLBM attack against Soviet ICBM silos involved the destruction of 376 USSR missile silos. And, in terms of collateral civilian losses, the USSR would sustain in excess of 2 million casualties, of which 50 percent (1 million) probably will be immediate (short term) fatalities. For reference, as shown in Table 4, the primary collateral cities in the Soviet Union are Tula (population: 610,000), Ivanovo (population: 465,000), and Perm (population: 1,075,000). It is certain that the detonation of more than 1,100 100 KT surface-bursts would inflict heavy casualties on the collateral civilian populations in the Soviet Union, in fact probably far in excess of these projections.

The second part of Phase II in SLBM targeting concerns the use of the Poseidon SLBMs, each of which has ten 40 KT warheads. The target in the Poseidon campaign will be 264 SS-11M3 ICBMs in the following four ICBM bases: Derazhyna, Svobodnyy, Drovyanaya, and Zhangiz Tobe, all of which were targeted by a total force of 336 Poseidon SLBMs. Although the Poseidon has a similar attrition rate to the Trident, the lower probability of kill and WLS of the Poseidon indicates that the targeting allocation scheme will be on the order of four-on-one. The difficulties that are implicit in such an attack are clearly formidable—especially in comparison with the already tenuous three-on-one allocation plan for the Trident. In a typical attack, such as against the Drovyanaya field, 124 Poseidon SLBMs were launched; of this number, 576 RVs detonated in each of the fields that contain 85 silos, for an effective five-on-one targeting scheme. The launch and detonation attrition rates in this strike were approximately 45 percent. Most important, in this attack by the Poseidon SLBMs, a total of 302 Soviet ICBMs were destroyed. We note that the Poseidon SLBM, which typically is considered to be a countervalue weapon, might be used to destroy the SS-11M3, which also happens to be well suited for strikes against countervalue targets in the United States. This phase of the countersilo attack involved more than 3,300 Poseidon RVs, yet only 1,584 Poseidon RVs actually detonated at the silos, which translates into a 45 percent success rate. From the Soviet perspective, this phase of the SLBM attack resulted in more than 700,000 casualties in the cities of Blagoveshensk, Chita, and Ust Kemenogorsk, half of whom would be expected to die quite shortly.

The last phase of the SLBM attack involves the use of the Polaris missile, of which a total of 80 Polaris SLBMs were launched against a handful of silos in the Zhangiz Tobe missile field that contains SS-11M3 ICBMs. Given the failure rate of the Polaris, as well as its relatively low probability of kill and WLS values against hard targets, the strike resulted in an effective five-on-one warhead allocation scheme. Perhaps the destruction of this ICBM field was not worth the use of 80 Polaris missiles, yet we nevertheless sought to explore the limits of the American countersilo capability, and therefore to know whether the US in fact could destroy remaining Soviet ICBM silos. An additional reason for the use of Polaris is that its short flight time minimizes the (already little) amount of warning time that is available to the USSR. While this hypothetical exchange is of doubtful real-world value, it again serves to test the limits of US counterforce capabilities, and thereby to demonstrate that even the entire US ICBM force and most of its SLBMs would not be sufficient for destroying the entire Soviet ICBM force if we assume what only could be seen as moderate levels of attrition. At least 86 Soviet ICBMs still remain to be targeted by US bombers, as is shown in the next section.

In summary, the second phase of the countersilo operations resulted in the destruction of 683 Soviet land-based ICBMs. For the United States, it meant the launch of 684 SLBMs: 252 Trident, 352 Poseidon, and 80 Polaris. Of the 6,120 warheads that were launched, approximately 1,600 detonated at the silos, for an aggregate attrition rate of 75 percent. In comparison with the 26 percent attrition rate of the ICBM attack in Phase I, the generally lower reliability rates of the SLBMs, in particular their lower level of readiness, was the primary reason for the fact that the level of failure was nearly double that of the ICBMs. And, in terms of the USSR, Phase II resulted in nearly 3 million civilian casualties from post-attack radioactive fallout, in which roughly 1.5 million would die within several months.

In retrospect, we wonder whether the destruction of nearly 50 percent of the USSR's land-based missile forces was worth the depletion of virtually the entire American SLBM force. If we consider that the land-based missile force is the largest component of the Soviet Union's nuclear triad, then it is apparent that the elimination of these primary Soviet counterforce targets should be of paramount importance to the United States. On a deeper level, however, there are those who will argue, with considerable persuasiveness, that the use of US SLBMs against land-based missiles reinforces deterrence by shifting from the assured destruction of Soviet cities to the destruction of counterforce targets. Others might argue, again with considerable force, that the entire US SLBM force should not be targeted against ICBM silos in the USSR or any other targets for that matter, because the SLBMs constitute an "urban-industrial withhold" of warheads for threatening retaliation against Soviet cities—if the USSR attacks American cities first. From this perspective, targeting all US SLBMs against urban populations in the USSR could contribute to a weakening of intra-war deterrence because so doing removes one incentive for deterring the Soviets from launching an attack on US cities. On both sides of this debate, it perhaps is beyond dispute that the SLBM strikes against Soviet silos would reduce US nuclear reserves to a level that may preclude effective intra-war bargaining for the termination of a nuclear war. Would the Soviet Union, for example, really consider the preceding nuclear strike as a "limited," surgical attack against its missile force when the attack involved more than 4,300 surface-burst nuclear detonations? It certainly is doubtful that they would, just as it is questionable whether the US would consider the preceding attack as anything less than all-out nuclear war. But we are jumping ahead of ourselves. Let us defer these questions for the moment.

Phase III: Bomber Strikes

Even after the nuclear strikes in Phases I and II, the Soviet Union still would retain roughly 86 ICBMs—26 SS-11M3s at the Zhangiz Tobe and 60 SS-13s at the Yoshkar Ola missile fields. To destroy this remaining group of ICBMs, we simulated the launch of several squadrons of US B-52 bombers (see Table 4). The fundamental problem with this tactic is that the effectiveness of Soviet air defenses is unknown, and this leaves considerable uncertainty about the number of bombers that actually would reach the Soviet missile fields. In one illustrative case, 23 B-52s were launched against the SS-13 missiles at the Yosh Karola field, but only 22 percent of the deliverable warheads reached the silos. This level of attrition is attributable to our assumptions about the effectiveness of the USSR's air defense system of surface-to-air missiles (SAMs), interceptor aircraft, and AWACs-type surveillance aircraft. In reality, we do not know how US bombers would fare if they attempted to penetrate the Soviet Union's air defense system. Accordingly, as in all previous examples, we based our analysis on a "middle level" estimate of the penetrability of Soviet airspace. If, in fact, the ability of the US bomber force to penetrate Soviet air defenses is significantly higher than the 22 percent that was postulated in this scenario, then the US nuclear reserve force of bombers would increase in an almost linear fashion. This, in effect, would increase the numbers of targets that could be attacked in other phases of the war.

For the USSR, Phase III meant the destruction of 86 ICBMs, as well as the roughly 1 million collateral casualties. For reference, the Soviet city of Kazan (population: 1,040,000) is the primary collateral civilian target for the Yosh Karola missile field. In the bomber phase of the countersilo attack, the targeting of 86 silos with 104 bomber-delivered SRAMs resulted in a warhead allocation scheme of slightly higher than one-on-one. In view of the relatively high probability of kill and WLS of the SRAM, this phase of the attack would have to be considered as one of the most efficient, assuming, of course, that we disregard the low penetration rate (22 percent) of the bombers through Soviet airspace. On that score, Phase III hardly appears to have been a paradigm of military effectiveness.

One issue that should be addressed is the advisability of assigning the bomber force to attack land-based missiles, given that ICBMs are time-critical targets (meaning that they should be attacked as quickly as possible before any retaliatory launch can be ordered). It is hard to defend the bomber allocation scheme on the grounds of optimality—indeed, assigning bombers to attack time-urgent targets is one of the least desirable elements in the US counterforce scenario. There is a reasonable probability that the ICBMs would have been launched from their silos well before the bombers ever could reach the Soviet missile fields. Several factors, however, might alter this tactical situation. First, the liquid-fuel status of the ICBMs that were targeted by the American bombers indicates that Soviet missiles may not be responsive enough to be launched before the arrival of the bombers. It may take several hours before the ICBMs could be fired from the silos, which may leave barely enough time for the bombers to strike. A second factor is the staggering level of confusion and uncertainty that will envelop the USSR's nuclear C3 system and its leadership after the effects of nuclear decapitation. Recalling that we chose to attack Soviet C3 centers before the silos, it is entirely plausible that the Soviet leadership might not be able to launch the SS-11M3 and SS-13 ICBMs before the bombers destroyed them. The effects of EMP from space-based nuclear bursts over the Soviet Union, in conjunction with the degrading effects of an attack on command posts, are such that the bombers may have adequate time to destroy the silos well before the Soviet military leadership could make the decision to fire their missiles. Still another uncertainty exists. It is the extent to which the Soviets have armored their electronic and computer-based command and control communications system, and the extent to which they still rely on tube-technology in their communication system, both of which significantly reduce the immunity of the C3 system to disruption from EMP than, say, silicon-based computer technology. Still a third possibility is that the USSR might launch some (or most) of its forces on receipt of tactical warning that the United States has launched an attack. Indeed, Marshal of the Soviet Union Ogarkov suggested that in the future the USSR will not accept the losses of the counter-attack strategy that was employed by the USSR in

World War II. Instead, the Soviet Union may be forced to launch a pre-emptive attack in order to forestall imminent American aggression. More-over, he observed that every technological breakthrough since 1945 has been an American initiative. Such a process drives the USSR to keep up and, at times, to achieve even a temporary military superiority, such as its pre-sent countersilo capability. If this process prevails there may come a point when the USSR must preempt in order to avoid the "use it or lose it" situation.

Countersilo Summary What did the United States gain from this attack against the ICBM forces of the USSR? Most important, the US achieved the destruction of virtually all 1,398 Soviet land-based missiles, and caused ap-proximately 8 million collateral casualties, half of whom are expected to die in the next 30–60 days. To destroy the roughly 1,400 ICBM silos in the USSR, the US launched 1,000 ICBMs, 684 SLBMs, and 39 bombers. More than 4,400 nuclear warheads would have detonated on Soviet soil, which accounts for the high number of civilian casualties. This attack used more than 85 percent of all deliverable US nuclear warheads, and destroyed an equivalent number of Soviet nuclear warheads. By all accounts, each side would appear to have sustained roughly equal losses of nuclear forces, al-though the USSR has sustained civilian losses from collateral nuclear effects that approach the enormous losses of World War II. (We still have not addressed the destruction of the numerous submarine and bomber bases in the USSR.) It is difficult to avoid the conclusion that, up to now, this coun-terforce attack against the USSR has disarmed the United States as much as it has eliminated Soviet forces. If we use the traditional standard of military success, which is that the attacker should destroy more enemy forces than it uses, then the American countersilo strike has been of dubious value. And for now a number of questions about Soviet retaliation also remain unanswered.

SOVIET BOMBER BASES

From any number of perspectives, nothing compares with the magnitude of a large-scale nuclear strike on the ICBM fields of an adversary. Any other counterforce strike pales by comparison with the sheer size, complexity, and timing of such an attack. Sometimes, however, it is easy to forget that in a comprehensive counterforce attack, the countersilo operation would be just one phase of a larger nuclear exchange that would aim for the destruction of the other legs of the Soviet Union's nuclear triad. Here, in the third major phase of a counterforce attack on the USSR, we examine the details of an American strike against bomber bases in the Soviet Union. This will involve the targeting of 219 Soviet strategic nuclear bombers at 25 bases scattered throughout the USSR. When one considers the potential offensive power of the bomber leg of the Soviet triad, it is no wonder that its destruction is critical if the United States is to execute a "successful" counterforce attack.

A word of caution is in order about the data and assumptions that are embedded in this analysis of the Soviet bomber force. It is easy to determine the rough size and composition (by bomber type) of the USSR's force of strategic bombers, for we know that the Soviets have three types of strategic bombers: BEAR, BISON, and BACKFIRE bombers. Using the same sources that were used to compile the data in the other sections, we have estimated that there are 105 BEAR, 49 BISON, and 65 BACKFIRE bombers in the Soviet arsenal at the time of this research (Spring, 1982). Beyond that point, however, some of the issues become somewhat murky. What, for instance, is the payload of the Soviet bombers in each of these classes? Even more difficult, where are the Soviet bombers deployed and how many are there at each base? As there are no available, unclassified answers to these and a host of other questions, to proceed from here, we must depend on a healthy degree of inference if we are to complete a relatively accurate composite picture of the Soviet bomber force. In defense of this admittedly rudimentary (but, infortunately, unavoidable) approach, we suggest that this uncertainty about, for instance, the number of bombers at individual bases may not alter radically the fundamental capabilities of the force, which, after all, are a direct function of the number of aircraft, about which there seems to be sufficient information. This subject is covered in more detail in the Appendix.

In reality, the Soviet bomber bases would be attacked at the same time as the other targets in a counterforce nuclear war, yet in this study we have separated the attack on the USSR's bomber bases into three phases that correspond to the types of US aircraft that were used in each phase. In the first phase, 21 B-52 bombers were targeted against ten bomber bases where 105 BEAR bombers are stationed. (See Table 5.) In view of the uncertainties that attend the penetration capabilities and survivability of the US bombers, our projections were that 12.5 percent (33) of the warheads of the attacking force would reach their assigned bomber bases. The destruction of the Soviet bomber bases, a soft target, was predicated on the detonation of at least one (but preferably two or three) air-burst nuclear warheads.[12] Air-burst detonations, which maximize the lethal radii of the warheads, were selected to maximize the probability that aircraft on the tarmac, as well as those escaping in the air from the base, would be destroyed. In this instance, air-bursts increase the probability that escaping Soviet aircraft might be blown down by the overpressure of the blast, as well as incapacitated by the effects of EMP and thermal radiation. While we considered using surface-bursts because the formation of craters would deny the Soviets any further use of the airfields (for a short time, anyway), it was determined that the risk of allowing Soviet aircraft to escape the bases would increase the threat of eventual retaliation against targets in the United States by those surviving bombers. This possibility suggested that the primary objective is the destruction of the *bombers*, not the bases.

The immediate effect on the USSR was the destruction of 105 BEAR

Table 5
US Attack on Soviet Bomber and SSBN Bases

Target	Bomber/SSBN	No.	US Weapon	No.	Total	Detonations	Yield	City	Casualties
Andizhan	BearA	11	B52A	2	24	3	200KT	Andizhan	330,000
Birobidzhan	BearA	11	B52A	2	24	3	200KT	Birobidzhan	67,000
Donetsk	BearA	8	B52A	3	24	3	200KT	Donetsk	2,050,000
Groznyy	BearB	12	B52A	3	36	6	200KT	Groznyy	375,000
Kuldur	BearB	12	B52A	2	24	3	200KT	Kuldur	21,000
Novopokrovka	BearB	11	B52A	2	24	3	200KT	Novopokrovka	67,000
Tula	BearB	10	B52A	2	24	3	200KT	Tula	610,000
Vinnitsa	BearB	10	B52A	2	24	3	200KT	Vinnitsa	313,000
Vladivostok	BearB	10	B52A	2	24	3	200KT	Vladivostok	-------
Voronezh	BearB	10	B52A	2	24	3	200KT	Voronezh	783,000
Bialystok	Bison	5	B52A	2	24	3	200KT	Bialystok	45,000
Gomel	Bison	5	B52A	2	24	3	200KT	Gomel	383,000
Kharkov	Bison	5	B52A	2	24	3	200KT	Kharkov	1,444,000
Kaliningrad	Bison	5	B52A	2	24	3	200KT	Kaliningrad	355,000
Kiev	Bison	5	B52A	2	24	3	200KT	Kiev	2,375,000
Lida	Bison	5	B52A	2	24	3	200KT	Lida	56,000
Minsk	Bison	5	B52A	2	24	3	200KT	Minsk	1,295,000
Ryazan	Bison	5	B52A	2	24	3	200KT	Ryazan	453,000
Ulan Ude	Bison	5	B52A	2	24	3	200KT	Ulan Ude	300,000
Vitebsk	Bison	4	B52A	2	24	3	200KT	Vitebsk	297,000
Anadyr	Backfire	11	B52A	2	24	3	200KT	Anadyr	11,000
Bologoye	Backfire	11	B52A	2	24	3	200KT	Bologoye	34,000
Boru	Backfire	12	B52B	2	12	1	1MT	Boru	62,000
Gorkiy	Backfire	11	B52B	2	12	1	1MT	Gorkiy	-------
Kirov	Backfire	10	B52B	2	12	1	1MT	Kirov	390,000
Tallinn	Backfire	10	B52B	2	12	1	1MT	Tallinn	430,000
Kamchatskiy	SSBN	15	TITANII	6	6	3	9MT	Kamchatskiy	215,000
Polyarnyy	SSBN	20	TITANII	6	6	3	9MT	Murmansk	381,000
Severodinsk	SSBN	20	TITANII	6	6	3	9MT	Archangelsk	385,000
Vladivostok	SSBN	20	TITANII	6	6	3	9MT	Vladivostok	550,000
Total	Bomber	219		53	588	73			12,546,000
	SSBN	75		24	24	12			1,531,000

bombers and civilian collateral losses of 4.6 million. Yet, a word of caution is in order. Since we have assumed that the Soviet Union has located its bomber bases near cities (for the same reason that US bomber bases are located near cities—the availability of physical and skilled resources), our projections as to collateral losses certainly are not beyond question. Indeed, it is safe to note that these figures for collateral damage, as shown in Table 5, probably minimize the real-world consequences of a counterbomber attack. In any event, the reader ought to view these figures with caution, for that is how we interpret them.

The second group of bomber bases in the USSR contain the 49 BISON bombers in the Soviet arsenal. As shown in Table 5, these aircraft are deployed at ten bases. A total force of 20 B-52 bombers were launched against these bases; 30 warheads (or 12.5 percent of the deliverable warheads on that group of bombers) detonated at the Soviet bases, resulting in the destruction of 49 BISON bombers. Again, it is worthwhile to note that all of these nuclear detonations were calculated to be air-bursts. In addition to the loss of aircraft, this phase of the counterbomber attack resulted in roughly 7 million collateral casualties. Although the nuclear detonations were air-bursts, meaning that the levels of radioactive fallout would be low, it is safe to assume that the projected proximity of the cities to the bases and the possibility of warhead misses indicates that there will be some degree of collateral damage to the Soviet population. While they probably are not of the magnitude of the collateral damage that will occur in the areas that are downwind of the Soviet ICBM fields, nevertheless there are indications that some losses would be sustained.

In the third phase of the counterbomber attack, the target set included six bomber bases where 65 BACKFIRE bombers are stationed. Attacked by B-52s carrying SRAMs and bombs, the model projected that the BACK-FIRE force would be destroyed. Facing the same Soviet air defense system as the earlier waves of US bombers, only 12.5 of the warheads on this attacking force of B-52s would detonate as air-bursts over the Soviet bases. Roughly 1 million collateral casualties would be sustained by the USSR, as shown in Table 5.

In summary, 219 BEAR, BISON, BACKFIRE bombers in the Soviet nuclear arsenal would be destroyed by an attacking force of 53 B-52 bombers. As a measure of the low penetration rate of the US force, an average of only 12.5 percent of the warheads actually were delivered to the targets. Beyond the loss of its bomber force, the Soviet Union also suffered the loss of more than 10 million collateral casualties from this strike. Using a rough measure of comparison, the US launched one bomber for every four Soviet bombers that it destroyed. Several factors might alter this outcome in directions both favorable and unfavorable to the United States. In the first instance, the Soviet Union might scramble its bomber force, even during the difficult circumstances of a counterforce nuclear attack. Whether the disruption of their command system and the associated phenomenon of EMP would interfere with the ability of the Soviets to release their bombers remains unclear. But should this happen, the outcome might be radically different, with the US losing far more bombers than it actually destroyed. For the US planner, the disposition of the Soviet bomber force will remain a highly uncertain variable in any analysis of the vulnerability of the Soviet bomber force.

In another instance, Soviet airspace might prove to be far more permeable than we have imagined, allowing larger numbers of US bombers to reach their assigned targets, and thereby resulting in overkill, with perhaps up to ten warheads being delivered against each of the bomber bases. In effect, this would allow US bombers to strike a number of secondary and tertiary targets in Eastern Europe and the Soviet Union (that were not covered in this model) after hitting the strategic bomber bases. On the broadest level, any number of factors could affect the strike against Soviet bomber bases, and thereby effectively alter the outcome of the attack, resulting in variable levels in wasting US bombers and increasing the survival of Soviet bombers.

To be fair, we have defined this model to provide attrition rates for the attacking force that result in the highest assurance of success, i.e., give the highest probability of destroying the target force. In this way, we have therefore asked whether the US in theory could destroy Soviet bombers as long as sufficient numbers of bombers are assigned to the mission. The tentative answer is "yes," if we recognize that the attrition rates for the US bombers and warheads are high—only one out of every eight warheads actually reached the assigned targets. For some, this calculus is too costly for the US, while for others it provides a conservative measure of the ability to destroy Soviet bombers. We, however, think that there is sufficient uncertainty in these calculations (or any calculation about counterbomber attacks) to suggest that the outcome can vary to a large extent from scenario to scenario. And the employment of the US strategic bomber force against Soviet bomber bases directly may not in fact be the best way to use these weapons, even if virtually all of the nuclear resources of the US have been used in a counterforce strike. While the use of gravity bombs might have some utility, in the future a better tactic might be to launch of a mix of airborne cruise missiles and SRAMs to blast a path through Soviet defenses, including interceptor bases, with simultaneous waves of ALCMs against the strategic bomber bases, i.e. to launch an attack from stand-off B-52s to conserve this recoverable resource while degrading the potential of the Soviet bomber force. There are in fact many other alternatives which we could have examined with this computer data base, but space precludes an analysis of such a multiplicity of futures. It is best at this stage to keep the strategic landscape austere rather than littering it with "a slum of possibilities."

SOVIET SUBMARINE BASES

The "invulnerability" of the SSBN (strategic submarine, ballistic nuclear) is for the present an uncontested, indeed an almost orthodox, element of conventional wisdom. Yet, as SSBNs, like all weapons systems, must report regularly to bases for routine maintenance and repairs, each SSBN base, therefore, becomes in effect a large repository of up to one-half of a super-power's deliverable SLBM force. Moreover, as a soft target, an SSBN base is a relatively easy target for an attacker to destroy. So it is with the four submarine bases in the USSR, which are located at Kamchatskiiy, Polyar-nyy, Severodvinsk, and Vladivostok. (We do not include the submarine base at Leningrad since to the best of our knowledge no ballistic missile sub-marines are stationed with the Soviet Baltic Sea Fleet.) There are approx-imately 10–20 ballistic missile boats at each submarine base during peace-time. Aside from the inherently greater control that the Soviet leadership can exercise over SSBNs in port, the relatively low readiness rates of Soviet SSBNs is a strong indication that Soviet SSBNs are less reliable than their American counterparts. All of this results in a set of highly lucrative targets for the US in a counterforce nuclear war: somewhere in the vicinity of 85–90 percent of all Soviet SSBNs normally are in port. Thus, if we assume that 75 out of the 85 SSBNs in the Soviet fleet are in port at any give time, the United States potentially may be able to destroy most of the Soviet SLBM forces in what, under ordinary circumstances, would be an extremely lim-ited component of an all-out counterforce attack.

Considering that an SSBN base is a soft target, the question becomes how might one plan an attack on one. Most structural elements at an SSBN base, such as the cranes, lifts, and associated support equipment would be de-stroyed by even low levels of overpressure. An air-burst, therefore, would be an appropriate tactic for the attack, for it effectively would destroy most of the critical support facilities at the base and would do so over a larger area. A submarine partially submerged in the water, however, might be substan-tially more resistant to the effects of overpressure than dock-side equipment, particularly because a submarine by design is encapsulated within a pressure hull to protect it from hydrodynamic (water) pressure. Theoretically, a near-by air-burst explosion might destroy the submarine and its SLBMs. But warhead guidance malfunctions, however, could result in final trajectories that increase the chances of a submarine's survival if the explosion occurs at a point just beyond the limit of lethal overpressure. These factors, and a host of other operational uncertainties, point somewhat convincingly to the sur-face-burst as the optimum tactic for an attack against an SSBN base.

To illustrate the effect of a surface-burst detonation against an SSBN base, imagine for a moment the immediate consequences of the explosion. If the warhead were to detonate in or just above the water at the base, large quantities of seawater would be vaporized instantly by the fireball. In effect, this detonation would leave a large "hole" in the water which, moments later, would be refilled by an immense inpouring of seawater, and followed by the subsequent blast wave that would be transmitted through the sea-water. Several more moments later, the base would be subjected to the effects of a tidal (shock) wave that would inundate all of the repair facilities and, quite possibly, crush the hulls of the submarines. Later, the radioactive seawater could prevent the base from being used as a repair or reloading facility. In short, the surface-burst appears to increase the probability of total, catastrophic, and virtually irrevocable damage to the SSBN base, at least on a timescale that is measured in *years*. It is for these reasons that we opted to use surface-bursts against Soviet SSBN bases in this model.

As shown in Table 5, a US strike against SSBN bases in the USSR was executed with the Titan II ICBMs. In anticipation of launch and detonation failures, each SSBN base was targeted with six ICBMs that, given the pre-dicted failure rates, meant three of the six 9 MT warheads were projected to explode as surface-bursts at each of the bases. This method, as the calcula-tions indicate, produced an extremely low probability that any SSBN at the base would survive the attack. At each base, roughly 15–20 SSBNs would be destroyed by a matrix of effects: overpressure, heat, and the shock effect of the tidal wave in the water. This tactic, of course, will alter significantly the extent to which the primary collateral targets are affected. From the data on civilian casualties in Table 5, our calculations indicate that roughly 1.5 mil-lion civilians would become casualties in an attack against the four Soviet SSBN bases. At least 50 percent or more of the civilian population will become fatalities within 30–60 days of the attack, as the radioactive fallout certainly will contaminate the submarine bases and adjacent areas for vary-ing lengths of time, depending, of course, on the fission–fusion composition of the warheads.

A typical Soviet base, such as the one at Polyarnyy, will suffer the loss of the 20 or so submarines that are stationed there, and the primary collateral city of Murmansk, which has a population of 381,000, would sustain heavy levels of damage from blast and fallout. Overall, the destruction of the SSBNs, the base, and the collateral city would be a likely event in an attack with the nine megaton warhead on the Titan II.

On an aggregate level, this attack against Soviet SSBN bases resulted in the loss of roughly 75 Soviet submarines that would be in port at the time (assuming a normal peacetime patrol rate), and 1.5 million collateral casu-alties. The loss of these SSBNs is significant because, of the total Soviet Union SSBN fleet of 85 boats, roughly 90 percent of its SSBN force would be destroyed. To achieve these losses, the US launched 24 single-warhead Titan II ICBMs, although the attrition rate of 50 percent resulted in the detonation of only twelve warheads—three surface-burst explosions at each of the four bases. The remainder of the Soviet Union's SSBN force, which normally patrols along the Atlantic and Pacific coasts of the US, will be examined next.

SOVIET SSBNS ON PATROL

Perhaps the most difficult as well as uncertain phase of a counterforce nuclear war will be against the SSBNs that are on patrol in the oceans. It would hardly seem rational for the US to accept the presence of these Soviet SSBNs, knowing the havoc that they can wreak, as one of the "regrettable" yet unavoidable costs of war. From what is known about Soviet SSBNs, they are on the whole rather noisy, easy-to-locate strategic targets, and—if we can believe published reports—subject to virtually constant surveillance and tracking by US naval forces around the world. In the Mediterranean Sea, and the Atlantic and Pacific Oceans, US naval forces are reputed to have Soviet SSBNs under nearly constant surveillance once they exit any of the straits near the four SSBN bases in the USSR. The critical question, there-fore, is whether the US could destroy Soviet ballistic missile submarines in a counter-SSBN attack using strategic nuclear forces. We think there is evi-dence to suggest that, indeed, the US *might* be able to destroy Soviet submarines on a scale that is convincing to the USSR, at least insofar as the threat to do so may raise Soviet concerns about the viability of this force. [13]

It is known that Soviet SSBNs regularly cruise along the eastern and western seaboards of the US in fairly well known and well defined patterns. We assume that, at the outset of a nuclear war, there will be some coordina-tion (the extent unknown) between US strategic and naval forces unless, of course, EMP disables the entire communication system. Using what will probably be rough indications as to the general locations of Soviet SSBNs, we have postulated that the 250 or so remaining bombers in the US arsenal could be targeted against Soviet submarines in what has been called the "barrage" attack. In general, a typical barrage attack is imagined to consist of a series of high-megaton range sub-surface nuclear detonations in the region where the SSBNs are projected to be. For instance, as shown in Table 5, a B-52 bomber could launch a barrage attack with ten, one-megaton warheads against a *Delta III*-class Soviet SSBN. If the location of the SSBN could be placed within a 50–100 square mile grid, then we estimate that there is a 50 percent probability that the barrage attack (using bombers in this instance) would destroy the submarine. [14] From what is known about the effects of underwater nuclear explosions that were conducted in the 1950s, the target submarine will be vulnerable to the intense, high-pressure wave that forms after the explosion. Sometimes referred to as the Van Dorn effect, the high-pressure wave from a one-megaton explosion will be lethal to a submerged submarine at a distance of between two and three miles from the explosion.

If the estimated location of an SSBN were bracketed with, say, megaton-range warheads, there is a reasonable chance of killing the submarine. This, at least, is how we have proceeded in this study.

If we recall from the section that addressed an attack on Soviet submarine bases, in which roughly 75 Soviet SSBNs were destroyed in port, that would leave some ten Soviet SSBNs at sea. For ease of analysis, we have assumed that these ten boats already would be on patrol along the US coasts, although in reality some of the submarines would be traveling to and from the patrol areas in order to replace submarines that are at the end of their normal patrol. This translates into the presence of between 7 and 10 SSBNs along the US coast. The central issue, therefore, is whether the remaining US B-52 and F-111 bombers could eliminate at least some of the Soviet submarines before they fired their SLBMs. While we can infer that some percentage of the Soviet SSBNs will be destroyed, it surely is beyond the limits of this model, or for that matter virtually any model, to place exact quantitative values on the calculus of a counter-SSBN exchange. This means, of course, that some Soviet SSBNs, which survived the US barrage attack that was launched from bombers, would retaliate at some later, unknown, time against selected US counterforce and countervalue targets. To make matters more difficult still, how will the United States know if a barrage attack against a particular submarine succeeded? It is doubtful that the US will be able to detect the wreckage of a submarine as did the destroyer crews in the first and second world wars. The evidence that a Soviet submarine (or submarines) survived the barrage attack will come in the form of a strike against US targets that will be launched with little or no warning. This may take the form of a tragic equation: The survival of the submarines that the US sought to destroy will be confirmed only by the disappearance of those cities that the US sought to preserve. All of this results in the somewhat unsettling conclusion that even in the best circumstances the US can never rest assured that the Soviet SSBN force had been destroyed. While the US can readily destroy very large fractions of the force with strikes on the submarine bases, it will never eliminate the Soviet SSBN threat altogether. Most important, this means that a counterforce attack on the Soviet SSBN force will never erase the fear that some boats may survive long enough to lay waste civilian and military targets in the United States. In this sense, we can hardly express satisfaction with the "outcome" of the counter-SSBN attack. From a military perspective, the strike could not be said to be "efficient" if the criterion is the destruction of *all* Soviet SSBNs. If, however, the strike results in the destruction of, say, 50 percent of the Soviet SSBNs, and thereby reduces the retaliatory potential of Soviet SSBNs by a like amount, then we feel safe in saying that the US counter-SSBN strike was a "theoretical" success. However, one measure of the outcome of the attack, for instance, which we address in Chapter 6, is the number of US casualties that the Soviet SSBN force could inflict on the United States both *before* and *after* the US counter-SSBN attack.

Soviet Launch on Warning

There is a distinct possibility that, in the midst of the American nuclear attack, the Soviet Union might retaliate during the attack. At any time, from receipt of the first tactical warning to just moments before the detonation of the first US warheads, the Soviets could launch all or portions of their strategic nuclear forces in order to prevent its destruction. Elements of the USSR's ICBM, SLBM, or bomber forces could be launched on warning of the attack, although it is most likely that they would launch their ICBMs, which are the most responsive in terms of the time it takes to launch, and represent the greatest fraction of the USSR's strategic nuclear warheads and deliverable megatonnage. While the liquid-fuel status of the Soviet ICBM force and the generally lower readiness of Soviet ICBMs, may increase the difficulties of executing a launch-on-warning response, recent Soviet references to the utility of LOW suggest that the Soviets may have this capability. The dominant issue, of course, is how a Soviet decision to launch on warning would affect the outcome of an American counterforce attack, and whether it would alter the general structure of such an American attack.

Let us recall that the US counterforce attack against the three legs of the Soviet nuclear triad absorbed a large fraction of the deliverable American nuclear warheads—on the assumption that the attacking force encountered relatively severe attrition rates. After this attack, one could express the outcome in terms of an effective kill ratio: the number of Soviet warheads or launchers that were destroyed by the detonation of a certain number of US warheads or launchers. What Soviet launch on warning effectively does is to decrease the effective kill ratio for the United States, and in some sense to defer the destruction of Soviet forces altogether, for the latter will be used to attack American targets. In a strict sense, a policy of launch on warning (or, for that matter, launch under attack) has a clear effect on the size of reserve forces. To picture this, consider the Soviet nuclear arsenal as a three-dimensional matrix, with each axis representing the force of ICBMs, SLBMs, and bombers. In a US counterforce attack, the size (or volume, if you will) of the Soviet nuclear matrix decreases paradoxically at roughly the same rate as the US nuclear force matrix shrinks. In a crude sense, an American counterforce attack collapses the US and Soviet nuclear force matrices in a proportional and simultaneous fashion.

Should, however, the Soviet Union launch its forces on warning, then the reserve of forces that is available to the Soviets increases and the effective US kill ratio decreases. It is noteworthy to mention that this is not a post-attack reserve force to which we are referring. Rather, it is an intra-war reserve force that must be used at the same time as the American attack. Soviet launch on warning ultimately would reduce the number of warheads destroyed by the US attack, and would expand greatly the number of American counterforce and countervalue targets that the Soviet Union could destroy. In a strict sense, Soviet launch on warning will not alter the final outcome of the US attack, for Soviet forces will be either destroyed or launched—neither outcome increases the size of the USSR's post-attack reserve force, nor paradoxically for the United States, who it is to be noted, launched most of its arsenal in the initial attack. However, launch on warning may provide some brief satisfaction for the Soviet leadership, who will have the knowledge that a broader array of US targets will be attacked than would have been possible without launch on warning. It seems entirely plausible to us that the Soviet Union would launch its forces on warning of a US attack if only, for no other reason, than to deny to the United States the possibility of achieving an uncontested counterforce attack.

SUMMARY

In thinking about the events postualted in this chapter, we sometimes lose sight of the reality of which we write. Lost in the haze and maze of numbers, warheads, casualties, and attrition rates, all of which constitute the typical technocratic jargon of nuclear war, it is an event that nonetheless should stagger the human imagination. Even a counterforce war, in all its theoretical, "surgical" cleanliness, will cause horrific levels of casualties. Thus, we are of two minds regarding the sequence of events in the preceding pages. There are the data about the event, and the consequences of the event. In looking at each, we seek to forget neither.

In examining the data on the exchange, we remind the reader that the US counterforce attack against the USSR occurred as a large-scale, coordinated action. While we segregated the war into five discrete phases (against command posts, ICBM fields, bomber bases, submarine bases, and SSBNs on patrol) in order to provide the greatest possible clarity in what is ordinarily a very complex event, in an actual exchange those targets would be attacked on a nearly simultaneous basis. What occurred in a sequential fashion in this chapter would, in reality, be seen as one unified, almost spasmodic military action. In terms of the results of the attack, the losses to the Soviet Union (and the US) would be enormous by any standard. If the assumptions about the calculus of nuclear war are essentially correct, the USSR would lose virtually all of its land-based command centers, ICBMs, bombers, and submarines. And of the SSBNs on patrol along the US coast, at least half of the 10 submarines would be destroyed. Thus, the USSR lost just about all of its strategic nuclear forces in this hypothetical US attack, with the possible survival of the scattered forces that statistically just might happen to escape the attack unscathed. To accomplish this task, the United States launched all of its ICBMs and SLBMs, and roughly one third of its bomber force. Excluding the warheads that were detonated in the oceans in order to kill SSBNs, approximately 4,500 nuclear weapons exploded in the Soviet Union, many of which were surface-bursts against the command posts, ICBM fields, and submarine bases. By any measure, the Soviet Union received an enormous "load" of equivalent megatons in this attack.

Paradoxically, we find in this study that the US probably succeeded in disarming the USSR in this exchange, but at the cost of its own near-total disarmament. On a general scale, this counterforce exchange translated into nearly symmetrical and simultaneous reductions in the US and USSR nuclear arsenals. It is worth recalling that the US used its entire ICBM and SLBM forces (with the exception of 52 Titans) in the countersilo phase of the war. Thus, it is no exaggeration to say that the US succeeded in disarming itself at the same time that it disarmed the USSR. Whether this outcome could be judged as "rational" quite clearly depends on the definition of rationality. While it might be rational to launch such an attack if it were clear to the US that the USSR was about to launch a preemptive attack against the United States, it hardly would be a paradigm of military rationality to do so without provocation in view of the unfavorable exchange ratio, not to mention the millions of collateral casualties in the Soviet Union. Even the logic of responding with a preemptive attack before the enemy could do the same might change, however, if the calculus suggested that the US could do no better than to disarm itself at the same time that it disarmed the Soviet Union. And aside from the arcana of exchange ratios, it is unlikely that the United States ever could remove the threat of a Soviet retaliatory attack against American cities from whatever forces survived the preemptive US attack.

One critical issue remains unclear. How might the Soviet Union react to a US counterforce attack? It clearly might launch its forces on warning of the impending attack, or just as plausibly, it might seek to ride out the attack. Theoretically, the Soviet response could range anywhere along the spectrum between immediate retaliation and delay. This being the case, we sought to address US capabilities without direct reference to Soviet retaliation. The effect of this approach was to simplify the analysis. While it is certainly true that this model is far simpler than the reality of such an attack, the point was to examine theoretical US counterforce capabilities. We had no intention of trying to resolve the nuances of timing and execution for a large-scale counterforce exchange, as this would go far beyond the capabilities of this model. To be explicit, the sole purpose was to explore the limits of US counterforce capabilities, always recognizing that in reality, unanticipated events could change the outcome in any number of directions. From this analysis, it is reasonable to infer that US counterforce capabilities are significantly less than those which would be required for such an exchange *and* the maintenance of an adequate post-attack reserve force for intra-war deterrence against an attack on American cities. This hypothetical exchange illustrated that "success" resulted in the reduction of US and USSR nuclear forces to a level of rough parity or equivalence.

On the human side of the scale, the costs to the Soviet Union would be catastrophic. Out of a population of 275 million, we calculate that the USSR would suffer the loss of between 35–40 million people as the result of their proximity to nuclear targets, warhead guidance malfunctions, and the residual effects of post-attack radioactive fallout. Though it is hard to say exactly how these factors would produce casualties, the evidence is clear that the fallout from thousands of surface-burst detonations will be the primary cause of the casualties. More than 4,000 nuclear warheads were detonated as surface-bursts, which is more than sufficient to induce large-scale civilian losses. Here, roughly 13 percent of the Soviet population was at immediate risk in this theoretical attack. This means that approximately half of the 37 million casualties (18–20 million) will die within 30–60 days as the result of their exposure to post-attack radiation. And if the Soviet civil defense program is effective (a highly doubtful proposition in an American attack that seeks to kill Soviet civilians), it might lower the level of casualties to 10–20 million. As there are no reliable data about civil defense in the USSR, our initial projections must remain until such time as we see compelling evidence to the contrary.[15]

To conclude, the costs of a limited American counterforce nuclear attack against the USSR would be staggering. With the exception of the cities that were targeted directly in order to destroy command posts, the war was aimed against military targets alone. Even this tactic, however, resulted in more than 37 *million* casualties. It is this "collateral" damage that in theory could be the provocation that induces the USSR to retaliate as best it can against US cities in order to balance civilian losses. We explore that possibility in Chapter 6.

4

USSR Counterforce Attack

Throughout history, much has been written about the emergence of empires, kingdoms and hegemonic political structures, with particular emphasis on the military sphere of activity. From the Chinese, Roman, and Aztec civilizations to the Napoleonic, Hitlerian, and Stalinist periods, a dominant theme has been the role of military power as the ultimate instrument of the state. Indeed, there is considerable justification behind the argument that the imprudent exercise of power, and military power in particular, has led to the extirpation of many political systems. Whatever the multiple factors or causes that have precipitated the "Decline and Fall" of empires, such as Assyria, which itself was a form of maddened militarism, Rome's conquest of the known world, or Nazi Germany's well publicized excesses, military defeat is almost always the proximate cause of decline of, or the death blow to, empires. Whether one observes Assyria, Carthage, the disastrous defeat suffered by Rome at Hadrianople in 378, or the devastation of the Middle East by Hulagu Khan in the thirteenth century from which the area never recovered, one sees that the death of nations and societies often has come from the sword.

Thus, a sobering thought is that, regardless of how decrepit a regime may be, it is the military dimension that usually proves to be the factor that hastens decline. This historical pattern may have special significance for us now in the present era, when we are witnessing the unparalleled growth of the military power of the Soviet Union. Most distressing of all, there is some evidence to suggest that wars frequently occur when a regime estimates that others will pose a formidable challenge to what it sees as its own evanescent superiority. In effect, this is the now popularized "use it or lose it" syndrome that has drawn so much notoriety in the nuclear age.

As we look back upon the last decade, it is readily apparent that the Soviet Union has created a formidable military apparatus. Although the USSR doubtless is plagued by many of the problems that typically exist within any military state, nevertheless there is the undeniable fact that the growth of Soviet military power has outdistanced that of the West. On this point there is little broad disagreement in the West. There is considerable debate, however, on the outcome of any military struggle between the US and USSR, not the least of which is in the field of nuclear war. Beyond the simple portrait of the large-scale destruction that a nuclear war will cause, the deeper issue is the comparative capabilities of the USSR and the United States in narrowly specified explicit scenarios of engagement. How, for instance, do the counterforce capabilities of the US and USSR compare today? Are there significant differences between the capabilities of the respective nations that bear scrutiny? At the most basic level, could one nation have an advantage that might lead to victory, however one wishes to define that idea in nuclear war?

If one thing remains clear, it is that the use of the term "victory" in the context of a nuclear war has lost much of its meaning, even for those who think in terms of the traditional military concepts of the offense and the defense, victory and defeat. It is also a word that signifies the great abyss that has grown between the dominant schools of thought in nuclear affairs. To be sure, the mere mention of the word "victory" hardly engenders endearment—either among those who are loathe to link the consequences of classical wars with those of nuclear wars, or those who disdain the idea that the outcome of nuclear armageddon can be simplified as a victory or defeat for the combatants who surely will be unrecognizable after a nuclear war of any intensity.[1] In the face of these monumental difficulties, we, albeit conveniently, will defer on such questions as to whether it is correct to use historical analogies when speaking about nuclear war. What we seek to do in this chapter is to explore the counterforce capabilities of the Soviet Union in exactly the same way that we examined the counterforce capabilities of the United States. In looking at the details of a Soviet counterforce attack against US C3 centers, ICBM bases, bomber bases, submarine bases, and SSBNs on patrol, we will develop a composite sketch of the Soviet Union's counterforce capabilities. Moreover, this structure will be a mirror image of US counterforce capabilities that will facilitate direct comparisons. Rather than the vague discussions about superiority or parity that all too often appear as "analyses" of the nuclear balance of power, this will provide a systematic basis for detailed comparisons that to date have not been publicly available.

As important as it is to understand the nuclear capabilities of the superpowers in what some have called the "age of vulnerability," there is perhaps greater value in an assessment of the counterforce potential of the Soviet Union. This is the case particularly in view of the widespread concern in the United States, Europe, and the Far East that the USSR has achieved some margin of nuclear superiority. What we find in this study is not reassuring for, in some measures, the Soviet Union does in fact possess greater capabilities than the United States. The real issue, however, is not superiority in the counterforce area, but rather the detailed comparison that this study represents.

A word about the sequence of events is in order. For reasons that include realism as well as ease of comparison, this analysis of a Soviet counterforce attack on the United States is structured along the same lines as the American counterforce attack on the USSR in Chapter 3. From an operational perspective, this targeting approach seems to be rather realistic. Quite expectedly, this approach simplifies the comparisons that some may wish to construct in order to examine US-USSR counterforce scenarios in terms of specific classes of targets, and thus highlights the differences that exist. Armed with this information, it will be possible to understand the difference between what could be called significant and insignificant advantages, and particularly how we should be able to recognize and dismiss the latter.

US COMMAND, CONTROL AND COMMUNICATION TARGETS

If there is a logic to fighting a nuclear war, it is that it probably will begin with an attack on the command centers that coordinate a nation's nuclear forces. Independent of any assessment of whether this is a prudent tactic for the attacker, there will be enormous pressures on the attacker, in this case the USSR, to concentrate one wave of the initial counterforce strike against American command and control targets. From the Soviet perspective, it may appear to be essential to destroy as many elements of the US command system as possible in order to lessen the chances of an all-out or a fully coordinated US retaliatory strike against the Soviet Union. The issue, however, of whether the USSR in reality can effectively destroy the US command system is not clear, and indeed cannot be resolved here, but we still seek to examine how the Soviet Union might attempt this in a counterforce attack, and the consequences of such an attack.

To begin with, we may note that the US command system for the control of nuclear forces is better understood and more fully documented than that of the Soviet Union. Surrounded in a veil of secrecy, it is difficult to know precisely how the Soviet command system works, in particular how—if at all—the system may be disrupted beyond the normal effects of EMP and proximate nuclear explosions. Indeed, in the case of the USSR, we do not really know for sure where the primary C3 centers are, nor how they might operate in a nuclear war. This, however, is not the case in the United States. From a number of sources, it is possible to construct a relatively accurate sketch of the US command system, and thereby to understand how the USSR might proceed to attack it. Again, we emphasize that many details about the operation of the US C3 system remain a mystery outside of the classified literature. The reason for this is quite simple: The more the adversary knows about one's command system, and therefore the strengths and weaknesses of the network, the easier it is to disrupt it.

On a general level, the US command and control system depends upon a network of positive and negative flows of information to the strategic nuclear forces. A positive control may be understood as the transmission of a binary stream of data that authorizes the launch (retaliatory or otherwise) of nuclear forces, whereas a negative control is a data transmission that prohibits launch. The permissive action link (PAL) system ensures that US nuclear forces will not be used without authorization (negative control), and that only the authorized individual, such as the President, may use nuclear forces (positive control). The security of the system is measured by its ability to operate with a high degree of confidence in fulfilling the requirements of positive and negative control. Using a complex network of microwave, laser, and low-to-high frequency signals, the command and central system transmits an emergency action message (EAM) to the triad that authorizes the release of nuclear forces. Should the system be disrupted before the transmission of the EAM, then the release of nuclear forces may be prevented for some (unknown) length of time. It remains unclear whether American nuclear forces, in particular the ICBM and bomber forces, can be released after some length of time if the forces are disconnected from the National Command Authority.[2] It is assumed that American SSBNs have independent launch authority, more for reasons of the difficulties and uncertainties that plague the US communication system than the fears of the threat of nuclear decapitation. Nevertheless, it is conceivable that US nuclear forces, such as the launch control center crews that control the ICBM force, can not launch their forces if they are unable to communicate with the NCA. Thus, in the context of a counterforce attack, one possible Soviet objective may be to destroy the US command system in a counterforce attack as soon as possible, and thereby in theory to reduce the probability of a fully coordinated US retaliatory response.

Like any system that contains centralized and vital parts, the greatest vulnerability of the US C3 system is in its fixed, land-based centers. Aside from the complex effects of EMP on the transmission system of the command system (such as the vulnerability of the hilltop microwave transmitters, and the fact that much of the pre-attack communication system for US nuclear forces is a subsystem of the unshielded commercial AT&T long distance telecommunications apparatus) and uncertainties about the consequences of a nuclear war on the C3 system, somewhat more can be said about the physical centers that form the critical nodes in the US command network. As shown in Table 6, we have identified five primary C3 targets in the continental United States that will serve as the focal point for this discussion. We do not include the capabilities of the mobile elements of the C3

Table 6

Soviet Attack on US Command Centers

Target	Sov. Weapon	No.	Total	Detonations	Yield	City	Casualties
NORAD	SS19M2	15	15	10	10MT	Col. Springs	296,000
Fort Ritchie	SS19M2	15	15	10	10MT	Frederick, MD	26,000
Mount Weather	SS19M2	15	15	10	10MT	Front Royal, VA	10,000
Grand Forks	SS19M2	15	15	10	10MT	Grand Forks, ND	------
Washington, DC	SS19M2	15	15	10	10MT	Washington,	3,025,000
Total		75	75	50			3,357,000

system, such as the Strategic Air Command (SAC) aircraft that are on continuous airborne patrol (Looking Glass) or other similar systems (e.g., NEACP, the President's "doomsday" plane), as the effect of a nuclear attack on these systems remains unknown at this time. Nor have we considered whether or not the NCA has planned for C3 redundancy. By this we mean a series of alternate command modes where national control could be shifted to a number of preselected Continental Army Command centers or to, say, Commander in Chief Pacific. While this appears a prudent series of arrangements, we do not know if such arrangements exist.

In this Soviet counterforce attack, we are concerned with the destruction of the five command complexes that are listed in Table 6. While we do not suppose for a moment that the destruction of these targets will render the US command system inoperable, it will give some idea of the requirements of a nuclear decapitation attack and the collateral consequences of such an attack. In this model, the American C3 targets were attacked by a small wave of Soviet SS-19M2 ICBMs. In reality, this attack probably would be preceded by a salvo of several SLBM warheads that were programmed to detonate 200–300 miles above the United States for the purpose of blinding momentarily US C3 ground- and space-based warning sensors. It was assumed that these C3 centers, most particularly the NORAD Cheyenne Mountain complex, are hard targets, and that their destruction would require the detonation of at least ten high-yield surface-bursts. While this assumption may be too rigorous, for just one ten megaton warhead might be sufficient, it is likely that a conservative military planner in the Soviet Union would accept this overkill as a necessity in view of the consequences of a failure in the attack. The SS-19M2 ICBM was selected for this attack on American command centers given that the yield and CEP of the warhead generates a 95 percent probability of kill against a hard target.

In this scenario, we assigned 15 SS-19M2 ICBMs to every command post in the United States, which is equivalent to launching a total of 75 missiles against the five targets. In view of the expected launch and detonation failure rates of the SS19M2 ICBM, ten RVs would be expected to detonate as surface-bursts at each target, i.e., 66 percent of the RVs assigned to the targets actually detonated at or near the command centers. The assumption is that the command posts would be destroyed by the detonation of ten 10 MT warheads. Perhaps the most difficult of the US C3 centers to destroy is NORAD, which is buried in Cheyenne Mountain under 1,700 feet of granite and is mounted on shock absorbing gimbals. It is reported that NORAD has a hardness (resistance to overpressure) of at least several hundred psi.[3] This means that, if Cheyenne Mountain could survive the detonation of one or two 10 MT explosions, it is highly doubtful that it could withstand ten such detonations. In short, it seems reasonable to argue that NORAD, as well as the other C3 centers that are listed in Table 6, would not survive the first-wave of a Soviet counterforce attack. One logical effect of this Soviet attack is the disruption of the network of sensors, computers, and human decision-makers that are supposed to coordinate US nuclear retaliation. Since the purpose of this study is not to assess how (or if) the US would respond to such a Soviet counterforce attack, we will conclude with the observation that the retaliatory mechanisms of the US would be in disarray and confusion. Whether this would preclude or diminish retaliation remains beyond the scope of this study.

What does not remain outside this study, however, are the collateral consequences of a Soviet attack on these specified US command centers. Measured in terms of the immediate and direct civilian populations that are near the C3 targets, a projection of the collateral losses from this attack will give us some indication of the magnitude of the attack. The reader should recall that these Soviet strikes were calculated to be surface-bursts, which means that each of the 60 nuclear detonations by the 10 MT warheads would produce a 2,700 foot wide crater at the point of impact. More important, these surface-bursts will inject millions of tons of ejecta into the atmosphere that will result in the formation of clouds of radioactive fallout that will be deposited downwind of the explosions. As shown in Table 6, the US will suffer collateral losses in excess of three million, 50 percent of whom will become fatalities within 30–60 days. The largest of the collateral targets, of course, is Washington, D.C., which is normally considered to be a prime C3 target. In Washington, after all, one normally would find the President and Cabinet, Congress, Joint Chiefs of Staff, and many of the US government and military officials who are in the chain of command. The concentration of these critical individuals means that Washington, which has a population of more than 3 million, is more than likely to be destroyed, for much the same reason that the US would attack Moscow in a counterforce attack.

As we look at the results of the attack by the USSR on the US C3 system, it is worthwhile to note that a small fraction of the Soviet ICBM force (75 warheads, or 5 percent) might be sufficient to disrupt the US command structure.[4] Beyond these three million civilian casualties, the United States would lose the complexes from which it otherwise would plan and execute a nuclear retaliatory attack. As was examined in Chapter 3, the potential advantages of nuclear decapitation are lucrative indeed, as long as one accepts the fact that a number of uncertainties still remain unanswered. For instance, is the US command system designed so that retaliation is certain even after a successful Soviet decapitation attack? Will American nuclear forces be launched after some specified period of "command disconnect"? So, while the USSR can follow up the attacks on the C3 centers with strikes against remaining American counterforce targets, it can never know the precise effect of decapitation on US retaliatory capabilities. Yet, from the Soviet perspective, there appears no other choice than to destroy C3 targets because of one simple and compelling reason: No matter how effective the Soviet attack in theory was, after decapitation it is certain that US retaliation will be less effective and threatening. Accordingly, the premise that a Soviet (or US) counterforce attack would be started with a strike on C3 centers seems sound. For the Soviets, this attack would require only a minuscule fraction of the Soviet nuclear arsenal, while for the United States, the consequences, in terms of control over its nuclear forces, would be severe. Civilian losses, moreover, would be relatively insignificant in comparison with the casualties that will be sustained in a large-scale counterforce attack, or naturally, an attack on American urban-industrial centers.

US ICBM FIELDS: COUNTERSILO STRIKES

If there has been a continuing theme in US defense policy over the last 20–25 years, it surely has been that the ICBM is the most important weapon in the US and Soviet nuclear arsenals. It should come as no surprise that the theoretical vulnerability of US ICBMs in a Soviet preemptive attack would be the cause of a bitter political debate. This threat, which probably has existed at least since the late 1970s, suddenly crystallized as the central defense issue in the 1980 presidential campaign. The phrase "window of vulnerability" came to symbolize, for conservatives and liberals alike, the waning years of American nuclear superiority over the USSR, and signaled the beginning of what few would deny has become a more unstable nuclear balance. It did not seem to matter that the American alert bombers at their bases have been vulnerable to an SLBM attack for quite some time; that half of the US submarine fleet that is in port at all times is at risk; or that the strategic nuclear command structure is highly vulnerable to a preemptive attack. Only when the vulnerability of the ICBM surfaced, and thus became a potent political force in 1980, did people begin to think about the significance of the vulnerability of several legs of the triad. To understand this phenomenon, it is important to see the ICBM as the benchmark for the durability of strategic forces, deterrence, and the global balance of power. Perhaps the burden on the ICBM is too great, its symbolic power far in excess of what it can bear. The reality, however, is that the threat of ICBM vulnerability started a revolution in nuclear forces, the effects of which we have only begun to feel. In short, the concept of the "window of vulnerability" probably in retrospect will prove to have been the single most critical issue in nuclear deterrence since the 1960 missile "gap" started the US on the path to large-scale deployments of ICBMs and the subsequent modernization of the nuclear arsenal.[5]

How can we explore the notion of a Soviet attack on US ICBM fields in a chapter on counterforce scenarios without at least some mention of the debate surrounding ICBM vulnerability? To be fair, before we examine the results of this computer model it seems prudent to say that few subjects are as contentious as this. From the start, some in the scientific and technical communities have criticized the idea of ICBM vulnerability as a patent absurdity.[6] How, they ask, can the Soviet Union execute an attack on US silos without the level of large-scale ICBM flight tests that are necessary to generate highly confident data about the *actual* performance of the missiles, warheads, and guidance systems? Without this type of information, a countersilo attack would be a technical folly of the worst sort, not to mention that it would be a catastrophic failure for the attacker. Some argue that even unimpeded access to operational data (such as data for ICBM flights over the North Pole, which as an untested trajectory, involves the unknown effects of magnetic and gravitational anomalies on the inertial guidance systems), would not resolve the fundamental uncertainty about the outcome of such an attack. In short, for the skeptics of counterforce attacks, even a discussion of ICBM vulnerability becomes a technological and perhaps quasi-theological dispute that is bound to mean a lessening in the stability of nuclear deterrence. Even worse, it may result in unnecessarily large and burdensome expenditures on nuclear forces that, in reality, are being wasted on solutions to a problem that might not have existed in the first place.

We certainly did not dismiss these concerns out of hand when the model was designed. As noted in the Appendix, the operant assumption is that an attack on ICBM silos will succeed as long as the attacker is willing to allocate enough RVs in the attack in the expectation that the attacking force will suffer relatively high attrition rates. Indeed, this approach is not entirely inconsistent with those who, albeit recently, have revised upward their estimates of the Soviet ability to destroy US ICBM silos, partly in recognition of the fact the scenario seems more plausible if one uses higher attrition rates and more accurate guidance systems than were used in earlier calculations.[7]

In this section of Chapter 4, we examine the theoretical ability of the USSR to launch an attack on US ICBMs. As the reader will see, the USSR's ICBM force encountered relatively high failure rates in the attack, which were not much different from the attrition rates of American nuclear forces in their attack against Soviet ICBMs. One result of this exercise is to provide a common set of references for comparisons between the countersilo capabilities of the US and USSR. To this extent, we are providing an approximate measure of the relative countersilo potentials of the US and USSR. Here, the issue is the theoretical ability of the USSR to destroy US ICBMs, and more important, just how the Soviet Union might execute this attack. The countersilo operation will be divided into four phases, corresponding to the fields of Minuteman IIIA, Minuteman IIIB, Minuteman II, and Titan II ICBMs.

Phase I: Minuteman IIA

The first phase of the Soviet attack on US ICBM silos focuses on the 300 Minuteman (MM) IIIA ICBMs that are stationed in two wings of 150 missiles

Table 7
Soviet Attack on US ICBM Fields

Target	ICBM	No.	Sov. Weapon	No.	Total	Detonations	Yield	City	Casualties
Grand Forks AFB	MMIIIA	150	SS18M4	55	550	307	500KT	Grand Forks, ND	99,000
Minot AFB	MMIIIA	150	SS18M4	55	550	307	500KT	Minot, ND	34,000
Malmstrom AFB	MMIIIB	50	SS18M4	19	190	105	500KT	Great Falls, MT	88,000
Warren AFB	MMIIIB	127	SS18M4	46	460	255	500KT	Cheyenne, CO	3,000
	MIIIB	73	SS18M2	50	400	222	900KT		
Ellsworth AFB	MMII	84	SS18M2	57	456	252	900KT	Rapid City, SD	93,000
	MMII	66	SS19M1	60	360	202	550KT		
Malmstrom AFB	MMII	150	SS19M1	135	810	454	550KT	Great Falls, MT	------
Whiteman AFB	MMII	94	SS19M1	85	510	283	550KT	Warrensboro, MO	13,000
	MMII	60	SS17M1	76	304	171	750KT		
Davis-Monthan AFB	TITANII	17	SS17M1	24	96	54	750KT	Tucson, AZ	479,000
Little Rock AFB	TITANII	17	SS17M1	24	96	54	750KT	Little Rock, AR	387,000
McConnell AFB	TITANII	18	SS17M1	26	104	57	750KT	Wichita, KS	411,000
Total		1052		712	4886	2723			1,607,000

at the Grand Forks and Minot Air Force Bases (AFB) in North Dakota. This group of ICBMs represents roughly 30 percent of the US ICBM force, and without doubt, is the most capable countersilo weapon in the US nuclear arsenal, a fact that makes the MMIIIA the highest Soviet priority target. In this attack, 55 Soviet SS-18M4 ICBMs were targeted against each group of 150 missiles, for a total of 110 attacking Soviet ICBMs in this wave. As shown in Table 7, roughly 307 of the 550 RVs that were launched detonated at each missile field. This equals more than 600 nuclear surface-burst detonations in the two ICBM fields for a two-on-one attack (2 RVs for each silo). Given this number of nuclear detonations, the attrition rate for Soviet ICBMs is 40 percent, i.e., 60 percent of the Soviet RVs performed as one would expect. Regardless of how this level of attrition may be judged, it results in the probable destruction of 300 MMIIIA ICBMs, and correspondingly, the depletion of 110 Soviet ICBMs, or roughly 8 percent of the Soviet ICBM force. Again, for reference it was assumed that this Soviet countersilo attack entailed a two-on-one allocation scheme of two RVs for each silo; and that the attack consisted of surface-bursts in a south-to-north targeting scheme of sequential explosions. It was assumed as well that some surviving MMIIIAs might be "pinned" down in the attack by a combination of nuclear effects: x-rays, blast, heat, and debris.

Beyond the miasma of details about how many Soviet and American nuclear forces were used and lost, there remains the matter of the collateral casualties for the populations that live in the areas immediately adjacent to and downwind of the missile fields. The primary collateral targets, Grand Forks and Minot, North Dakota, which have populations of 99,000 and 34,000, respectively, are calculated to have been destroyed by the post-attack radioactive fallout, resulting in roughly 135,000 casualties.[8] As noted earlier, we assume that 50 percent of these casualties will die within 30–60 days from exposure to the radioactive fallout. As a normal event in a statistical sense, it is possible that one or more nuclear warheads inadvertently may have struck the cities, which would result in still higher numbers of immediate dead. While these figures for collateral casualties do not seem particularly high at this point in a nuclear war, the reader is urged to pay close attention to the magnitude of civilian casualties that will occur in what are essentially "pure" counterforce (non-civilian) attacks. Table 7 alone shows the projected civilian losses from an attack on American ICBM fields only.

Phase II: Minuteman IIIB

In the next phase of the USSR's countersilo attack on the US, the targets will be 250 Minuteman IIIB ICBMs. Fifty of the MMIIIB are deployed at Malmstrom AFB in Montana, while the remaining 200 ICBMs are at Warren AFB in Colorado. The first 50 MMIIIB missiles at Malmstrom AFB were targeted with 19 SS-18M4 ICBMs; of the 190 RVs launched, 105 or 55 percent detonated in a two-on-one warhead allocation scheme. The destruction of the remaining 200 MMIIIB ICBMs at Warren AFB becomes a bit more complex, principally because the remaining 46 SS-18M4 ICBMs in the Dombarovskiy missile field are not numerically sufficient for the attack. Of the 46 SS-18M4 ICBMs that were launched, 255 of the 460 RVs detonated on target, which resulted in the loss of 127 MMIIIB ICBMs. Therefore, it is estimated that 73 MMIIIB ICBMs would survive the attack. To accomplish the destruction of the 73 MMIIIBs, 50 SS-18M2 ICBMs were launched as part of the wave of attacking Soviet ICBMs, of which 222 RVs, or 55 percent, detonated in the ICBM field. As a summary of the attack, 200 MMIIIB ICBMs were destroyed by a total of 115 Soviet ICBMs (65 SS-18M4 and 50 SS-18M2 ICBMs), and roughly 480 nuclear surface-burst detonations. In terms of collateral losses, it is projected that Great Falls, MT (population: 88,000) and Cheyenne, CO (population: 3,000) would be destroyed in the Soviet strike, and that there would be approximately 90,000 immediate civilian casualties in this attack on the two missile fields in the American mid-west.

Phase III: Minuteman II

Four-hundred fifty MMII ICBMs in the US nuclear arsenal are deployed in wings of 150 each at Ellsworth AFB in South Dakota, Malmstrom AFB in Montana, and Whiteman AFB in Missouri. In comparison with the capabilities of the MMIIIA and MMIIIB, the MMII probably ranks third on the Soviet list of countersilo targeting priorities. Despite its lower ranking in this hypothetical list of targeting priorities, it nevertheless is a critical target from the Soviet perspective because of its prompt launching and targeting capabilities. To begin with, the first group of 150 MMIIs at Ellsworth AFB was targeted by a wave composed of 57 Soviet SS-18M2 ICBMs. Of the 456 total RVs launched, 252 or 55 percent detonated at the missile field for an effective three-on-one attack. This attack resulted in the destruction of 84 MMII ICBMs. Then, surviving 66 MMIIs were targeted by 60 Soviet SS19M1 ICBMs; 202 RVs, or 56 percent of the RVs that were launched, detonated in this three-on-one attack. It is important to reiterate that the ratio of RVs to individual silos is a function of the RVs' probability of kill and Warhead Lethality Score (WLS). This scoring is, in turn, a function of an equation which relates CEP, yield, cratering effect, and launch and detonation reliability rates to produce a warhead allocation scheme. As shown in Table 7, there are 360 RVs on the 60 SS-19M1 ICBMs, as each SS-19M1 ICBM carries 6 RVs. The primary collateral city, Rapid City, South Dakota (population: 93,000), was presumed to be inundated by the post-attack radioactive fallout that would settle downwind of the missile field.

The 150 MMII lCBMs at the Malmstrom AFB in Montana suffered a similar fate. Of a total of 135 Soviet SS19M1 ICBMs that were launched against Malmstrom AFB, 454 or 55 percent of the RVs detonated at the field in a three-on-one allocation scheme. Since Malmstrom AFB was targeted in Phase II by virtue of the 50 MMIIIB ICBMs that were deployed there, no additional collateral casualties would be calculated in this attack. Finally, the 150 MMII ICBMs at Whiteman AFB were targeted by 85 SS-19M1 and 76 SS-17M1 ICBMs. As shown in Table 7, 283 of the 510 SS-19M1 RVs, and 171 of the 304 SS-17M1 RVs, actually detonated at the silos in three-on-one attacks. The primary collateral target for Whiteman AFB is Warrensboro (population: 13,000), which of course would be calculated as an immediate civilian loss.

As a summary of the targeting in Phase III, the Soviet Union launched more than 400 ICBMs against 450 MMII missile silos in the US. Even though the average attrition rate for the Soviet land-based missiles was 55 percent, there were approximately 1,300 surface-burst explosions in the states of South Dakota, Montana and Missouri. In terms of the USSR, this means that roughly 30 percent of its land-based ICBM force was used in this attack. For the US, more than 40 percent of its land-based missiles were destroyed, and more than 100,000 collateral civilian casualties were sustained in this Soviet countersilo attack. It is uncertain whether we can judge this exchange ratio to be advantageous for the USSR. Since, however, the USSR used more than 1,300 warheads for the destruction of less than 500 point targets, it might seem to be a somewhat inequitable exchange ratio for the USSR. On the other hand, this phase of the Soviet attack would result in the destruction of approximately 2,100 American ICBM warheads, which for an attacker might seem to be militarily significant. This, however, involves a judgment as to the significance of exchange ratios in determining the value of the attack. Properly speaking, this is a matter for the reader to judge.

Phase IV: Titan II

The final phase of the Soviet Union's countersilo attack against the US hardly seems more than trivial: roughly 50 Titan II ICBMs are at stake. While this small force of aging, obsolete ICBMs does not seem significant in comparison with the other 1,000 Minuteman ICBMs in the US force, the 9 MT warheads on the Titan II ICBMs could cause enormous damage to several dozen large urban targets in the USSR. They also could be used against soft C3 targets by virtue of their large radius of damage. In any event, the three wings of 17 Titan II ICBMs at Davis-Monthan AFB in Arizona, Little Rock AFB in Arkansas, and McConnell AFB in Kansas were targeted by waves of 24 SS-17M1 ICBMs. As shown in Table 7, roughly 54 RVs, or 56 percent of those launched, detonated at the three missile fields in

a three-on-one attack. By most measures, this loss of ICBMs is hardly significant in terms of military utility. In terms of collateral civilian losses, however, the results would be disproportionately devastating. More than 1.1 million civilians are calculated to be casualties from the effects of post-attack
radioactive fallout in the three primary cities: Tucson, Arizona (population:
479,000); Little Rock, Arkansas (population: 387,000); and Wichita, Kansas
(population: 411,000). In rough terms, the destruction of 5 percent of the US
ICBM force resulted in the immediate loss of more than 1 million people.

Countersilo Summary The countersilo phase of the USSR's counterforce
attack on the United States resulted in the destruction of 1,052 US ICBMs
and approximately 1.6 million civilian casualties.[9] To accomplish this task,
the USSR launched a wave of 700 ICBMs (approximately 50 percent of its
ICBM force) and nearly 5,000 RVs, of which 2,700 detonated. The mean
attrition rate in this scenario was 45 percent—in other words, 55 percent of
the RVs launched operated successfully. This means that the USSR, even if
we assume fairly substantial levels of missile attrition, could destroy the
entire US ICBM arsenal with about half of its land-based ICBM force.
Looking ahead to the remaining phases of the USSR's counterforce attack on
the US, the USSR still has roughly 700 ICBMs and intact bomber and
submarine forces for use against American targets. This capability translates
into a degree of strategic (as opposed to "unrestricted") superiority in the
unlikely event that the USSR ever attempted this kind of attack. The US, by
comparison, would virtually disarm itself in a similar countersilo attack
against the Soviet Union. This, of course, does not mean the the Soviet
Union would do such a thing, for the US still has significant countervalue
(city-busting) capabilities on its submarines at sea (a subject that we will
explore in Chapter 5). Nevertheless, the fact remains that the USSR theoretically could destroy US land-based ICBMs in a preemptive attack if we
assume a moderate level of attrition as well as general uncertainty about the
outcome of the attack.

Perhaps the central issue in this discussion of a Soviet countersilo attack
against the US is the rationality of the attack. How rational would it be for
the USSR to launch an attack on US ICBM silos if that attack would require
as many as 5,000 RVs for the destruction of 1,000 targets? The easiest answer
is that this worst case scenario suggests that the USSR, in using so much of
its ICBM force, hardly achieves significant results—unless the elimination
of the US ICBM force is a critical objective for the USSR's military leadership. A different way of looking at this issue is to realize that, even if the
attrition rates in reality were significantly less than we show here, the USSR
still would have to expend thousands of warheads. In either case, the rationality of this attack depends on the importance that the Soviets assign to
the destruction of American ICBMs. Seeing that US ICBMs present the
greatest threat to the array of hard-target sites in the USSR, it is not hard to
understand that their prompt elimination not only reduces US retaliatory

options but also diminishes the size of any US counterattack against cities or military targets in the USSR. American ICBM fields thus are targets of enormous value to the USSR.

In the sterile atmosphere of this intellectual (and hypothetical) analysis of nuclear war, who can argue with the conclusion that rationality has a very different meaning from that which would prevail in the peacetime environment. In peace, there are no immediate pressures to make decisions that may have far-reaching and catastrophic consequences. Yet, in a crisis that might lead to a nuclear war, it seems likely that the definition of rationality might change slowly and imperceptibly, so that what once seemed absurd or foolish in academic discussions now would represent a realistic choice. Then, to a Soviet decision-maker the prospect of launching half of its ICBM force in order to destroy the US ICBM force might seem more rational than it ever could have been in the past. It is at this point that the preceding scenario of a Soviet countersilo attack on the US missile fields might seem all too realistic and plausible. Yet, to some this defense of admittedly improbable scenarios that are based on crisis irrationality is not compelling because it seems to forget that the underlying uncertainty about the outcome of such an attack would never disappear, even in the worst of crises. Not even the USSR would fall prey to the worst of contemporary sins, that of believing in the technological quick-fix of a preemptive nuclear attack on the United States. To this line of thought, which seems compelling in that it argues fundamentally for a human predisposition for rational thinking in crises, we offer the observation that it is hard to dismiss this scenario on the grounds that humans will recognize foolishly self-destructive behavior for what it is before they attempt it. Thus, the case for the preceding countersilo scenario rests fundamentally on the argument that, if the USSR were to fall prey to the worst of temptations in a nuclear crisis, then this is but one example of what might happen. Admittedly, this rationale is tautological in character. It justifies futurological scenarios on the presupposition of systemic human irrationality, and, that human irrationality all too often can make otherwise foolish actions appear to be rational. Right or wrong, there are too many historical instances wherein the unthinkable seemed perfectly rational to the participants at the time. The Battle of the Somme in 1916, for instance, comes immediately to mind.

By the standard of a US countersilo attack on the USSR, which seemed far more complex and intricate because all legs of the US nuclear triad were launched, the USSR's countersilo attack on the US was a somewhat more straightforward and simple operation. It, after all, involved the launch of several hundred Soviet missiles against ten ICBM fields in the US, whereas the US attack on Soviet silos required the launching of many more American ICBMs, not to mention the SLBMs and bombers that were involved in the scenario. Whether this fact allows us to deduce something of truly monumental proportions remains to be seen. There is no doubt, however, that the mechanics of a countersilo attack are far simpler for the USSR, if all other factors, such as technology, remain equal. In reality, such a countersilo attack would be a highly complex and delicate operation that involves the coordination of thousands of RVs, wherein even relatively minor errors could have catastrophic results for the attacker. This is not, therefore, meant to lessen the difficulties that are inherent in any such attack, but only to infer that such difficulties probably are greater for the US. Thus, to speak about US-USSR countersilo capabilities is to discern a significant disadvantage for the US. In comparative terms, we find that the allocation of RVs in a countersilo attack is less complex, in terms of planning, timing, and execution, for the USSR. While this scenario is hardly a paradigm of simplicity for the Soviets, theirs is an easier task. It is difficult to know whether this would change the fundamental logic of deterrence that emphasizes the uncertainty of the outcome. In a crisis, the USSR might be tempted to launch this attack, thinking as they did that the greater simplicity of the task gives them an advantage (however fleeting) that the US does not possess. And in the deepest sense, the logic of crisis behavior and thinking is what we should be concerned with here, for who in normal times would consider these activities as anything other than suicidal? So, in the narrow sense of plausibility, this worst-case scenario is far more realistic than some might otherwise have dared to imagine.

US BOMBER BASES

In recent years the vulnerability of US bomber bases has emerged as a serious challenge to the survivability of the alternative legs of the triad. By any standard, a bomber base (and its aircraft) are inherently vulnerable to nuclear attack because it is a soft target. Most of the bombers and structures at the bases can withstand a maximum of between 5–10 psi overpressure, which would be found at the outer edges of a weapon's lethal radius. This means that even if the warhead detonates at the maximum permissible distance from the base (so that the detonation occurs near the outer edge of the warheads' lethal radius) the base will be subjected to levels of overpressure that are capable of destroying or damaging bombers. For instance, the 950 KT warhead on the SS-11M3 ICBM has lethal radii of 5.1 and 8.3 nautical miles for surface-burst and air-burst detonations, respectively. An escaping aircraft at the limit of 5 miles from the surface-burst explosion would encounter between 2–4 psi, which is more than enough to cause structural damage to the bombers and, quite possibly, might cause the bombers to crash. If the bomber had an average escape speed of 200 mph, then the aircraft would be vulnerable to blast effects (this does not include thermal pulse or neutron flux) for the 3 minutes it would be within the lethal radius of the weapon. Even in the case of a surface-burst, which might be used in order to disable the base and thereby prevent later use, the base and its bombers could be destroyed quite easily. Moreover, if the preemptive attack is such that warning time is limited to extremely low levels, aircraft on the ground as well as escaping bombers could be destroyed quite easily. For these reasons the bomber bases in the United States are vulnerable to destruction in a Soviet counterforce attack, particularly if the attack (as in this case) is initiated by an attack on the US command and warning system that momentarily blinded the United States with EMP. US bomber bases in any case were not designed to provide even nominal levels of protection against overpressure from nearby nuclear explosions. Thus, we see the issue of bomber vulnerability as an important, and threatening, dimension of a massive counterforce attack.

Table 8 shows the results of a Soviet strike against US bomber bases as well as the location of and type of aircraft stationed at the 26 bomber bases in the continental US (SAC bases in NATO countries were excluded from this study). There are at the time of this writing 379 US bombers: 319 B-52s and 60 FB-111s. Based on available targeting information, the 319 B-52s are deployed at 20 bases scattered throughout the US. Interestingly, the 60 FB-111s are deployed at six bases, all of which are in the northernmost tier of states (Maine, New Hampshire, New York, Michigan, and Washington). This, of course, is the result of the shorter range of the FB-111. In any event, it was assumed that the bombers are distributed uniformly at the bases, so that an average of 16 B-52s and 10 FB-111s will be at each base. Although the aircraft are moved about from time to time, they still land at the few available bases. Thus, the law of average distribution will hold. In a typical attack, the bomber bases were targeted with either two 600 KT warheads on SS13 ICBMs or two 950 KT warheads on SS11M3 ICBMs. To compensate for the expected attrition of the Soviet ICBMs, four of the single-warhead ICBMs were launched against each bomber base in anticipation that roughly half of the four warheads would detonate. Despite the smaller lethal radii of the warheads, this attack was calculated on the basis of surface-bursts, so that the cratering of the runways would effectively prevent any further use of the bases. An alternative tactic would be to air-burst the warheads to increase the lethal radii of overpressure, as this would magnify the risks of aircraft "blow-down." This effect occurs when bombers escaping from the base are knocked down by the blast of nearby nuclear explosions. One tactic, for instance, is to calculate the likely bomber escape routes in order to detonate the warheads where they will destroy as many bombers as possible. In reality, some US bombers would survive a surprise Soviet counterforce attack as the result of attack uncertainties, variations in escape time, and a host of other imponderables.[10] If it is assumed, however, that the Soviet attack on US command centers effectively blinded the warning system, then one can see how large numbers of bombers could be caught on the ground or near their bases. This assumes as well that the bombers are sufficiently hardened against EMP. Thus, in this typical scenario most of the US bomber

Table 8
Soviet Attack on US Bomber Bases

Target	Bomber	No.	Sov. Weapon	No.	Total	Detonations	Yield	City	Casualties
Altus AFB	B52A	16	SS13	4	4	2	600KT	Altus, OK	27,000
Barksdale AFB	B52A	16	SS13	4	4	2	600KT	Shreveport, LA	359,000
Beale AFB	B52A	16	SS13	4	4	2	600KT	N/A	------
Blythesville AFB	B52A	16	SS13	4	4	2	600KT	Blythesville, AK	25,000
Carswell AFB	B52A	20	SS13	4	4	2	600KT	Fort Worth, TX	351,000
Castle AFB	B52B	16	SS13	4	4	2	600KT	Merced, CA	34,000
Dyess AFB	B52B	16	SS13	4	4	2	600KT	Abilene, TX	130,000
Ellsworth AFB	B52B	16	SS13	4	4	2	600KT	Rapid City, SD	------
Fairchild AFB	B52B	16	SS13	4	4	2	600KT	Spokane, WA	328,000
Grand Forks AFB	B52B	16	SS13	4	4	2	600KT	Grand Forks, ND	------
Grissom AFB	B52B	16	SS13	4	4	2	600KT	Peru, IN	13,000
Johnson AFB	B52B	16	SS13	4	4	2	600KT	Goldsboro, NC	36,000
March AFB	B52B	16	SS13	4	4	2	600KT	San Bernardino, CA	104,000
Mather AFB	B52B	16	SS13	4	4	2	600KT	Stockton, CA	320,000
McConnell AFB	B52C	16	SS13	4	4	2	600KT	Wichita, KS	------
Minot AFB	B52C	16	SS11M3	5	5	2	950KT	Minot, ND	------
Offutt AFB	B52C	16	SS11M3	5	5	2	950KT	Omaha, NB	589,000
Robins AFB	B52C	16	SS11M3	5	5	2	950KT	Warren-Robins, GA	43,000
Travis AFB	B52C	11	SS11M3	5	5	2	950KT	Berkeley, CA	112,000
Wurtsmith AFB	B52D	16	SS11M3	5	5	2	950KT	Oscoda, MI	7,000
Bremerton AFB	FB111A	10	SS11M3	5	5	2	950KT	Seattle, WA	------
Loring AFB	FB111A	10	SS11M3	5	5	2	950KT	Limestone, ME	2,000
Plattsburgh AFB	FB111A	10	SS11M3	5	5	2	950KT	Plattsburgh, NY	25,000
Griffis AFB	FB111B	10	SS11M3	5	5	2	950KT	Rome, NY	47,000
Pease AFB	FB111B	10	SS11M3	5	5	2	950KT	Portsmouth, NH	24,000
Sawyer AFB	FB111B	10	SS11M3	5	5	2	950KT	Marquette, MI	75,000
Total		379		115	115	52			2,654,000

force was destroyed in the attack; that is, most of the 379 aircraft are counted as casualties in the exchange. For the US, this represents a significant loss of its total number of warheads and the equivalent megatonnage of the force. And, in terms of collateral damage to primary urban centers, there would be more than 2 million civilian casualties.

In this attack the USSR launched a total of 115 ICBMs (60 SS-13 and 55 SS-11M3), in which 52 RVs or 45 percent of the warheads detonated at the 26 bases. In terms of the USSR's ICBM force, roughly 8 percent of the launchers and a relatively insignificant fraction of ICBM RVs were used. Although the USSR could have allocated a larger number of warheads to the US bomber bases, the effects of nuclear decapitation and EMP raise the theoretical possibility that a large fraction of the bomber force could be destroyed in a surprise attack. The USSR could have targeted SLBMs against US bomber bases, just as SLBMs were used during the initial salvo on the command centers. The shorter flight times of SLBMs, however, does not outweigh the fact that Soviet SLBMs generally are considered to be less reliable than its ICBMs. An alternative scenario in which SLBMs, instead of ICBMs, are targeted against US bomber bases decreases the amount of warning time for the US and therefore in all likelihood increases Soviet confidence in the outcome of the attack. Nevertheless, in this scenario Soviet ICBMs were allocated against US bomber bases in order to increase their confidence in the outcome of attack. It should be recognized that the difference between using ICBMs and SLBMs involves a tradeoff between warning time and weapon reliability.

US SUBMARINE BASES

Perhaps the most vulnerable counterforce target in the US is the submarine (SSBN) base. Not only is it a soft target and therefore vulnerable to overpressure, but the SSBNs in port cannot flee rapidly (in anything less than several hours) from the base once it is learned that a nuclear attack is imminent. Thus, the high value of the SSBN base is a function of the number of boats in port at any time and the number of SLBMs in the boats. At a typical US SSBN base, for instance at Bangor, Washington, under normal (non-generated) alert conditions, there might be four SSBNs in residence. If each boat carried 16 SLBMs, the base could house 64 SLBMs and up to 640 SLBMs RVs—assuming 10 MIRVs per launcher. This extremely high concentration of offensive nuclear warheads leads to a Soviet attack that logically would assign a high value to the destruction of the SSBN base in a counterforce nuclear war. A further incentive to the USSR is the relative vulnerability of the SSBNs. Like the port repair facilities, docks, and related equipment at the base, the SSBN is not a hard target. Although there are no unclassified data on the hardness of US SSBNs, it is doubtful that a submarine can withstand more than 100 psi if the same attack phenomena that

Table 9

Soviet Attack on US SSBN Bases

Target	SSBN	No.	Sov. Weapon	No.	Total	Detonations	Yield	City	Casualties
Bangor	SSBN	4	SS17M1	2	8	3	750KT	Seattle, WA	1,524,000
Charleston	SSBN	4	SS17M1	2	8	3	750KT	Charleston, SC	399,000
Kings Bay	SSBN	4	SS17M1	2	8	3	750KT	Brunswick, GA	20,000
Guam, PH	SSBN	4	SS17M1	2	8	3	750KT	Guam, PH	81,000
Holy Loch	SSBN	4	SS17M1	2	8	3	750KT	N/A	
Total		20		10	40	15			2,024,000

applied to the US preemptive attack on Soviet SLBM bases apply in this attack. In any event, US SSBNs in port, SLBMs, as well as the associated maintenance and repair facilities at an SSBN base, are highly vulnerable and lucrative targets in a nuclear war for either side.

The assumption in this Soviet counterforce attack on the five US submarine bases (see Table 9) is that each of the bases contains four submarines on non-generated alert. Some combination of Poseidon and Trident SLBM submarines would be distributed at these bases, the exact distribution being a function of the mix of Poseidon and Trident SLBMs in the force.

This Soviet attack was composed of waves of two SS-17M1 ICBMs, each missile carrying four 750 KT warheads. Based on the predicted attrition rates, three of the eight ICBM RVs would be expected to detonate as surface-bursts at the submarine bases. The surface-burst was selected in order to maximize the lethal effects of the shock waves in the air and the water, just as in the US attack on the Soviet bases. Moreover, the fallout from a surface-burst would contaminate the SSBN base area for a considerable time, making repairs to the SSBNs and the reloading of SLBMs an extremely difficult operation, even months or years after the attack. This attack hardly would be a clean affair, yet it would eliminate the possibility of reusing the base, particularly if the two sides became engaged in a protracted nuclear war.

The immediate losses to the US nuclear arsenal would be enormous: 15 of 31 SSBNs (45 percent) would be destroyed, probably before any of the submarines could escape to sea where they would be essentially immune to destruction. On a rough scale, this represents the loss of somewhere between 2,000 and 2,400 US RVs, resulting in by far the most economical Soviet attack in terms of the number of warheads destroyed versus the number of warheads launched.

The magnitude of this favorable attack ratio for the USSR is apparent when one considers that only ten ICBMs (for a total of 40 RVs) were expended for the destruction of approximately 2,000 US SLBM RVs. In a typical attack against a US SLBM base, say at Bangor, Washington, four SSBNs would be destroyed by the effects of the 750 KT surface-burst explosions from SS-17M1s. As noted, the pressure waves from the bursts would either crush the hull of the SSBN if it were close to the point of detonation, or possibly beach the submarine. The bases would be cascaded by thousands of tons of highly radioactive water, and thereby would contaminate (if not eliminate) the base as a potential site for operations in a protracted war.

One unfortunate consequence of the decision to use surface-bursts to maximize the probability of SSBN destruction is the higher levels of damage that will be inflicted on collateral US cities. Based on the populations that are adjacent to US SSBN bases, roughly 2 million civilians will become casualties from the radioactive debris. In summary, the USSR attack on US SSBN bases resulted in the immediate loss of nearly half of the SSBN force and high civilian casualties.

For its part, the USSR launched an insignificant number of ICBMs (or RVs) in the attack, despite the heavy losses sustained by the US. As a soft and vulnerable array of targets, SSBN bases are the most lucrative targets in the US on the basis of the exchange ratio: 40 RVs launched to 2,000+ RVs destroyed, or an exchange ratio in excess of 1:50. From a strategic perspective, it is probably impossible to avoid the vulnerability of SSBN bases in an enemy attack, although it is feasible to avoid the collocation of SSBN bases with civilian urban centers. Even this might prove difficult to do given the symbiotic relationship that obtains between military bases and cities in terms of the latter's supplies of economic resources and skilled manpower.

US SSBNS ON PATROL

The SSBN on patrol remains the most secure leg of the US nuclear triad, and is likely to be so for the foreseeable future. In comparison with Soviet SSBNs, the US fleet of 31 SSBNs probably are quieter and less detectable than their Soviet counterparts in terms of either acoustic or non-acoustic methods of SSBN detection. Today, the physical and electronic systems for muffling the acoustic and non-acoustic emissions of the SSBNs are reportly so sophisticated that anecdotally, in the estimate of one US ASW commander, US SSBNs literally can be undetectable to the sensing systems even when within visual sight of the ASW crew on the mission.[11] It is hardly an exaggeration to say that all evidence points convincingly to the invulnerability of the US SSBN force, although the secrecy that surrounds the Navy's submarine program makes it difficult to verify this situation. Yet, one need not look very far to find a plethora of affirmations that the Soviet ASW program is not likely to find US SSBNs when they are on patrol in the oceans. From the standpoint of a chapter on a Soviet counterforce attack on the US, the issue would be closed with respect to Soviet attempts to target US SSBNs on patrol. Even those who do not take issue with the vulnerability of US missile silos would find it difficult to contemplate seriously the possibility that the Soviet Union could launch effective attacks on US submarines. From virtually all sides of the nuclear debate, and one does not have to look hard for signs of debate and disagreement in this field, there is near certainty about the survivability of US ballistic-missile submarines. While we do not challenge this proposition in any fundamental way, something ought to be said about targeting SSBNs. It is not difficult to understand why this is the case.

Even when we consider the large number of warheads on bombers or ICBMs, the SSBN fleet still remains the single largest concentration of nuclear warheads on one platform. An *Ohio*-class SSBN, for instance, could carry up to 240 nuclear warheads, which are more than enough warheads for targeting the 50–75 largest cities in the USSR, depending on one's assumptions about the allocation of warheads and their reliability. In general, the

SSBN on patrol is such a lucrative target that a Soviet nuclear war planner could not ignore the submarines altogether. It is clear that, from a practical point of view, a Soviet planner surely would be remiss not to consider an attack on US submarines, but whether the Soviets could succeed in this ambitious mission, is a matter of deep concern and dispute. In the late 1970s, some in the Pentagon (William Perry, to name but the most prominent) argued that US SSBNs *could* be vulnerable to a barrage attack by Soviet ICBMs or SLBMs. This Soviet option, as noted earlier, might lead to the destruction of a fraction of the US SSBN force that is normally at sea. Of the 31 boats, roughly 16–17 are on patrol at any given time, with the remainder, of course, in port, which places them in a vulnerable position.

It is enormously difficult to predict how many US SSBNs might be destroyed in a barrage attack by Soviet land-based ICBMs. A substantive discussion of this subject would entail access to "code-word" information that obviously is not available in this analysis. Neither can we begin even to estimate the effect of the recent espionage coup by the Soviets in the Walker case that was discovered in the summer of 1985. From the sketchy reports that have appeared in the media, the damage may be very serious. Still, on the most general level, it does seem fair to suggest that a small number, perhaps between two and four US SSBNs, could be destroyed as part of a Soviet counterforce attack. Applying the laws of conservative (oftentimes called "worst-case") analysis, the attrition of several US submarines through conventional and nuclear ASW methods is an eminently reasonable assumption for an American or Soviet planner. By its very nature, it avoids the sort of "crisis" conclusions, such as the view that the entire SSBN force is in perilous danger, that so often serve as evidence of an analyst's conviction, rather than a studied assessment of the problem. While it may be true that the American SSBN force is in mortal danger from Soviet interdiction, there are no conclusive data to support such a claim. Nor, for that matter, are there data to suggest the opposite, that US SSBNs are completely secure from destruction by the USSR. Confident that the truth lies somewhere in the middle, the conclusion here is that the US should expect to lose a small number of its SSBNs that are on patrol from a Soviet counterforce attack. It seems reasonable to project that the vast majority of the SSBN force probably will survive long enough to execute a retaliatory strike against military or urban targets in the USSR. In Chapter 5, we will explore the capability of the US SSBN force in one dimension: an attack against countervalue targets in the USSR based on the SSBNs that might survive a preemptive Soviet attack.

High-Risk States in Countersilo Attacks

In a nuclear war, not only would the entire nation suffer enormous human and physical losses, but the globe *might* undergo a prolonged period of post-

Table 10
US High-Risk States in Countersilo Attack

State	ICBM	No.	Base
Arkansas	TITAN	17	Little Rock AFB
Arizona	TITAN	17	Davis-Monthan AFB
Kansas	TITAN	18	McConnell AFB
Montana	MMIII MMII	50 150	Malmstrom AFB
Missouri	MMII	150	Whiteman AFB
North Dakota	MMIII MMIII	150 150	Grand Forks AFB Minot AFB
Wyoming	MMIII	200	Warren AFB
South Dakota	MMII	150	Ellsworth AFB

war cooling as a result of the millions of tons of dust that might be injected into the stratosphere from surface-burst explosions and fires. Somewhat expectedly, this "nuclear winter" scenario remains highly uncertain. What is less uncertain, however, is that selected states in the US will suffer far more than others in the event of a countersilo nuclear war. For political and economic reasons, US ICBM bases were constructed in eight states that are primarily in the midwestern quadrant of the continent. As shown in Table 10, five of the eight states (Montana, Missouri, North Dakota, South Dakota, and Wyoming) are home to the 1,000 Minuteman ICBM silos. Excluding the three states (Arkansas, Arizona, Kansas) where the 52 Titan ICBMs are deployed, the states where the Minuteman ICBMs are deployed will be inundated by thousands of nuclear explosions, most of which will be surface-bursts. Depending on the assumptions about the structure of the attack, somewhere between 3,000 and 4,000 RVs will detonate in these states. The proximity of these missile bases to civilian centers, and the fact that these bases are collocated with large urban populations, indicate that the populations in these and adjacent states will be decimated by post-attack radioactive fallout and the occasional warheads that land near (or in) cities. It is, therefore, appropriate to designate these five states as high-risk areas, and to note that these states will receive the brunt of the effects of a Soviet nuclear attack. Even if a nuclear war were to be terminated after a purely counterforce exchange, there would be staggering levels of destruction in these high-risk states, and in the states that are immediately downwind. It is estimated that between 10–40 million Americans would die in a countersilo war (see Tables 7–9) with losses nearer to the high side of the estimates. These states would receive a disproportionate share of the civilian losses by virtue of their proximity to lCBM bases, which are by any definition prime, high-priority targets in a Soviet nuclear attack.

US Launch on Warning

One of the responses that the United States might select during a Soviet counterforce attack is to launch its forces on warning, particularly the ICBM force. Aside from the salutary effects of launch on warning on stability, the more immediate concern here is with the effects of launch on warning on the outcome of a Soviet counterforce attack. Again, thinking in terms of the nuclear forces matrix and the effective kill ratio, a Soviet counterforce attack with ICBMs can destroy effectively the vast majority of the American nuclear triad. Rather than resulting in the near-complete disarming of the Soviet Union, an effective Soviet attack could leave large elements of its nuclear triad intact for later use as a post-attack reserve force. The fact that portions of the Soviet arsenal will not be launched during a preemptive counterforce attack raises the importance of launch on warning for the United States because this would threaten to destroy those portions of the Soviet triad that otherwise would escape unscathed during the attack. If executed properly, US launch on warning can restore some balance to the reserve forces of the two nations, particularly if the United States attacks the remaining ICBMs, SLBMs, and bombers in the Soviet arsenal that were not launched originally.

Perhaps the crucial difference between launch on warning for the United States and the Soviet Union is the magnitude of the forces that would not be launched in a Soviet counterforce attack. A substantial fraction of the ICBM, SLBM, and bomber forces still would be available to the Soviets after a successful preemptive attack against the United States, and it is this force that constitutes the prime targets for US launch on warning. In some senses, the United States can restore some balance to the post-war balance of forces by destroying the Soviet reserve forces that otherwise would survive. Thus, from the American perspective, launch on warning has great utility because it keeps US and Soviet reserve forces on an equal level, and thereby denies the Soviets the hope of destroying US forces and retaining a reserve force that is large enough to deter the Americans from further reprisals against both counterforce and countervalue targets in the USSR. It goes without saying that launch on warning can be a destabilizing policy in a crisis because of the inherent pressure to retaliate on the basis of warning, rather than empirical confirmation of an attack. Still, that difficulty notwithstanding, launch on warning for the United States can lessen any advantage that the USSR might have after a counterforce attack by virtue of reversing what otherwise would be an asymmetrical balance of forces that favors the Soviet Union.

SUMMARY

What we have just examined is a detailed account of how the USSR might execute a counterforce attack against the United States. This subject is by no means simple or straightforward, for it requires judgments as to how the USSR might think and act under circumstances of tremendous pressure and risk. This estimate, then, is based on the assumption that the Soviets, if they were serious about fighting a counterforce nuclear war, probably would think in rational, almost economic, terms about the conduct of the war. Stripped of all the latent emotion and passion, not to mention the quasi-theological quality of the debates that surround the theoretical possibility of counterforce scenarios, this is a purely technical prediction of how the USSR might attack counterforce targets in the United States if the objective is to execute a fully disarming attack. This is not to say that this is how the USSR might allocate warheads or that this particular sequence of events is correct. Rather, our objective was to understand the mechanics of a counterforce war, and particularly the relationship between different types of targets and their importance to the adversary.

For instance, the decision to attack C3 targets at the outset of the war reflected our judgment that decapitation is a credible option that could disrupt the US command system just long enough to cause confusion or hesitation in US retaliation. A Soviet military planner, accordingly, could well have the same expectations. In any event, a brief review of the results of this hypothetical counterforce attack by the USSR is in order.

In the opening phase of the exchange, the five primary complexes in the US C3 network were destroyed by a wave of SS-19M2 ICBMs. From a tactical perspective, the 10 MT warheads on the SS-19M2 were calculated to be surface-bursts in order to ensure the destruction of the sites. The precursor to this attack on C3 targets was a series of high-altitude nuclear explosions that were launched from Soviet SSBNs that detonated over the continental US, which created an intense field of EMP (at least 50,000 volts/meter) that temporarily blinded US sensors. The primary concern here, however, remains the destruction of the American C3 centers, and the level of collateral civilian casualties, which was estimated to be in the range of three million. Incidentally, it was assumed that Washington, D. C., which is one of the more critical C3 centers, would have been destroyed in the attack by ten 10 MT warheads. While this may be too many warheads, a conservative military planner would be compelled to allocate more warheads than necessary, particularly in an attack with a system for which there is no operational analogue or experience. The second phase of the counterforce war concerned the targeting of the ICBM fields in the US. Roughly 50 percent of the USSR's ICBMs were launched, creating a wave of nearly 5,000 RVs. Expected ICBM and RV failures, however, resulted in the detonation of approximately 2,700 RVs, for a 2.7:1 attack. It is difficult to predict whether an overall five-on-one (5 RVs launched per silo destroyed) attack scheme is an excessively conservative (or pessimistic, depending on one's perspective) estimate for the performance of Soviet ICBMs). Let us say that these particular results have the effect of minimizing the countersilo potential of the USSR. Yet, uncertainty about the operational reliability of Soviet systems forces us to place a premium on the expectation that there will be some attrition of weapons in a nuclear war. In the event that Soviet weapons are significantly more reliable than we have assumed in these projections, then this increases the magnitude of the Soviet countersilo potential, and gives the USSR a larger reserve force of ICBMs (not including bombers and SLBMs) after the exchange. The mean attrition rate in this scenario was 44 percent, which hardly seems to be an unreasonable estimate in view of our lack of operational experience with ICBMs. If, for example, the Soviet ICBM force were 90 percent reliable, then the attack on US silos could have been carried out with substantially (60 percent) fewer RVs.

Discounting questions about the timing of the attack, the scenario indicates that, even assuming nearly catastrophic attrition rates, the USSR could destroy the US ICBM force with roughly half of its ICBM force. If one recalls that the US launched waves of ICBMs, SLBMs, and bombers to destroy Soviet ICBM silos alone, then the magnitude of the Soviet capability becomes apparent. In relative terms, the US used most of its strategic forces to accomplish what the USSR achieved with half of its ICBM force. By any standard, we consider this to be an "edge" or "margin of superiority" in the narrow context of scenarios of nuclear war, which, admittedly, are of uncertain real-world value. Nevertheless, this limited indication of *relative* counterforce capabilities is perhaps the most significant.

In the remaining phases of the counterforce attack, Soviet ICBMs destroyed or disabled large portions of the US bomber force and submarine fleet at their respective bases. Based on these exchanges, the USSR eliminated most US strategic forces, with the exception of 16 or so SSBNs at sea, a couple of which were calculated to be lost in the exchange. Prompt civilian collateral casualties amounted to roughly 10 million—in truth, we expect that this number would double, triple, or even quadruple depending on the weather and wind conditions that exist at the time of the attack. On a general level, these collateral figures seem to accord well with numerous other estimates of the damage to urban populations that would result in a pure Soviet counterforce nuclear attack. It hardly matters whether these estimates are ultimately accurate, for on a long-term basis the final number of casualties probably will be several times greater than the number of prompt casualties.

There are numerous pitfalls and obvious dangers that confront those who attempt to project the outcome of a nuclear war, particularly a counterforce nuclear war in which there are so many variables and imponderables. Yet, we should not lose sight of the purpose behind this exercise: to project how the USSR might fight counterforce nuclear war, and what the outcome of such a war might be. From this perspective, perhaps this analysis will shed some light on the targets, allocation schemes, and general results of an attack of this magnitude. To proceed beyond this level of analysis to predictions about the timing or intricacies of an attack would be a dangerous, not to mention foolish and unscientific, exercise. By staying within the limits of this model, we can infer with a reasonable degree of confidence that the USSR has a substantially greater counterforce capability than the US. This fact emerges quite sharply from the scenarios that were depicted in Chapters 3 and 4. Irrespective of the particular details of the scenario, the fact is that the USSR retains a greater reserve force of ICBMs, SLBMs, and bombers after a counterforce attack than does the US after a similar exchange. Does this mean anything?

Who can say whether this "paper" advantage has real-world significance? In reality, an exchange limited to counterforce targets would cause such large-scale civilian casualties, and, quite possibly, might escalate into unrestrained countervalue ("city-busting") attack (see Chapters 5 and 6), that the war we have described would signify large-scale systemic destruction, and, in theory, might have adverse effects on the global ecological and climatological system. Thus, if we stay on the level of political and military realism, this Soviet "advantage" probably does not sway the global balance of power to any measurable degree. This advantage, however, most certainly does influence the ephemeral level of politics, where behavior is calculated not only as the product of military power, but also on the basis of confidence and that imperceptible sense of superiority. Masked by the frequently cited Soviet penchant for inferiority (which, parenthetically, we think is often overstated), it would be hard to ascertain whether this theoretical advantage might translate into more assertive Soviet behavior. Perhaps this level of speculation goes beyond the aims of this study. Nevertheless, it seems to us that the USSR has a definite edge over the US when it comes to the ability to destroy counterforce (hard) targets in a nuclear war.

_____ 5 _____

Soviet Countervalue Attacks

The last strand of peaceful coexistence snapped during the bitter winter of 1984, plunging the United States and the Soviet Union into a nuclear nightmare from which the world has yet to awaken. On January 8 of that year, nuclear warheads totalling more than 4,000 megatons destroyed military and industrial targets in the United States, killing close to 100 million people. Destruction ranged from the large industrial centers on the coasts and Great Lakes to small farming communities close to the great missile silos and military bases. The Northeast Corridor, from north of Boston to south of Norfolk [Virginia], was reduced to a swath of burning rubble.

—*The Day After Midnight: The Effects of Nuclear War*

In this grisly scenario of nuclear war, the violence was not confined to counterforce strikes, for it escalated quite rapidly past the threshold of a limited counterforce nuclear war. Hundreds of US cities, both large and small, had been obliterated by the Soviet nuclear attack that caused 100 million casualties. This is, in abbreviated form, what we shall consider here. The only difference is that this study will provide a more detailed view of the critical effects of a countervalue nuclear war, from a limited attack on New York City to an all-out "city-busting" attack against hundreds of American cities by the Soviet Union.

For a war such as this to begin there must have been a catastrophic failure of deterrence. For decades, the essential and irrevocable foundation of nuclear deterrence has been the ability to destroy the countervalue (urban-industrial) centers of the opponent. A nuclear war, therefore, could become a large-scale slaughter of civilian populations in what is euphemistically

111

known as an "urban-industrial" exchange. This threat, alone, can raise the cost of a nuclear war beyond that which even the most calloused of policymakers could accept or contemplate. In general, the consequences of a "city-busting" attack are known to be so appalling that even a limited attack would be a catastrophe of unparalleled proportions, a fate far worse than that which has happened in the innumerable wars throughout the millennia. It appears, at least on the basis of recent studies, that a nuclear war which concentrated on the destruction of urban centers could, through the resultant ash and smoke, cast a global pall that could exterminate all human life in the ice age that would ensue almost immediately.[1] While this scenario makes for good drama, few really accept the "nuclear winter" apocalypse as anything more than a remote theoretical possibility. Yet it seems to symbolize the almost universal fear of nuclear annihilation. Today, almost everyone accepts the logic of nuclear deterrence: that a nuclear war, in some form, will disintegrate into an unrestrained assault on US and Soviet cities.

It is difficult to imagine what the aftermath of a countervalue nuclear war would look like, principally because there are no examples in history that can be cited for describing carnage on this scale. What we do know is that all of the features of modern civilization will collapse in an instant: Government, schools, hospitals, homes, libraries, museums, industries, universities, research centers, and public utilities will be gone. Even worse, somewhere between 50–100 million people will die from the prompt effects alone. To be sure, this future is stark enough to terrify even the most resolute of souls. Yet, this is the undeniable reality of the present and the face of the future. Today, the US and USSR have the "ability" to start us on the path to destruction of this magnitude in less than 30 minutes. Whether deliberate or accidental, rational or irrational, there is nothing we can do to change this one essential, and inescapable, part of the political fabric of the twentieth century. Neither anguish or anger, nor fear or contempt will erase this feature of the contemporary landscape of international relations. So well entrenched is this mode of thinking in the conscious of the leadership in the US and USSR that the prospects for change are remote—if measurable in any real sense.

In this chapter we examine how the USSR might fight a countervalue nuclear war. This is done on three levels. The first section of this study explores the effects of a nuclear attack on New York City, providing a "microscopic" view of a nuclear war. This will serve to highlight in detail what a nuclear attack will mean for a large urban center, and thereby put in perspective much of what will happen to the tens or hundreds of other cities in the US urban-industrial complex as the result of a more comprehensive Soviet nuclear attack. The second section addresses a large-scale Soviet assault on the urban-industrial infrastructure of the United States in much the same way that a nuclear planner would approach the problem. US cities will be viewed as a series of potential targets, measured primarily in terms of their potential human and economic importance to the United States.

More specifically, alternative sets of targets will be created by grouping cities in terms of their population and contribution to the economy. While there are only some 300 or so American countervalue targets in this study, the target sets will provide an indication of the process by which the USSR might wage a nuclear war against population centers if the objective is to maximize damage. Finally, in the third section, we will examine the residual nuclear capabilities of the USSR that survived the US counterforce attack (see Chapter 3). The assumption is that since surviving Soviet nuclear forces might attack American cities, in this analysis it will be useful to estimate the extent of damage that the USSR could create in a retaliatory countervalue strike.

Each of the three instances gives an approximation of the shape of these explicit types of countervalue nuclear war. Certainly, the USSR could attack a major US city, such as New York, and thereafter terminate the exchange, having demonstrated the political resolve to fight such a war, and having recognized that further attacks would be futile and suicidal. It is easy to imagine that the carnage of a nuclear attack on New York alone might cause the leadership in the US and the USSR to stop the war, if in fact this would be possible, before things really got out of control. Alternatively, the USSR from the start of the war could wage a nuclear campaign against the hundreds of major urban centers in the US instead of attacking counterforce targets. Finally, the USSR could use the nuclear forces that happened to survive a preemptive US attack in order to incinerate as many US cities as it can. While these general alternatives establish the basic options that the USSR might follow in a nuclear war, neither any nor all of these options are intended to be inclusive of all that might happen in the event of a failure of deterrence. To be sure, this is, in the aggregate, a sufficiently comprehensive outline of the alternative nuclear disasters that the USSR can wreak upon the United States in the immediate and foreseeable future.

From a technical perspective, it is far easier to analyze the effect of a nuclear attack on a population center than a military target.[2] The well defined, discrete physical parameters of a nuclear explosion—whether airburst or surface-burst—cause fairly predictable levels of damage to urban structures and humans that are standardized for most cities. Accordingly, it is relatively easy to predict how a nuclear explosion may affect a city (in terms of casualties), at least in comparison with the highly uncertain effects of a nuclear attack against ICBM silos or C3 targets.

HYPOTHETICAL ATTACK ON NEW YORK CITY

In the 1964 movie "Fail Safe," a crisis brought on by a US technical mishap and deliberate radar jamming by the Soviets sent a squadron of US bombers on a one-way, and as it turned out, suicidal mission into the Soviet Union. The target was Moscow, which eventually was destroyed by the detonation of two ten megaton nuclear air-bursts over the Kremlin. Rather than face an inevitable all-out nuclear war, the US President ordered a US bomber to drop two ten megaton weapons on New York City. The film ended just seconds before the two warheads detonated—scenes of normal urban life filled the screen with the sights and sounds of life in New York City just moments before the world would end for its inhabitants. Nothing can match that chilling and helpless feeling as the viewer hopelessly watches as one of the world's largest metropolitan centers is about to be incinerated. Beyond doubt, everyone wondered what would happen to New York City: how many would die, would anyone survive, what would be left after the fires stopped burning?

Once we begin to shift from the emotional horror of the attack to the necessarily arcane mechanics of nuclear war, this vision loses much of its power. But the power of this image in reality lies with what really would happen to New York. We begin by addressing this fundamental question.

In this computer model, we have made a number of assumptions about the effects of a nuclear explosion and the structure of a city. In this example, the New York City standard metropolitan statistical area (SMSA) has a population of approximately 9 million, and an area of 1384 square miles that include Manhattan, the boroughs, as well as parts of suburban Connecticut and New Jersey. Here, the 9 million people are assumed to be more or less evenly distributed in the city, a fact that seems to correspond well with the daily migration of people in and out of the metropolis. Clearly, the number of casualties will vary by the time of the attack: At night, the larger number of people in the peripheral urban areas would lower the number of casualties, while during the day, the higher concentration (density) of people in the business district would increase the number of casualties in the city. By distributing the population evenly throughout New York, we can avoid the distortions in casualty estimates that would arise from the fact that the population in a major urban area is subject to wide fluctuations during the course of a day. This method provides a better baseline estimate of casualties in a nuclear attack on an urban target because it standardizes the time of the attack and therefore produces a normalized estimate of the distribution of people within the city.

The various attacks that are described are assumed to have the following constraints:

—The population in New York City had no warning of the attack and, therefore, no chance for sheltering or evacuation. The attack on New York City had no precursors.

—The attack occurred during the night when the population would be more evenly distributed than the daytime.

—The weather was clear. This means that the nuclear explosion was not attenuated by clouds, moisture, or precipitation.

—The warhead detonated at the optimum height of burst (HOB) for the yield specified.

—In all cases, ground zero was the Empire State Building in Lower Manhattan. In an air-burst, the warhead detonated more or less directly over the building. A surface-burst would detonate within several hundred meters of the structure.

—The population had no opportunity for relocation, evacuation, or sheltering. People, therefore, were afforded only such protection from weapon effects as structures might provide.

—The warheads were not designed to maximize fallout or direct radiation, such as the enhanced radiation ("neutron") bomb. While the normal mechanisms of a surface-burst would cause radioactive fallout, the fallout was not enhanced through weapon design techniques.

—Most important, these estimates of casualties should be viewed as just that: *estimates*. In any nuclear attack, there are numerable uncertainties and imponderables associated with the event that could have a drastic effect on the outcome of the attack.

Nuclear Weapons Effects

The detonation of a nuclear weapon in an urban area, or any area for that matter, will produce a number of damaging effects.[3] Many of these phenomena will damage people and physical structures, such as buildings, either individually or through a synergistic combination of effects.

Blast When a nuclear weapon detonates, it is followed by a rapidly expanding and intensely hot (and radar opaque) sphere of ionized gas. This plasma is the fireball, which radiates energy in numerous wavelengths of the electromagnetic spectrum. As this fireball expands it compresses the air in its path to produce a region of greatly increased atmosphere pressure. Known as overpressure, this region produces the well known blast effect of a nuclear detonation. The intensity of the blast wave decreases the farther one is from the explosion. In the vicinity of the fireball, overpressure (which is measured in pounds per square inch above normal atmosphere pressure of 14.7 psi), can be upwards of 100,000 psi. Farther out from the epicenter of the burst, it can be as low as 2–5 psi, but it still is capable of destroying ordinary steel and concrete buildings and injuring people. In New York City, or any urban center, the blast wave can crush or destroy urban structures, such as the buildings, bridges, and power plants that are found in cities and industrial areas. The blast wave also can shatter materials, such as glass and concrete, which become flying debris (shards) that can kill or injure people and decimate structures. While the human body can withstand overpressures up to 30 psi, unlike buildings that typically collapse with overpressure in the vicinity of 5–10 psi, many of the casualties will be the result of flying debris. Glass, for instance, can cause fatal lacerations to people who are in the open and exposed to the clouds of debris that will envelop the outer zones of the affected areas.

In general, the blast wave will destroy or topple many buildings, killing or entrapping the people within them. In an urban area, the effects of blast probably will cause the greatest damage to the population and the physical structures therein.[4] Depending on yield of the weapon, and specifically weapons yields that are greater than one megaton, a large fraction of the total casualties will be derived from the blast wave.

Direct Radiation As the detonation of a nuclear weapon produces an intense field of ionizing alpha and gamma radiation, the population near the explosion will receive varying dosages depending on their exact distance from the burst. Typically, one would not expect direct radiation to be a major cause of casualties, principally because modern buildings would absorb most of the radiation. More important, the population that is within a lethal range, which means that they will receive dosages greater than 600 rems, probably will be killed by the effects of the blast. By most standards, the direct radiation from an air-burst will not be one of the major causes of human casualties. So, in the case of New York, the casualties that are caused by direct radiation will be minimal in comparison with those that will be caused by blast and the other complex mechanisms of a nuclear explosion in an urban center.

Thermal Radiation A nuclear detonation generates a pulse of thermal radiation that varies in intensity with the distance from the explosion. One of the primary effects of thermal radiation is the creation of widespread fires, which are started by the deposition of heat energy on flammable substances. Wooden structures and nearby forested areas, for instance, can be ignited by the thermal radiation of a nuclear explosion even at great distances from the explosion. In terms of casualties, people who are exposed in the open can receive first-, second- or third-degree burns, depending on their precise distance from the explosion. A large number of casualties also will result from the massive conflagrations that can be started within an urban area. In the worst case, a firestorm, which may develop if the wind and weather conditions and combustible materials are appropriate, could reduce New York City to a mass of burning rubble, thereby killing most of the people in the area who would die from the resultant heat and lack of oxygen. Still, it remains highly uncertain whether a nuclear explosion will cause large-scale fires. The absence of sufficiently combustible materials in a modern city, which is constructed of steel and concrete, can lessen the chance of fires. Another more uncertain factor is the blast wave. At present, there is some debate about whether the blast wave will extinguish many of the fires that are started by thermal radiation. It is by no means clear how the blast wave will interact with fires, so the damage and casualties that are attributable to fire remain uncertain.

As a modern city, the structures in New York probably would not be the source of fires because they are not particularly good sources of combustible materials. However, supplies of petroleum distillates, such as natural gas and liquid fuels, certainly could be ignited by thermal radiation, and continue burning for a considerable time—perhaps weeks or months. Aside from the human casualties that will occur in these fires, many people at great distances from the city will be burned, particularly those in the open, as they are the most vulnerable to thermal radiation.

EMP Electromagnetic pulse (EMP) is an intense field of energy that has the effect of overloading and burning out electronic equipment. With minor exceptions (such as those wearing electronic heart pacemakers, for instance), EMP has no direct effect on humans. EMP, however, will be the cause of considerable dislocations of public utilities, cars, computers, telephones, and a host of other electronic systems that constitute the infrastructure of the modern technological society. A conservative estimate is that this effect alone could disrupt all the communications and transportation systems in New York. While the collateral effects of EMP, such as the disruption of power, could cause casualties, the level is likely to be relatively low. In any event, there will be a significant number of casualties for those who are trapped in subways and elevators, and thereby unable to escape—to the extent that escape is possible in a city that is burning and in ruins after a nuclear attack. Worse yet, the loss of power will reduce the ability of various public services (police, fire, emergency medical personnel) to function properly. And any response that can be assembled will be hindered by the inability to communicate or move within the city.

In summary, EMP will have little direct effect on people. The real loss, however, will be to the infrastructure that supports a modern urban area, particularly a city like New York, which is the financial center of the United States. EMP probably will erase the unprotected or unshielded computer data banks that constitute the memory or the repository of a substantial portion of the world's financial information.[5]

Radioactive Fallout In an attack that uses an air-burst detonation, there will be negligible casualties from fallout, although some of the bomb components that are vaporized in the explosion eventually will settle to the surface. Thus, in an attack against New York, radioactive fallout would be an insignificant problem—unless the weapon was detonated as a surface-burst.

By contrast, a surface-burst detonation will produce large amounts of radioactive fallout from the material that was vaporized where the warhead detonated. At this point, a crater will be formed where the fireball vaporizes earth and dirt that come in contact with the fireball. This debris, which is contaminated with radioactive matter, will settle back to the surface downwind of the explosion as post-attack radioactive fallout. In this case, people downwind of the explosion who are exposed to the fallout would become casualties. Since we are assuming that New York was attacked by air-bursts, radioactive fallout will have an insignificant effect on the number of casualties.

Effects Summary

By far the most significant factor in a nuclear explosion is the blast wave, for it will be the dominant cause of the level of casualties. The other effects, while spectacular and exceedingly lethal by themselves or in combination, pale in comparison with the effect of blast. The blast wave will do most of the structural damage to the city, and thereby produce most of the human fatalities and casualties. One exception to the "rule of casualties" is the effect of the fireball. In this region, buildings and people will be vaporized by the fireball. The population within the immediate vicinity of ground zero (an area that is proportional to the yield of the warhead) never will be affected by blast. In this region of the explosion, casualties will be caused by the fireball. Beyond the region of the fireball, however, it is analytically and conceptually correct to relate human casualties primarily to the blast wave of the detonation.

Attacks with Varying Yields

Exactly how the Soviets might structure an attack on New York would depend on the assumptions about the conditions at the time of the attack and the objectives of the attack. Clearly, the Soviets could strike the city with any number of different yield warheads—from the 500 KT to the 20 MT warheads that are available in the Soviet nuclear arsenal. The magnitude of damage will vary significantly across this spectrum of attack contingencies that are a function, in the ideal case, of the purpose of the attack. In one case, the Soviets could select a lower-yield warhead so that damage would be confined to Manhattan. After a nuclear war of some duration, the attacker may not have the desired warheads available in its arsenal. Seeing that the lower-yield weapons were depleted in the countersilo strikes, the Soviets might use a 20 MT warhead, even though this will cause significantly higher levels of damage than they may want to achieve. In any event, the effects of attacks on New York with 500 kiloton, 1 megaton, and 20 megaton warheads will be examined in terms of the limited case of the level of prompt casualties. We make no attempt to project the long-term effects of such attacks on the population or the ecosystem of New York, for this goes beyond the capabilities of this, or any, methodology with which we are familiar.

500 Kiloton Warhead The lowest yield in the USSR's strategic nuclear arsenal is the 500 kiloton warhead on the SS-18M4 ICBM. With roughly 1,750 such warheads in the arsenal, it is conceivable that a warhead of this yield might be used in an attack against New York, despite the high probability that these warheads would be used in massive countersilo attacks on US ICBM fields. If it is assumed that the warhead is detonated at the optimum height of burst, it will have areas of damage of 145 square miles for an air-burst and 53 square miles for a surface-burst, in terms of the 2–3 psi overpressure gradient. This represents lethal radii of 6.8 and 4.1 nautical miles, respectively, for the 500 kiloton warhead.

For a 500 KT air-burst over New York, there would be roughly 327,000 dead and 622,000 wounded people in a population of 9 million. (See Table

Table 11
Casualties in New York City for Selected Yields (Air-burst)

Yield	Dead	(%)	Wounded	(%)
500KT	327,000	(3.6)	622,000	(6.8)
550KT	350,000	(3.8)	655,000	(7.6)
750KT	409,000	(4.5)	776,000	(8.5)
950KT	476,000	(5.2)	905,000	(9.9)
1MT	512,000	(5.6)	973,000	(10.7)
6MT	1,600,000	(17.6)	3,030,000	(33.4)
10MT	2,300,000	(25.4)	4,410,000	(48.6)
20MT	3,620,000	(39.9)	5,443,000	(60.1)

11.) This means 3.6 and 6.8 percent of the population would be killed and wounded on a prompt basis. There is no certain way of knowing how many will die later, but most estimates range between 1 and 2 times the number of immediate casualties. If we assume that the 500 KT warhead was detonated as a surface-burst, the casualties would fall to 120,000 dead and 240,000 wounded, or 1.3 and 2.6 percent of the target population. A surface-burst produces fewer prompt casualties, in part because the lethal radius of the burst is smaller due to the cratering effect of the burst. For reference, such a warhead would dig a crater roughly 300 meters (1,000 feet) in diameter and 30 meters (100 feet) deep. The highly radioactive fallout, and the contaminated crater area, would more than compensate for the smaller number of blast-related injuries. At least as many people would die or suffer from the short-term (less than 60 days) effects of radiation, not to mention the somatic effects (biological or genetic) of the fallout. It is readily apparent that an air-burst is more effective against a large urban area than a surface-burst, especially in view of the fact that the same yield warhead, if used as an air-burst, produces at least double the casualties. For this reason it is generally conceded that a countervalue attack will consist of air-bursts, which parenthetically means that there will be virtually negligible levels of post-attack fallout in areas downwind of the target. Not only is the air-burst attack "cleaner" and more lethal to larger numbers of people, but it is in a perverse sense the "economic" option.

One-Megaton Warhead In the Soviet arsenal, a one-megaton nuclear warhead is found on the SSN-18 SLBM, among a number of other launchers. On the basis of the proximity of New York to the SSBN patrol zones to the

US Atlantic seaboard, we can infer that the SSN-18 SLBM might be a logical weapon for an attack on New York. The one megaton warhead also establishes the baseline case in this study.

Air-burst over New York, a one megaton warhead would produce roughly 500,000 dead and 1,000,000 wounded, i.e., 5.6 percent dead and 10 percent wounded. The 2 psi overpressure ring reaches 8.5 miles from the burst point, covering approximately 227 square miles in New York. In the alternative case of a surface-burst explosion, the prompt casualties would be 200,000 killed and 400,000 wounded. A surface-burst of this yield would form a crater 380 meters (1,250 feet) in diameter, which is the length of nearly 5 city blocks, and as a surface-burst, a warhead of this yield has a lethal radius of 5.2 miles at the 2 psi overpressure gradient.

There is no evidence on the basis of which we could infer that a one megaton warhead is the most likely weapon to be used in an attack on New York. Nevertheless, the large number of megaton-range warheads in the Soviet arsenal is but one compelling reason to consider the effects of a one megaton explosion. It is difficult to avoid the suspicion that the Soviets deployed such a large number of warheads in the megaton range in order to optimize an attack against American cities. Since US cities are large, well-dispersed metropolitan regions, large yield warheads are the most practical. This case of a one megaton burst is a good example, especially if one considers that the Soviets could allocate several such warheads in order to maximize civilian casualties and economic losses.

20 Megaton Warhead Yet another realistic scenario for a Soviet attack on New York City is the use of a very high-yield warhead. The 20 MT warhead on the SS-18M3 ICBM, which is probably reserved for use against hardened command posts, provides a good example of the effects of this type of attack.

For a 20 megaton air-burst, the radius of the 2 psi ring is approximately 23 miles, which corresponds to an area of damage of almost 1,700 square miles. And, for a surface-burst, the radius of the 2 psi ring is 14 miles, or 615 square miles of damage. An air-burst over New York of this yield produces roughly 3.6 million dead and 5.4 million wounded, i.e., 40 percent dead and 60 percent wounded. Unlike the effects of the 500 KT and 1 MT explosions, the 20 MT detonation affects the entire population of the city on a prompt basis. In the case of a 20 MT surface-burst, there are 1.4 million dead and 3 million wounded. A surface-burst of this yield would produce a crater 1,000 meters (3,400 feet) in diameter and 100 meters (340 feet) deep. A crater of this size would be roughly 13 city blocks long, or about the distance from Central Park South to 47th Street.

By any measure, the effects of a 20 megaton air-burst explosion would be catastrophic, even in comparison with the damage caused by the 500 KT detonation. An explosion of this yield would cover the entire metropolitan area with at least 2 psi of overpressure, and would cause significant levels of damage well out into the suburbs in Connecticut and New Jersey. While we can say that a 500 KT explosion would cause enormous damage to New York, the 20 MT warhead would all but annihilate it. The destruction is virtually complete, as all areas of the city would be either in ruins or engulfed in flames. In time, even most of the 5.4 million who survived the 20 MT air-burst would die from the usual causes.

Summary There is no way that we can visualize or adequately express the enormous damage to New York that these different nuclear attacks represent. Perhaps the best way to see the damage that is expected in a nuclear attack is to compare different yields and the resultant number of casualties. As shown in Table 11, the number of *prompt* dead ranges from 300,000 for a 500 KT air-burst to 3.6 million for a 20 MT air-burst. (The ICBMs or SLBMs that are deployed with warheads of these yields are listed in Table 2.) It is to be remembered that this projection includes only casualties in New York— no other city has been attacked. Thus, a nuclear war that involved the detonation of *one* nuclear warhead translates into prompt casualties (dead and wounded together) between 1 million and 9 million depending on the yield of the warhead. It is important to emphasize this point in a discussion that involves the detonation of potentially *thousands* of nuclear warheads. In New York, just one 500 kiloton warhead will create more casualties than all the war casualties that the United States has sustained since the Revolutionary War. It is estimated that the US has suffered 700,000 casualties in all its wars, including Vietnam. This is to say that, even in the context of large-scale counterforce and countervalue exchanges with thousands of warheads and hundreds of targets, the effects of a single detonation should not be taken lightly, particularly when it would be a catastrophe of unprecedented proportions for the afflicted city.

LARGE-SCALE COUNTERVALUE DESTRUCTION

In most typical scenarios of nuclear war, at least during the past decade or so since the deployment of Soviet ICBMs that are capable of destroying US silos, the conflict is postulated to have been initiated by a Soviet countersilo strike. In scenarios of this type, the opening attack was followed by further attacks on the bomber bases, C3 posts, and submarine forces in the continental United States. After this phase of the war, the analysis usually focuses on the loss of some portion of US nuclear forces, and the equally dismal prospect that the USSR will retain substantially larger reserve forces that can be used as a threat against US cities in response to any American counterattack. It is only at this point, after the Soviet counterforce attack and the eventually uncontrolled metastasis and disintegration of the war, that either side begins to contemplate countervalue nuclear attacks. Indeed, it seems clear that both the United States and the Soviet Union are so well versed in this logic that it would be easy to become embroiled in a war against urban centers that would serve no rational purpose. And should a nuclear war evolve first into a limited, and then later into an unrestrained, campaign against cities, we all know with great clarity what the consequences will be. Millions will die, industries will be destroyed, and in one brief moment the essence of this civilization will cease to exist—with little likelihood of post-war recovery.[6]

If we were to restrict this analysis to the scenarios that are most common in strategic thought, this study perforce loses some of its power. For instance, it is entirely conceivable (although admittedly unlikely in the extreme) that the USSR would concentrate its attack on US urban centers— most especially after a US counterforce attack. Surviving Soviet ICBMs, SLBMs, or bombers could be used in an attack against the primary counter-value targets in the US, in which the countervalue base of the United States would be treated as no more than another potential set of targets. From this scenario it is easy to analyze the extent of the destruction of the urban population of the United States. On the broadest scale, this section addresses the aggregate capabilities of the Soviet Union in an attack on a class of targets that, while often viewed as an aberration in nuclear targeting, in reality constitutes the ultimate dimension of nuclear deterrence. In the extreme case, the ability to destroy the urban infrastructure of the adversary is more important than counterforce capabilities—if one accepts the logic behind, and the arguments for, mutual assured destruction. For now, let us examine a purely countervalue nuclear war in which the Soviet Union unleashes its full nuclear arsenal on the 150 million Americans who live in the 300 largest cities in the United States.

US Cities: Demographic Analysis

In this study, the countervalue target base for the United States contains 304 cities with a total population of 149 million people. Using 230 million as the approximate population of the United States in 1984 (at the time of this writing), the target base represents approximately 63 percent of the human and, by inference, a marginally greater percentage of the economic resources of the United States.

At first glance, a target complex of this magnitude is a rather unwieldy and large entity with which to deal. How does one approach the problem of planning a nuclear attack, when there are more than 300 potential targets covering 400,000 square miles (11 percent of the area of the US) with an immediate population on the order of 150 million? One method is purely notional: to select the largest and best-known cities as the initial focus of the attack, and later to allocate available forces to cities that seem to be worth-while targets in terms of their population or economic potential. Hardly rigorous or scientific in its methodology, this approach nevertheless will guide the planner in the (roughly) correct direction. In terms of MAD, this approach will result in the destruction of the American civilization, rendering "unacceptable" levels of destruction on the cities that are the subject of the attack.

A more appropriate way to plan an attack against US cities is to rank the potential targets by order of importance. Using population as the critical variable, we could organize US cities into countervalue "target sets." As shown in Table 12, US (as well as Soviet) cities are arranged into seven groups of targets by population. In terms of economic output, as numerous studies, such as the Office of Technology Assessment Study "Effects of Nuclear War" have found, the economic significance of a city tends to be very closely related to its population.[7] Thus, a larger city has a larger output of goods and services than a similar, smaller city. While the model loses some of its validity in the case of highly specialized industries, it provides a useful, albeit rough, measure of the importance of a city. Table 12, therefore, provides discrete groups of potential targets based not only on the relative size of the cities, but also in terms of their *relative* economic output.

In the United States, category one targets are cities which have a population greater than 1 million. There are 34 such urban areas, the largest, New York, has a population of nine million, and the smallest, Columbus, Ohio, has a population of 1.1 million. These 34 cities have a total population of roughly 85 million, corresponding to nearly 60 percent of the people in this countervalue target list. Even in this relatively small number of cities, we will find a substantial fraction of the economic resources of the United States, probably somewhere in the vicinity of 30–40 percent of the US gross national product. For the Soviet planner, this list of 34 cities would be a highly lucrative set of targets—assuming, naturally, that it is either necessary or desirable to execute the countervalue option during a war.

One of the more distinguishing demographic features of a modern state is the high concentration of people and industry in a relatively small number of cities. The United States is no exception. In this sample, 71 cities, which have populations greater than 500,000, account for more than 100 million people, or 74 percent of the countervalue population in this study and 40 percent of the total US population in 1984. Despite the large area of these urban targets, this concentration amounts to a vulnerability of people and resources to a nuclear attack that is, in the face of modern sociological and political forces, as unavoidable as it is regrettable. (This simple fact accounts for the uncertainty, as well as the systemic pessimism, about the effectiveness of ballistic-missile defense, wherein the lion's share of the US population lies in a relatively small number of area targets that eventually will be hit.)

As shown in Table 12, as the population of the cities decreases, the number of cities in the subsamples increases. For instance, consider urban areas with populations between 100,000 and 250,000. There are 78 cities in this group that account for less than 10 percent of the target population in the US; yet, the 78 cities represent 25 percent of the cities in the study.

Table 12
Distribution of US and Soviet Cities by Population

Population	United States			Soviet Union		
	No. Cities	(%)	Population (%)	No. Cities	(%)	Population (%)
1,000,000+	34	(11.1)	84,659,000 (58.6)	24	(7.8)	43,617,000 (40.4)
750,000-1,000,000	16	(5.3)	11,213,000 (7.8)	6	(2.0)	5,125,000 (4.7)
500,000 - 750,000	21	(7.0)	11,323,000 (7.8)	16	(5.2)	9,015,000 (8.3)
250,000 - 500,000	63	(26.7)	22,111,000 (15.3)	70	(23.0)	24,582,000 (22.8)
100,000 - 250,000	78	(25.6)	12,088,000 (8.4)	157	(51.2)	23,860,000 (22.1)
50,000 - 100,000	20	(6.6)	1,511,000 (1.1)	18	(5.8)	1,128,000 (1.0)
Less than 50,000	72	(23.7)	1,396,000 (1.0)	15	(5.0)	544,000 (0.5)
Total	304		144,301,000*	306		107,871,000**

* = 63% of total US population in 1984: 230,000,000.
** = 39% of total USSR population in 1984: 275,000,000.

From the peculiar vantage point of a Soviet war planner, the destruction of the smaller, and more numerous, cities in the United States will offer diminishing returns. As the war envelops more of the smaller cities, the number of targets increases, thereby raising the number of warheads that are required for an effective attack. How effective is it for the USSR to attack the 78 or so US cities that have populations between 100,000–250,000 if the total number of affected people (and industries) is only 8 percent of the target population in this study, and only 5 percent of the total US population? The case is even more compelling if we consider the 92 cities that have populations less than 100,000. In this case, the target population is 1 percent of the countervalue base in this study, and less than one percent of the total population of the United States. This demographic fact leads to the inescapable conclusion that the Soviet Union most likely will concentrate its attack on the largest US cities, as this will require the least number of warheads, but accomplish the greatest destruction. In economic terms, this is the cost-effective route.

There always will be exceptions. It is not unusual for many small, isolated towns in the US to contain some highly critical industrial resources, such as the precision ball-bearing factory (for missile guidance systems) in Peterborough, New Hampshire. In a decentralized economic system, industries like this, which are key components in a high technology society, frequently are located in obscure cities and towns. A classic example is the dispersion of the computer industry, in which major and minor computer and software corporations are scattered all throughout the United States, with a greater concentration in California and the Northeast. The Soviet Union well may target these isolated pockets of technology—to the extent that they are aware of their existence—in order to exacerbate post-attack recovery (whatever one means by that phrase) through the shortage of critical industries, resources, and people. Whether this approach in Soviet targeting can create "bottlenecks" in the recovery of the US economy is not certain, given the enormous difficulties of understanding the complex mechanisms that will exist in the post-attack environment. To date, no convincing evidence exists to confirm the theory that targeting critical nodes in the US (or USSR) economy will impede recovery beyond that which will be expected after a generalized nuclear attack. Numerous studies, however, have grappled unsuccessfully with this very issue for some ten or more years.

Comprehensive Urban Attacks

In the first part of this chapter we addressed the effects of nuclear attacks with warheads of different yields on New York. This, typically, is how the consequences of countervalue attacks are presented, on the assumption that to understand the results of a hypothetical attack on a major urban center is to appreciate the costs of a large-scale countervalue nuclear war. There is considerable merit in this approach, for its directness and unambiguity as to the effects of a nuclear explosion reduce many of the arcane technical disputes to the level of irrelevant, possibly nonsensical, disputes among the ordained "priests" of nuclear science. Too frequently, however, this is where the analysis stops. From the horrible effects of an isolated nuclear attack, some assume incorrectly that we can deduce what hundreds or thousands of such explosions will mean for a society. In a word, the "event-level" leap from the specific to the general is not difficult, especially when the subject is nuclear war.

By contrast, in this study we are concerned with the consequences of a large-scale Soviet attack on US urban centers in which hundreds of targets, rather than the isolated few, are attacked. One objective was to reach beyond the assertion that the effect of a nuclear attack on New York is "x" million dead, or that 100 million would die if the USSR attacked 25 urban areas with weapons of specified yields. At this lower level of analysis, it is difficult to extrapolate beyond the effects of isolated attacks to the effects of a large-scale countervalue attack on all, or virtually all, of the urban centers in the United States. Accordingly, this study examines the consequences of a countervalue nuclear attack on 300 urban areas in the United States. The assumptions are the same as those employed in the analysis of the attack on New York City. Analytically, however, the 300 US urban areas are viewed as one large target, with all, or selected segments, of the Soviet nuclear arsenal targeted against it. Based on these calculations, two broad cases serve to illustrate the vulnerability of the cities in the United States.

Attack With 500 Kiloton Warheads With nearly 3,500 500 KT warheads in the Soviet Union's nuclear arsenal, there is the possibility that large-scale attacks against US urban targets might be launched with warheads of this yield. On the assumption that the USSR attacked the 300 US urban centers with 500 KT air-burst warheads, what level of casualties will the Soviets inflict? Shown in Graph 1, the detonation of 3,000 500 KT warheads will result in approximately 60 million deaths and (not shown) 87 million wounded on a prompt basis. The figure of 60 million dead represents 40 percent of the target population in this study (149 million) and 26 percent of the total American population. In this attack, the warheads were distributed evenly over the 300 cities to create uniform 2 psi overpressure level, so that the effects on each city in the sample would be roughly equivalent. One problem, however, is that the efficiency of this attack would be reduced by the coverage of the 100–150 smaller cities that in effect greatly increased the number of warheads required even though the results—measured in terms of casualties—showed only a marginal increase. A different way of looking at the problem is that of diminishing returns. The curve of casualties in Graph 1 is steeper in the beginning because the rate of casualties in the first 30–50 cities was significantly greater than the rate of casualties in the remaining 250–270 cities. For the attack planner, the destruction of the smaller cities is

Graph 1
Prompt US Fatalities: 1 Megaton and 500 Kiloton Air-Bursts*

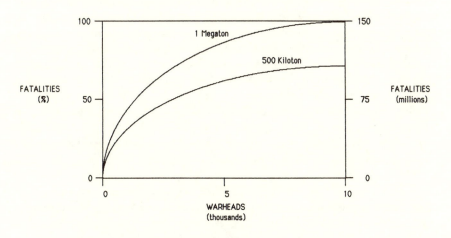

* This assumes a Soviet attack against the 307 largest urban-industrial areas
  in the United States, having a total population in excess of 150 million. All
  warheads detonate at the optimum height of burst.

more costly in terms of the number of warheads expended—in some cases
the area of damage would exceed the area of city several times—because the
attacker inflicts more relative damage in smaller cities; and thereby uses
more nuclear firepower against smaller urban targets. This simple fact provides one powerful argument for the "assured destruction" of a relatively
small number of US cities (or Soviet cities, as we shall see in Chapter 6)
based on the high concentration of people in a small number of targets.
Perhaps the criticism of MAD, which is that it implicitly sanctions attacks on
urban targets on the grounds that it meets purely economic criteria, is
misplaced. Despite the apparently unpalatable quality of MAD, sometimes
likened to "burning down cities," there is some vindication for those who
argue that this vulnerability of the US population, even a limited attack
against 50 cities, reinforces the fundamental and inescapable logic of
deterrence.

Attack With One Megaton Warheads There are roughly 1,700 warheads
in the Soviet arsenal that have a yield in the one megaton range, and are
found primarily on SLBMs, bombers, and several ICBMs. These warheads
are quite distinct from the more lethal (and generally lower yield and higher
accuracy) hard-target kill RVs, which, as significantly less accurate RVs, are
well suited for the targeting of urban areas. Using the same sample of 300
cities in the United States in this analysis, as in the preceding section, here

we examine the effects of a Soviet nuclear attack on US countervalue (urban) targets with one megaton warheads.

As in the last section, the American urban areas were aggregated into one target, which has a uniformly distributed population. As shown in Graph 1, such an attack on the United States would cause approximately 50 million deaths and 100 million wounded on a prompt basis. This represents the death of one-third of the US population that was used in this study, and 21 percent of the total US population. In the hypothetical case of an unlimited number of one megaton RVs in the Soviet arsenal, the detonation of 10,000 such warheads would kill on a prompt basis all of the 150 million people in the 300 urban areas. In comparison with the attack that used 500 kiloton warheads, the detonation of roughly twice the number of 500 kiloton warheads would produce an equivalent level of population losses.

This is clearly a case of a targeting inefficiency due, in large part (as noted earlier), to the problem of targeting smaller urban areas with warheads that are of greater yield than necessary. As is the case with 500 kiloton warheads, the initial attack with one megaton warheads would cause significant and large-scale urban losses. However, as the attack includes an increasing number of small urban areas the number of resultant casualties begins to decline in relative terms. At the extreme end of the curve in Graph 1, additional increments of one megaton warheads has only a minor effect on the total number of fatalities in the attack, suggesting that an effective attack on urban areas ends somewhere in the lower to middle sections of the curve. It should be emphasized that these are the number of prompt dead, and that this study does not attempt to calculate the losses of population and industry that will accrue over a protracted length of time in what is known euphemistically as the "post nuclear" environment. A reasonable estimate is that long-term fatalities will be at least equal to the number of prompt dead. Of course, the eventual number of dead could be higher still, perhaps in the vicinity of more than twice the number who were killed immediately.[8] Our confidence in projections of the number of casualties that will result eventually in the post-nuclear environment is extremely low, influenced in large measure by the enormous uncertainty about the structure of a society after a nuclear war, not to mention the limited (if not nonexistent) availability (and quality) of care for the wounded. Still higher uncertainty surrounds the biological effects of long-term exposure to low-level radiation and the nature of the climate in a post-nuclear world. Accordingly, we thought that it would be too risky to proceed beyond estimates of prompt levels of casualties, for to do so would introduce systemic estimates that are no better, and perhaps far worse, than educated guesses.

Soviet Countervalue Targeting Capability

It is natural to ask how much damage the Soviet nuclear arsenal could inflict on urban areas in the United States in the case of an unrestrained

Table 13

US-USSR Distributed Countervalue Attacks: Casualty Estimates

	Air-burst		Surface-Burst	
	Dead	Wounded	Dead	Wounded
United States*				
Total	113,587,000	34,690,000	62,445,000	85,832,000
Deliverable	82,485,000	65,792,000	35,631,000	67,998,000
Soviet Union**				
Total	111,075,000	None	111,075,000	None
Deliverable	111,075,000	None	111,075,000	None

* United States:
   Population: 148,277,000
   Area: 400,000
   Density: 370 persons/sq. mile

** Soviet Union:
   Population: 107,871,000
   Area: 23,000
   Density: 4,700 persons/sq. mile

countervalue nuclear war. Typically, scenarios of nuclear war concentrate on the counterforce option, in many cases to the virtual exclusion of counter-value analyses. There is a good reason for this oversight: nuclear strategy, at least since the 1970s, has been concerned with the possibility of a disarming strike against nuclear forces that, in theory, could shift the balance of reserve forces in the favor of the attacker. Although often viewed as an aberration in some circles of nuclear policy (usually those who castigate the assured de-struction misson, which means the destruction of urban areas), in other circles the "popularity" of the deterrent effect of countervalue exchanges has faded with the recent fixation on counterforce wars. Even though there is considerable emphasis on the counterforce option in US thinking and policy, it still is clear that a nuclear war could disintegrate into an unrestrained slaughter of American civilians. Soviet irrationality, or catastrophic errors in targeting, once again in effect could make urban areas the lucrative and high-confidence targets that they were in the formative years of nuclear policy.

One way of looking at the Soviet nuclear capability against US urban areas is to aggregate the areas of damage of all warheads in the Soviet arsenal into a cumulative, force-wide area of damage. As shown in Table 13, the total area of damage for all Soviet nuclear warheads in this study is 1.4 million square miles for air-burst detonations at the optimum height of burst, which means that the Soviet Union can blanket 1.4 million square miles with at least 2 psi overpressure. In the case of surface-burst detonations, the Soviet nuclear arsenal can cover approximately 500,000 square miles, which is about one-third of the area affected by an equal number of air-bursts. This example, however, is based on the somewhat unrealistic assumption that all of the warheads in the Soviet Union's strategic nuclear arsenal would reach their assigned targets or that all of these warheads would detonate once they reached the targets. In reality, the total arsenal would face attrition from the numerous mechanical and environmental factors that effectively lessen the magnitude of any nuclear attack. A more realistic value for the coverage of the Soviet arsenal will subtract the fraction of the warheads that are expected to fail, based on the launch and detonation reliability rates of the weapons in the Soviet arsenal. Based on this approach, the *deliverable* area of damage for air-burst detonations is 750,000 square miles, which is roughly half of the theoretical capability of the Soviet arsenal. In the case of surface-bursts, the coverage falls from 500,000 to 280,000 square miles. Using these more real-istic values, further light can be shed on Soviet countervalue capabilities.

The air-burst case is examined first. In the event that the entire Soviet nuclear arsenal worked perfectly, the USSR could kill more than 110 million people on a *prompt* basis, or 76 percent of the 150 million people in this sample, and wound an additional 35 million in this highly stylized attack. In the opposite example, where the Soviet arsenal performs in accordance with the limits imposed by the reliability rates, the level of US countervalue casualties would be 82 million prompt deaths, or 55 percent of the target population, and 65 million wounded. This example illustrates the pronounced effect of launch vehicle attrition on the level of resultant civilian casualties in a nuclear war. The second case is the surface-burst. The idealized nuclear attack using surface-burst detonations would kill promptly 62 million and wound another 85 million civilians, which represents a 42 percent level of fatalities.[9] If one takes into account the expected attrition rates of Soviet nuclear forces, the expected level of damage declines to 35 million prompt deaths, 67 million wounded, and a remaining 44 million who will not be harmed directly in the attack. The level of damage in this example is roughly 25 percent. We emphasize, again, that these calculations are based on prompt damage and do not include estimates of prolonged deaths for those who are injured in or deprived by the effects of the nuclear attack.

COUNTERVALUE RETALIATION: SOVIET SSBNs

In the aftermath of a US counterforce attack against the Soviet Union (see Chapter 6), the Soviets would be faced with two basic options. The first would be to retaliate against as many US counterforce targets as their surviving forces allow in the hope of reducing US reserve forces to as low a level as possible. The strength of this option lies in the fact that it lessens US retaliatory capabilities and avoids the destruction of civilian populations as a premeditated course of action. Yet, the smaller number of RVs, primarily on the SLBMs, limits Soviet retaliatory options to the destruction of a minuscule number of military targets, at best a few command posts, or submarine and bomber bases. Given the scale of the initial US counterforce attack, and the staggering military and human losses associated with it, counterforce reprisals by the Soviet Union would have only a marginal effect on US nuclear forces and the US society at large.

The second option, by exclusion, therefore, is a retaliatory strike against countervalue centers in the United States. The surviving SLBMs in the Soviet arsenal, numbering roughly 350 after the US attack, are sufficient for an assured retaliatory response that will result in the destruction of most major population centers in the United States. As shown in Table 14, Soviet SLBMs (SSN5, SSN6, SSN8, and SSN18) that were on SSBNs at sea at the time of the US attack would be expected to survive the US attack. Of the 85 SSBNs in the Soviet fleet, the roughly 20 that survived this attack would give the USSR a reserve force of 254 SLBMs carrying 344 RVs with yields in the one megaton range. The accuracy of these RVs, while clearly insufficient for the destruction of hard targets, would be more than sufficient for urban-industrial targeting. Later, the resulting level of US casualties from this attack will attest to the "sufficiency" of the Soviet reserve force when it comes to countervalue retaliation.

Distributed Countervalue Retaliation

As explained in the last section of the chapter, a countervalue response can be distributed equally over the 300 SMSAs in the United States. The

Table 14
Soviet Countervalue Retaliatory Attack

| SLBM | Soviet SSBNs At Sea | | Total RVs | Area of Damage | | Attrition Rate | | |
	SSBN	MIRVs		AB*	SB**	Delivered	AB	SB
SSN5	4	1	12	2,724	1,020	.21	572	214
SSN6	7	1	112	25,424	9,520	.23	5,847	2,189
SSN8	6	1	76	13,756	5,016	.42	5,777	2,106
SSN18	3	3	144	32,688	12,240	.49	16,017	5,997
Total	20		344	74,592	27,796		28,213	10,506

* AB = Air-burst
** SB = Surface-burst

effect is to spread the nuclear warheads evenly over the cities in order to estimate the consequences of an attack that seeks to inflict casualties in as many cities as possible. The opposite method is to concentrate the attack on just a few cities in order to kill as many people as possible in those sample cities.

The residual force of Soviet SLBMs, using the distributed attack method, has the theoretical capability of targeting roughly 120 RVs against US urban areas in the expectation that the United States will suffer more than 3 million prompt dead and 7 million wounded—excluding delayed effects from the attack. An obvious problem with this tactic is that the attack does not maximize casualties in selected urban areas, but rather weakens the attack by distributing the warheads over large and small cities alike. The effect is to distort the attack by concentrating more RVs on insignificant urban areas (populations less than 50,000), when by contrast the same allocation of RVs against large urban targets would increase the number of prompt casualties. This, then, is the preferred method.

Concentrated Attack on Selected US Cities

A rational opponent, faced with roughly 120 deliverable RVs in an arsenal of 340 surviving warheads, probably would concentrate the retaliatory attack on the major urban centers in the United States. This will ensure the highest level of casualties and thereby maximize the destructive (deterrent) potential of the reserve force. This, at least, is what the United States probably would estimate for a Soviet response against American urban centers.

Based on the destructive potential of the residual SLBM RVs, an optimum attack might concentrate on the following US cities: Boston, New York, Washington, Chicago, Los Angeles, and Detroit. The first three cities (Boston, New York, and Washington) were targeted by the SSN5, SSN6, and SSN8 SLBMs, respectively. Two one megaton RVs from the SSN5 SLBMs were detonated as air-bursts over Boston, which would result in 500,000 prompt dead and 185,000 wounded civilians. Similarly, the 25 one megaton RVs detonated over New York resulted in 7.4 million dead and 1.6 million wounded people. This attack represents "overkill," yet it demonstrates that New York would be utterly destroyed by just one variant of a retaliatory strike. Indeed, the immense economic and cultural significance of New York and the surrounding suburban areas might justify the decision to allocate more warheads than is theoretically necessary. In any event, an attack of this type and magnitude would inundate the city beyond the point of repair or recovery. Finally, 31 SSN8 RVs were detonated over Washington, D.C., and the surrounding region, which would result in 1.7 million prompt fatalities and more than 1 million casualties. The significance of Washington, both as the center of the US government and a vital command center, also suggests that this "blanketing" attack would have high value to the Soviet planner. It would mean the utter destruction of the US capital and the federal government, with the exception of those government agencies (Transportation, Defense, and so forth) that had managed to disperse their personnel and resources throughout the nation to "survivable" command posts, or had made provisions for the establishment of emergency command centers.

The remaining 70 SSN18 SLBM RVs were allocated equally against the cities of Chicago, Los Angeles, and Detroit. Each of the urban areas, in the case of the detonation of 23 air-bursts, would sustain roughly 45 percent fatalities. In Chicago there would be 3.2 million dead; 3.0 million dead in Los Angeles; and 1.9 million dead in Detroit—all on a prompt basis. If the attack were based on surface-bursts, the level of prompt dead would fall to roughly 20 percent, although post-attack radioactive fallout would increase the number of dead, perhaps up to twice the original number of dead. In each of these attacks, the cities were blanketed with uniform overpressure levels of at least 5 psi, which is more than sufficient to cause large-scale and thorough destruction of the industrial and human resources within these cities.

The countervalue retaliatory option has been called a modern-day Sword of Damocles, an appellation that seems justifiable in view of the consequences of a limited nuclear attack on only six urban areas in the United States, which would kill more than 17 million people. The central point, that we sometimes tend to forget, is that even an apparently successful US counterforce attack against the Soviet Union could not forestall a retaliatory attack by Soviet SLBMs. The detonation of roughly 100 one megaton nuclear weapons—*approximately one percent of the USSR's strategic nuclear arsenal of 8,000 RVs*—would result in roughly 18 million prompt deaths. This, in the judgment of any reasonable person, constitutes consequences that are so unacceptable as to nullify the potential gains from a counterforce attack against the Soviet Union. Just the USSR's residual nuclear forces on the SSBNs at sea that happen to survive a surprise attack have the potential to inflict this level of damage. Moreover, there are no analyses with which we are familiar which suggest that less than 100 Soviet SLBM RVs would survive even a near-perfect US surprise counterforce attack. More to the point, most analyses predict that a much larger number of Soviet RVs would survive, which eventually could be launched against the United States. In a crude sense, this is the "stuff" of which deterrence is made.

SUMMARY

It is not so difficult to become mesmerized by the mechanisms of counterforce scenarios and the impression that such wars could be a surgically "clean" event. Nothing is so illuminating, or so disruptive of the view that nuclear wars could be managed, than an excursion into scenarios of countervalue nuclear war. The irreducible fact is that a nuclear war, no matter how carefully it may be planned or executed, can at any time become a slaughter of millions of people and the destruction of an entire civilization. Whether it be called deterrence, mutual assured destruction (MAD), essential equivalence, or a countervailing policy, the final result always appears to be the same: the extermination of the urban populations of the United States and the Soviet Union as well as the populations of Europe, China, and Japan. This, at least, emerges as more than a distinct possibility from the calculations in this chapter that focus on the effects of urban targeting.

It is equally simple and complex, stark and illuminating, that nuclear war probably never can escape the epithet that it will become an annihilatory exercise for its participants who, paradoxically, may believe that the war can be held at the counterforce level. The truth of this position ultimately depends on the human factor: how will American and Soviet leaders behave in a nuclear crisis? (See the afterward by Michael Caruso on the nuclear war crisis exercises that were conducted at Saint Anselm College and Harvard University's John F. Kennedy School of Government in 1984.) Will they fall prey to the temptation, either through ignorance or revenge, to attack cities in the hope that this demonstration of "resolve" will be interpreted by the other as a desire to terminate the war at this threshold? It is more likely that the first act of "resolve" will be seen historically (many decades or centuries after the war) as the first of many similar actions. How it begins then will be an historical irrelevancy. The fact is that, if it does, everything as we know it will come to a crashing halt.

Perhaps a hint of despair can be detected in these remarks. To be frank, how else should one feel after thinking about "so many routes to Hell?" In reality, each of the sections in this chapter is far more than a mere hypotheticality. The United States and the Soviet Union have these options readily at their disposal today, to be executed in less than one hour at any time. If the ultimate question is whether the US and USSR would execute these options, we must profess ignorance as to the answer. From a detached perspective, we think it is more than likely that urban areas will be annihilated at some point if a nuclear war were to begin. Quite simply, it is difficult to imagine a nuclear war that did not regress into a wholesale slaughter of civilian populations, for reasons that would include, but not be limited to, perceptions of "winning and losing," "balancing urban losses," "demonstrating resolve," and "command and control confusion."

6

US Countervalue Attacks

There had not, except in Russia, been slaughter as great as in the first World War, but the material destruction [in the second World War] had been unparalleled. City after city had been destroyed; the centers of industrial towns and capitals were rubble. Factories were flat, dams were broken, railways wrecked, canals empty, mines flooded, and even an ancient power station, if it was still working, was a priceless asset.
—*H. G. Wells, The Outline of History, 1949*

A conservative estimate is that the number of Soviet fatalities in the Second World War exceeded 20 million, which is some 100 times more than the 200,000 Americans who died in that same war. A historical study of the losses in war, in which the Soviet losses between 1941–45 are but one statistic, reveals that there are numerous precedents for wars in which the losses have been in the millions. In "Russian" history, the Mongol Empire slaughtered millions from Europe to China in what may have been one of the bloodiest periods in post-Roman history. The Thirty Years War (1618–48) that ended with the Peace of Westphalia was estimated to have killed between 20 and 30 percent of the German, and on a lesser scale, European populations. So, it is not unheard of for a war to kill millions of people, combatants and noncombatants alike. History is replete with untold examples of such annihilatory behavior.

This brief excursion into the history of war is not meant to suggest that we, or those in the Soviet Union, ought to take comfort in the thought that a nuclear attack on the Soviet Union might result in human losses that are well within the historical norm for warfare. Rather, the point is that a nuclear war may be just one more instance in which combatants have engaged in annihilatory behavior. The significant difference is that a nuclear war will kill its victims much more quickly—probably several orders of magnitude more quickly than did the wars in the pre-nuclear age. As horrible as a nuclear war certainly will be, it is true (and distressing) to realize that mankind has fought wars that resulted in millions of dead, the most recent example being the 50 million who died in World War II.

From the perspective of the Soviet Union, war has been a regular event in its history, at least since the Mongol hordes terrorized Europe and Asia in the 12th and 13th centuries. From this experience, some have attributed a barbaric instinct to the Russian people, in partial deference to the violence that has characterized Russian and Soviet history.[1] This has led to an institutionalized affinity for violence on the part of the Soviet populations that has permeated contemporary Soviet behavior and organizations, such as the KGB, which has maintained a well earned reputation for ruthlessness. What will be imagined here is a war that will eradicate the present Soviet civilization and institutions as thoroughly as the Mongol hordes indelibly stamped their mark (which we still see in Soviet culture) on Russia and central Asia nearly 700 years ago. The effects of a US nuclear attack on the Soviet Union today will be as significant as—and in fact incomparably greater than—the devastation caused by the tribes of Genghis Khan almost a millennium ago.

It was observed in the preceding chapter that a nuclear war is not likely to begin, although it certainly may end, as a countervalue exchange. It is more than likely that the destruction of urban centers in the Soviet Union will be preceded by American nuclear attacks on Soviet nuclear forces, unless the United States was responding to a Soviet counterforce attack with an assault on Soviet cities. Not the least of the reasons for the avoidance of urban targets is that, in circumstances when nuclear forces can be eliminated through selected nuclear strikes, laying waste to urban areas will not be a useful endeavor. Yet, beyond the opening salvos of a nuclear war, the unsettling fact is that the US nuclear arsenal, as presently structured, is designed primarily for retaliation against soft military and urban targets. To be fair, we should say as well that the United States could target as many Other Military Targets (OMTs) as possible, including conventional theater-projection forces in the Western Military District (WTVD) and Eastern Europe. While an attack of this type would not strictly speaking be directed against Soviet countervalue centers, the effects may be nearly indistinguishable, for in the Soviet Union, much like the United States, these potential targets are collocated with Soviet urban centers. This collocation may produce staggering levels of civilian casualties, whether from direct weapons effects or radioactive fallout. Thus, large-scale US nuclear attacks against OMTs in the USSR, which are the most important variant of soft counterforce targets, will involve strikes against areas that are so closely collocated with urban populations that the Soviets may not be able to differentiate between direct and unintended civilian casualties. In effect, the USSR will pay a heavy price indeed for the collocation of its urban and military targets in ways that are reminscent of the potential costs to the United States of the collocation of its ICBM silos and urban centers, which are in or near (as well as upwind) of two-thirds of its urban population. In any event, it is clear that the Poseidon and Trident SLBM forces, which are the mainstay of US retaliatory forces, are not the optimum type of weapons for use against hard military targets. (We sidestepped this point in Chapter 3 when Poseidon and Trident SLBMs were targeted against Soviet silos; the reason was that the scenario required more RVs than the US ICBM force could offer.)

In a strict sense, the US nuclear arsenal compels the United States to retaliate against the USSR's urban areas if the economic criterion of efficiency (which is to destroy most efficiently what you can) dominates the allocation of surviving RVs. Is it reasonable to strike Soviet hard targets with surviving forces when that same force can cause far more destruction against urban targets, and thereby reinforce the reluctance of the Soviet Union to start a counterforce war from the outset? Thus, it is not hard to defend the plausibility of countervalue scenarios; all one has to do is look at the US arsenal, particularly surviving forces after a Soviet attack, to see that escalation to urban destruction is an inevitable reaction in a nuclear war.

As in Chapter 5, this chapter will be organized into three sections. In the first section, we will examine the effects of hypothetical US attacks on Moscow for nuclear warheads of various yields. Not only will this provide a baseline analysis for the general consequences of different attack options, but also will enable us to construct comparisons with the results of similar attacks on New York. As always, a detailed picture of nuclear destruction in one urban area seems to allow one to keep the consequences of a large-scale countervalue nuclear war in perspective. The second section will examine the capability of the United States in a large-scale attack on the 300 largest urban areas in the Soviet Union. The critical assumption in this case is that the United States would concentrate its nuclear forces on strictly urban targeting. And the third section will analyze the countervalue capabilities of the US nuclear arsenal based on the forces that survived the Soviet counterforce attack that was detailed in Chapter 4. This analysis then is but one illustration of the assured retaliation mission for US nuclear forces after Soviet preemption.

From these broad scenarios of nuclear war, we seek to analyze the general capabilities of the United States in an attack that centers on urban areas in the USSR. Beyond that issue, this approach will provide a sketch of a large-scale exchange against cities in the Soviet Union, and thereby provide an outline of the consequences of what we understand to be one dimension of US nuclear policy.

HYPOTHETICAL ATTACK ON MOSCOW

In the Soviet Union, Moscow is the undisputed center of Soviet government, business, and culture. In fact, the significance of Moscow pales in comparison with that of any other city in any other nation. In any real sense of the word, Moscow epitomizes what we understand as the Soviet Union, for it is the focus of the Soviet national style and ethos. And it has been so since the reign of Peter the Great (1689–1725), perhaps even more so since V.I. Lenin and the 1917 Revolution, and all of his successors, including General Secretary Gorbachev. More than any other city in any other nation (except, possibly, Beijing in the Peoples Republic of China) in the modern world, Moscow symbolizes its nation. It is by virtue of this predominance in the national lifestyle of the Soviet Union that we have selected Moscow as the target to illustrate the effects of a nuclear attack. On a somewhat lesser scale, Moscow also forms the center of the USSR's military apparatus, as the (apparent) existence of a large number of hardened command posts within the city limits indicates. From any number of perspectives, Moscow is the logical target of an American nuclear attack.

A demographic analysis of Moscow is in order. First, however, we must stress that the data about Soviet urban areas is uncertain, due in large part to the failure of the Soviets to release detailed information about the composition of their urban centers. Despite this difficulty, we have in large measure circumvented this potentially fatal problem. (See the Appendix for an explanation of the sources and methods used to compile data on Soviet cities.) It appears that, in 1984, Moscow, or rather the entire Moscow urban area, had a population of roughly 8.4 million in an area of some 1763 square miles with a population density of 4,700 persons per square mile. The central core of Moscow covers approximately 339 square miles. Beyond the central urban core, there is the Green Belt area which has an area of 666 square miles. Finally, the peripheral suburban and industrial region (noting that industrial resources are distributed throughout the city) comprises an area of roughly 700 square miles. Thus, there is an immediate urban area of 1763 square miles, which we will use as the target in these hypothetical nuclear attacks with warheads of differing yields. On a technical note, the less densely populated areas in the periphery of Moscow, of course, are not as critical as the targets in the central city and Green Belt regions. Still, these areas will be included in the nuclear attack calculations that project the casualties in a countervalue strike.

As in the similar attacks on urban areas in the United States, the population within Moscow is assumed to be evenly distributed throughout the greater metropolitan area. As in a normal urban area, this assumption is consistent with the daily migration of people within Moscow, although the predictably lower population density in the outer reaches of the city may cause these casualty predictions to be on the low end of the scale. Still, the assumption that there is an even distribution of people within the city will avert the problem of having to estimate the location of the people at the time of the attack. This approach will result in casualty projections that "smooth out" the pernicious (with respect to predictability) effects of population shifts during the course of daily commuting of Muscovites to and from home and work. In reality, the migration of Muscovites during the day will shift the number of casualties either up or down, depending on the time of the attack.

In the nuclear attacks on Moscow, the following constraints are assumed to be the case:

—The population in Moscow had no warning of the attack and therefore no chance for sheltering or evacuation. The attack on Moscow had no precursors.

—The attack occurred during the night when the population would be more evenly distributed than the daytime.

—The weather was clear. This means that the nuclear explosion was not attenuated by clouds, moisture, or precipitation.

—The warhead detonated at the optimum height of burst (HOB) for the yield specified.

—In all cases, ground zero was the Kremlin in central Moscow. In an air-burst, the warhead detonated directly over the building, whereas a surface-burst detonated as close to the structure as possible.

—The population had no opportunity for relocation, evacuation, or sheltering. People, therefore, were afforded only such random protection from weapons affects as structures might provide. Despite assertions about the Soviet Union's civil defense program, these estimates discount the effects of the program.

—The warheads were not designed to maximize fallout or direct radiation, such as the enhanced-radiation ("neutron") bomb. While the normal mechanisms of a surface-burst would cause radioactive fallout, fallout was not enhanced through weapon design techniques.

—Most important, these estimates of casualties should be viewed as just that: *estimates*. In any nuclear attack, there are innumerable uncertainties and imponderables associated with the event that could have a drastic effect on the outcome of the attack.

In terms of the specific effects of a nuclear explosion on Moscow, the readers should refer to the section on Nuclear Effects in Chapter 5. We have applied the same assumptions, as well as roughly the same yield warheads in the attacks on Moscow as in the attacks on New York, so that direct comparisons may be made between these two major urban centers. Perhaps the most significant difference lies in relative importance: by any standard Moscow is *the* indispensable city in the Soviet Union. Its political, military, economic, and technological preeminence in the USSR is far in excess of the value of New York to the United States. This asymmetry, however relevant it might be in pre-war terms, will be an irrelevance after the war begins.

Attacks With Varying Yields

It is virtually impossible to predict how the United States might structure an attack on Moscow. Exact scenarios depend on the events (if any) that

Table 15
Casualties in Moscow for Selected Yields (Air-burst)

Yield	Dead	(%)	Wounded	(%)
40KT	41,000	(0.5)	78,000	(0.9)
100KT	74,000	(0.8)	140,000	(1.6)
170KT	113,000	(1.3)	215,000	(2.5)
200KT	120,000	(1.4)	225,000	(2.6)
335KT	145,000	(1.7)	275,000	(3.3)
600KT	271,000	(3.2)	515,000	(6.1)
1MT	373,000	(4.4)	708,000	(8.4)
9MT	1,580,000	(18.8)	3,000,000	(35.7)
24MT	3,500,000	(41.6)	4,870,000	(58.4)

precede an attack on Moscow, such as the availability of warheads and the yield of those warheads. However, once it has been established that Moscow will in fact be targeted, possible courses of action may be classified into general options that range from the "demonstrative," low-level attack to the all-out annihilatory attack. This continuum, otherwise stated, runs from the low-yield to the high-yield weapon and, therefore, the corresponding level of damage that will be sustained by the city. As will be seen, a US nuclear attack on Moscow with single warheads of these specified yields can kill, on a prompt basis, somewhere between 40,000 and 3.5 million people (see Table 15). This analysis, of course, is limited to the instance in which a single warhead is detonated over the city. A far more likely case would be the near simultaneous detonation of multiple warheads, of whatever yield, over Moscow that would increase the level of casualties far beyond what is projected here. In a sense, the continuum of plausible nuclear attacks on Moscow varies from the limited to the annihilatory. In less technical terms, these scenarios range from the sublime to the ridiculous.

In the following sections, the effects of these alternative nuclear attacks on Moscow will be examined. Different yield warheads (335 kilotons, one megaton, and 24 megatons) will be detonated in hypothetical attacks on Moscow, from which we can project the resulting level of fatalities and casualties. Of lesser importance, it will be possible to compare the general effects of these attacks with the effects of nuclear attacks on New York City. With the exception of the 335 kiloton warhead that will be used against Moscow (in comparison with the 500 kiloton warhead that was used on New York City), the attacks will be based on weapons of approximately the same explosive power. Bearing in mind that two nuclear attacks, even with warheads of the same nominal yield, can have substantially different results, it still remains useful to compare the effects of similar strikes. Thus, these attacks on Moscow provide a baseline study of the consequences of nuclear attacks on a large-scale urban area in the Soviet Union. While it is true that Moscow has more relative and absolute urban sprawl than the other cities in this sample of Soviet cities, this anomaly, paradoxically, reinforces the similarity to the attacks on New York City, and thereby provides a common demographic basis upon which to compare the effects of nuclear attacks on American and Soviet cities.

335 Kiloton Warhead In the current US nuclear arsenal there are 300 Minuteman IIIA (MMIIIA) ICBMs, each of which is MIRVed with three 335 kiloton RVs. From the vantage point of optimality, the MMIIIA RVs probably would be far more appropriate in strikes against hardened targets, such as the USSR's SS-18M4 ICBM silos, than they are for urban targeting. In fact, the 900 MMIIIA RVs might form the first wave of an American countersilo attack against the Soviet Union. Be that as it may, the issue before us here is the effect of the detonation of one 335 kiloton RV against Moscow. As shown in Table 15, the air-burst RV has an area of damage of approximately 88 square miles, which corresponds to a lethal radius of 5.3 nautical miles. If we assume that Moscow's population of 8.4 million is distributed uniformly over 1,700 or so square miles, there will be 145,000 deaths and 275,000 casualties on a prompt basis. The number of dead represents roughly 2 percent of the population, and the wounded is approximately 3 percent. Now, as has been noted earlier, these casualty projections can shift by a significant amount depending on a variety of factors that include the precise distribution of people in the city. If, for instance, the population of Moscow happened to be concentrated in the central urban area, the number of fatalities and casualties could increase by as much as a factor of two. As it stands in this scenario, more than 400,000 Muscovites either were killed or wounded in an attack with one 335 kiloton warhead. Parenthetically, if all three RVs on a MMIIIA ICBM were detonated at the same time over Moscow, it would result in 430,000 prompt dead and 820,000 wounded, or a total of 1.2 million casualties. Thus, on a rough scale, the detonation of each of these three warheads produces an average of 400,000 prompt fatalities and casualties.

Destruction of this magnitude seems almost incomprehensible, yet it must be emphasized that this is the consequence of the detonation of *relatively* small nuclear warheads. In comparison with warhead yields in the 1–20 megaton range, the casualties are, in some cases, an order of magnitude (10 times) less than that which would be caused by the larger RVs. To be sure, this is not to trivialize what has happened in this scenario. Yet, the consequences of megaton-range weapons will be far worse than the consequences of this particular attack.

One Megaton Warhead A one megaton warhead is a rather average yield weapon in the USSR's nuclear arsenal. In the US arsenal, however, it would be one of the largest, yet numerically one of the least significant, weapons. For a number of disparate political and military reasons, the United States deployed warheads that are on the lower end of the yield scale. Warheads in the 40–335 kiloton range are the most common yields, on both ICBMs and SLBMs alike. In spite of the relatively lower yields of US nuclear warheads, the United States does have 450 one megaton warheads on MMII ICBMs and approximately 1,000 on B-52 and FB-111 bombers. Historically, the megaton-range warheads are among the oldest in the US arsenal, with the designs dating back in some cases as much as 20 years.

In studies of the effects of a nuclear attack on a large urban area, defense analysts typically select a one megaton warhead to illustrate the effects of an "average" nuclear explosion on an urban area. If one were to select an average yield warhead from the US arsenal the choice would shift to weapons in the 100–200 kiloton range, whereas in the Soviet arsenal the one megaton warhead would be fairly representative of the weapons that are available. Nevertheless, for reasons that probably include the "neatness" of a one megaton value, it has become the baseline weapon. To be consistent with precedence (insofar as it exists), therefore, the one megaton RV will be examined here.

A one megaton warhead that is air-burst has an area of damage of 227 square miles, i.e., a lethal radius of 8.5 nautical miles. On a prompt basis, a one megaton air-burst over Moscow will kill approximately 370,000 people instantly and wound another 700,000. More than 4 percent will die immediately, while an additional 8 percent will be casualties. Since roughly half of the wounded will die within 30 days, nearly 10 percent of Moscow's population will die from the effects of a one megaton air-burst. To be consistent with what has been said, the ultimate number of fatalities may be much higher still as a result of the post-attack shortages of health care facilities, food, and shelter. On a still longer timescale, say months, the severe climatic conditions of the famed winter of the Russian steppes at the northern latitudes would be expected to kill an even larger number of people in the post-attack period. If we exclude these essentially "incalculable" facets of a nuclear attack, the immediate population affected (either dead or wounded) is more than 1 million, which equals roughly 12 percent of the population of Moscow as of 1984.

24 Megaton Warhead It is clear that in the earlier days of the US nuclear arsenal, selected B-52 bombers carried 24 megaton warheads. Some studies today, however, suggest that US B-52s no longer carry warheads of this yield. With this caveat in mind, nevertheless let us proceed to examine the effects of a 24 megaton explosion against Moscow, on the assumption that US bombers still may have such weapons as part of their deliverable payload. In the event that these weapons are no longer in the US arsenal, this hypothetical case still will provide a useful comparison with the effects of a 20 megaton explosion over New York City.

Even in the nuclear age, when our senses quite easily can become dulled by weapons of mass destruction that can affect hundreds of square miles, a 24 megaton warhead is indeed a weapon of staggering power. In an air-burst at the optimum HOB, such a weapon can cover 2,300 square miles with at least 2–3 psi overpressure. In terms of lethal radius, a 24 megaton warhead produces these psi levels more than 27 miles from the center of the explosion. The fireball alone would be more than three miles in diameter. On any scale, a 24 megaton warhead is a weapon with stupefying destructive powers. In this case, the detonation of such a weapon over Moscow would inundate the entire urban area. The explosion would kill 3.5 million people instantly, and would wound the remaining 4.8 million civilians. In other words, the explosion would kill 42 percent of Moscow's population and wound the other 58 percent. Beyond the nominal 30 days after the explosion, more than half of the surviving 4.8 million casualties would die. And months after the attack, the synergistic effects of blast, heat, fire, radiation, as well as blast-induced deprivations (shortages of food, shelter, water, and medical aid) probably would kill those who survived the initial explosion. This warhead effectively would eradicate all life in the greater Moscow metropolitan area in less than a year as the entire city would be reduced to a barren, desolate landscape. In stark terms, this is what might be meant by the often-abused phrase of nuclear "overkill."[2]

In summary, the detonation of a 24 megaton warhead over Moscow would have cataclysmic and probably irreversible consequences for the city. Should anyone survive this attack, it would only be those who happened to be sheltered in one of the 50–100 hardened *military* shelters in the region. Not available to ordinary citizens, these shelters, some speculate, will be occupied by the high-ranking military, party, and specialized elites who, in theory, will be essential for the reconstruction of the USSR in the post-attack ("recovery") phase.[3] In reality, an effective attack on Moscow would target these shelters as well with surface-bursts in order to destroy the elites who might otherwise have been expected to survive. A more sophisticated view would suggest that the threat of destroying these leadership shelters will have an undisputed and sobering deterrent effect on the Soviet Union's leadership. In any event, aside from the ancillary requirements of targeting the leadership, the detonation of a 24 megaton air-burst will signify the near-total destruction of Moscow and its environs.

Summary It is difficult to cover all reasonable contingencies when it comes to nuclear attacks on a large urban area, in this case Moscow. The best one can hope to achieve is a series of approximations about the yield of the weapons and the resulting casualties. In a study on nuclear war, we can be neither precise nor exact in our projections, for a number of variables can have a significant effect on the outcome of the attack. These projections of casualties, based on the detonation of warheads with differing yields, were meant to provide no more than broad estimates, for in reality the United States could have used any number of warheads, in any combination, to

Graph 2
Prompt Soviet Fatalities: 1 Megaton and 40 Kiloton Air-Bursts*

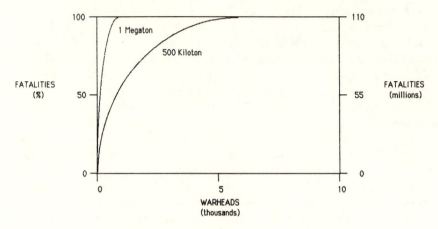

* This assumes a U.S. attack against the 306 largest urban–industrial areas
in the Soviet Union, having a total population in excess of 110 million. All
warheads detonate at the optimum height of burst.

produce the desired results. For these reasons, we have calculated the
prompt Soviet fatalities for single warhead detonations for each type of warhead in the US arsenal. (See Graph 2.) From the graph, we can derive
estimates of the casualties that would result from air-bursts of the specified
yields, as well as approximations of the consequences of a nuclear attack
depending on the delivery system that was used. Still, this outline provides
only a rough indicator of the effects of a nuclear attack and as such is not to be
construed as a comprehensive measure.

LARGE-SCALE COUNTERVALUE DESTRUCTION

In the early 1960s, then Secretary of Defense Robert McNamara first
elaborated the now infamous rule of nuclear deterrence. Simply stated, if
the United States could destroy roughly half of the Soviet Union's population
and two-thirds of its industry in retaliation, then this prospect of "unacceptable damage" surely would deter the Soviet Union from attacking the United
States in the first place. This countervalue retaliatory policy, or "assured
destruction" as it was called, came to be the basis for nuclear deterrence.
Logically and emotionally, the power of this policy lies in its starkness: the
deliberate and unequivocal annihilation of Soviet urban areas in reprisal for
Soviet nuclear aggression. One of the favorite symbols of this policy was the

predicted relationship between the level of civilian and economic destruction and the number of exploding nuclear warheads. Later, McNamara released studies which showed that the US could annihilate the Soviet Union as long as it retained 400 equivalent megatons (EMT) after any conceivable Soviet first-strike attack. Whether these figures are correct is not the point here. What is of monumental importance is whether the United States actually would slaughter Soviet civilians, as opposed to an attack against Soviet nuclear forces, in response to a Soviet nuclear attack. The clear and unavoidable answer is that there is every indication that the United States would follow this policy, despite the fact that the Soviet Union likewise would retaliate immediately against US cities. The entire chain of events reminds us of a tragedy of errors. A nuclear war that began as the result of accidental, unintentional, or third-party factors could shift to the unrestrained slaughter of innocent people. Somewhat surprisingly, this evolution (in fact, regression) in nuclear strategy is traceable to a technological factor: the inability to hit anything other than large, sprawling targets, such as cities, wherein delivery system inaccuracies are irrelevant.

There can be no doubt about the US capability for assured retaliation against Soviet cities. As we will see, the combined Poseidon and Trident SLBM forces present a credible countervalue threat to Soviet population centers. Here, the issue is how the United States might approach the task of destroying urban centers in the Soviet Union. Following the same methods of analysis that were outlined in Chapter 5, we will examine the mechanics of a large-scale US attack on the 300 largest urban areas in the Soviet Union. The contrasts between the US and Soviet countervalue target bases will, as the analysis shows, be stark and revealing, particularly in terms of the greater relative vulnerability of the USSR's urban population to US nuclear attacks.

Soviet Cities: Demographic Analysis

In 1984, the Soviet Union had a total population of 275 million. In this study, we have concentrated on the 306 Soviet cities that have a combined population of slightly less than 110 million, which represents 40 percent of the USSR's total population. The selection criterion for this sample of Soviet cities was (as in the American urban target list) roughly the 300 largest urban areas in the Soviet Union. To be explicit, in this study we are not concerned with the 160 million or so civilians who reside in the remaining rural areas or very small towns. Thus, as in the section on the United States, the focus of this analysis is the immediate urban population of the Soviet Union, i.e., those who were included implicitly in the McNamara "curves" of population fatalities in an assured destruction attack.

In comparison with the urban-industrial population in the United States, the urban population of the Soviet Union is less dispersed.[4] Using the data from this study, roughly 40 percent of the USSR's total population is concentrated in 300 cities, whereas in the United States the same number of cities contains more than 60 percent of the total American population. Aggregating the total US and Soviet urban populations and areas into a uniform scale, the population density in this sample for the United States (less than 400 persons per square mile) is one order of magnitude (ten times) less than the population density for the Soviet cities in this sample (4,700 persons per square mile). Looking at these Soviet population and cities, it is obvious that Soviet cities are smaller in terms of area than their US counterparts, and therefore that they are more densely populated. On a demographic note, the cities in the Soviet Union tend to have less urban sprawl than US cities, as the population in a Soviet city typically remains more tightly clustered around the urban core area. Perhaps one reason for this striking asymmetry is the relatively smaller number of automobiles in the USSR, which has the effect of concentrating the population's residences in the immediate urban core and thus closer to their work locations. If Soviet citizens are unable to purchase as many cars per capita as Americans, then they will be forced to stay near mass transit depots, which typically are distributed within the central city. As a result, the Soviet Union has not experienced the tremendous surge of urban or suburban sprawl that occurred in the United States during the 1950s and 1960s. Insofar as nuclear targeting is concerned, the effect is to have more densely populated urban "pockets" scattered throughout the Soviet Union, rather than the diffuse and amorphous web of urban areas in the United States that, in one case, blend together from Boston to Washington to form one distended metropolitan area.

In the Soviet Union, the urban population is scattered, almost helter-skelter, from the western and southwestern quadrants of the USSR to the southeastern quadrants in what is known as a crescent-shaped belt. By far the most important (i.e., largest) urban targets in this study are clustered in the western quadrant of the Soviet Union. The extent of this concentration in the western regions of the Soviet Union was a significant factor in the high level of collateral casualties that were sustained by the USSR in the U.S. counterforce attacks on Soviet ICBM silos. Indeed, the collocation of urban and military targets in the USSR is a function of the economic need to locate military centers within the "grids" of electric power and the supply of skilled manpower.

Perhaps the most useful approach to be taken in a large-scale attack on Soviet urban areas is to stratify Soviet cities into target subsets as a function of their population, just as we did in Chapter 5 for American cities. This approach will allow us to group Soviet cities into target classes by virtue of their size, and, therefore their relative importance, to the Soviet political and economic system. And aside from the obvious advantage of separating Soviet cities into discrete target classes, this approach also allows us to make direct and easy comparisons between the US and USSR cities in terms of the effects of large-scale nuclear attacks.

It is apparent that the largest cities probably would be the highest priority targets in a large-scale nuclear attack. The impact on the Soviet Union of the destruction of a large urban area, such as Moscow or Leningrad, will be significant, especially for a totalitarian state, which tends to concentrate political and economic power in a relatively small number of cities. Moscow, for instance, rightly is considered to be the most important city in the USSR—its importance is far greater than that of any comparable city in the Soviet Union. While the party and government organizations are located in Moscow, the archives of the CPSU (Communist Party of the Soviet Union) among other resources are located in Leningrad. Thus, the loss of either city would constitute a catastrophe of immense proportions for the tightly centralized Soviet government.

The first group of Soviet urban areas is composed of the 24 cities that have a population in excess of 1 million (see Table 12). As noted, the largest city in the Soviet Union, Moscow, has a population of 8.4 million, while the smallest in this sample is the city of Omsk (population: 1,014,000). The sample of cities with a population greater than 1 million has a total population that is in excess of 40 million, a value which corresponds to 40 percent of the total urban population in this study and 15 percent of the USSR's total population. Yet, the real significance of the 24 cities that have more than 1 million people is measured best in terms of economic output. A rough estimate is that these cities contribute upwards of 20–25 percent of the USSR's gross national product in selected categories, such as manufacturing and power production. For the potential nuclear antagonist, this subdivision of cities would be a lucrative urban-industrial target in the USSR. In terms of relative importance, these same cities probably are more essential to the Soviet economic system than their counterparts in the United States. Indeed, a concentrated attack on these 24 cities alone might well suffice as an assured destruction strike on the Soviet Union.

For a number of complex demographic and historical reasons, there are always more middle- to small-sized cities than large ones. In the Soviet Union, there is a distinct tendency to concentrate urban populations in a small number of large cities, with 46 urban areas having populations greater than 500,000. Still, the Soviet Union is more heavily populated with hundreds of cities and towns that have populations between 100,000 and 500,000 people. If we look at the percentage of total population in this sample of cities, the 46 largest urban areas (populations in excess of 500,000) contain more than 50 percent of the people in this study, as shown in Table 12. Yet, 80 percent (245) of the 306 cities in this sample that fall in the 50,000–500,000 population bracket have 46 percent (50 million) of the total urban population (107 million). From this data we can infer that, like the United States, the Soviet Union is populated with a large number of average-sized urban areas that have the effect of radically increasing the number of potential urban targets in the Soviet Union. Thus, the first group of 46 targets has a target population of 57 million, while the second group of 245 targets has a roughly equal population. This suggests that the destruction of the first 50 million Soviet civilians in this sample of urban areas can be achieved by attacking one-fifth as many targets as would be required for the destruction of the second 50 million people.

It was noted earlier that there is a more exaggerated tendency in the United States to concentrate people in the handful of largest urban areas. More than 70 percent of the US urban population in this study resides in the 71 largest cities, whereas in the USSR only 50 percent reside in the 46 largest cities. In the case of the Soviet Union's urban population, the number of middle-sized cities is striking, particularly the more than 150 cities in the 100,000–250,000 population group. Aside from the major urban areas, this sample of cities constitutes the core of the urbanized population in the Soviet Union. We might think of this group of cities as the second echelon of targets in an assured destruction attack by the United States. Of equal economic significance still are the 70 cities in the 250,000–500,000 bracket that also will figure as a dominant part of such an attack.

In large-scale urban exchanges the theoretical possibility that there may be "bottlenecks" of critical resources in the Soviet economy has prompted some to search for urban targets that are more important than others. We do not address this possibility directly, as these calculations are based on an equal distribution of people in, and the allocation of weapons against, the Soviet urban targets.

In summary, the function of this stratification of cities is to create manageable subsets of targets from the hundreds of available cities. As a conceptual tool, this approach helps one to organize the urban resources of the USSR into discrete packages that can be compared directly with the US target list. The population of a city is an excellent measure for assigning a value to the importance of that city, not excluding the fact that there are, of course, many other methods for ranking the priority of urban targets, such as the location of critical resources or the existence of power grids within a region. In view of the level of detail that is being used in this study, this population index will be a useful measure of the relative importance of the Soviet cities, and thereby serves to establish a general framework for the analysis. In the next section, the effects of large-scale nuclear attacks on Soviet urban centers will be examined. The consequences will be projected for US strikes on Soviet cities that employ 40 kiloton RVs on the Poseidon SLBMs and one megaton RVs on selected ICBMs and bombers. This will provide a baseline estimation of the capabilities of the United States in a countervalue nuclear exchange.

Comprehensive Urban Attacks

Let us suppose that the United States were to launch a massive nuclear attack against 306 cities in the Soviet Union. Given the total target population in these urban centers, which is in excess of 100 million, it is estimated that somewhere between one-half and two-thirds of Soviet industry will be damaged. Here, we will examine the consequences of two hypothetical scenarios:

—an attack with 40 kiloton warheads, which corresponds to the capabilities of the US force of Poseidon SLBMS.

—an attack with one megaton warheads on selected ICBMs and bombers.

As in Chapter 5, it is assumed that each of these attacks will be limited to warheads of the specified yields.

Attack With 40 Kiloton Warheads Perhaps *the* classic scenario in nuclear war studies is the retaliatory attack that is launched by US submarines against cities in the Soviet Union. Poised as the inexorable and forbidding ultimate deterrent force, the US SLBM force typically responds to some (rarely specified or truly credible) hypothetical Soviet action by unleashing thousands of warheads on Soviet urban centers. The result is as awesome as it is sudden: roughly 50–100 million Soviet casualties and the utter disruption of the Soviet Union's political and economic system. Here, we seek to analyze the major component of this attack, which is the countervalue capability of the roughly 3,500 40 kiloton RVs on the US Poseidon SLBM force.

Each Poseidon SLBM carries ten 40 kiloton warheads that have a CEP of 463 meters. A 40 kiloton RV has an area of damage of 25 square miles for an air-burst, and 10 square miles for a surface-burst. We will consider only the air-burst in this study. The issue is the resultant casualties in the Soviet Union from an attack with 40 kiloton air-bursts, which are shown in Graph 2. In an attack in which thousands of 40 kiloton warheads are distributed evenly over 306 Soviet cities that cover a total target urban area of 23,000 square miles, it would require roughly 6,200 RVs to kill the 107 million people in the target cities on a prompt basis.[5] The assumption is that the RVs would have to be detonated uniformly over the cities to create the maximum possible overpressure. In reality, however, this example is somewhat misleading because there are only 3,500 Poseidon RVs in the US arsenal at this time. A better question, therefore, is the level of damage that 3,500 Poseidon RVs could cause in the Soviet Union. It is estimated that 3,500 40 kiloton RVs, using the same attack assumptions, could kill some 85 million civilians instantly and wound the remaining 23 million in this sample of urban centers. This is an effective "kill rate" of 78 percent of the urban population in the 300 or so largest urban areas in the USSR. Of course, roughly half of the wounded will die within 30–60 days, resulting in a final kill rate that approaches 90 percent.

The dimensions of this US capability are more pronounced still when one considers that this attack excludes the Trident SLBMs, as well as other residual legs of the nuclear triad. Despite this potential for causing massive levels of damage to Soviet cities, there is one fact that puts this capability into sharper focus. It is the inherent inefficiency of an attack that considers large and small cities alike as equal targets. In this calculation we have assumed that all Soviet urban targets are aggregated into one large target with the total population uniformly distributed throughout, just as we have aggregated the areas of destruction of all the 40 kiloton RVs into one large area of damage. This approach has several effects. First, it tends to underestimate civilian casualties because in reality the people would be clustered within their respective cities, and therefore the population density would be less uniform than we estimate. Second, the aggregation of the areas of damage tends to overestimate the number of casualties because the method includes people in the area affected by the bursts even though they might reside between the circles of destruction that would be caused by the explosions. The net effect of this approach is to simultaneously inflate and deflate casualty levels. To some extent, these approaches probably cancel each other out.

The inevitable inference from this analysis is that the retaliatory power of US Poseidon SLBMs is more than sufficient for the annihilation of the USSR's urban population. Whether or not assured destruction is a palatable state of affairs in nuclear policy is an entirely different matter, for the inescapable fact is that the United States possesses the ability to destroy most major Soviet cities. In short, the assured destruction of Soviet cities still is a viable policy option for the United States at the present.

Attack With One Megaton Warheads There are roughly 1,500 one megaton warheads in the US nuclear arsenal, which are deployed on Minuteman II ICBMS, B-52s, and FB-111 bombers. This number of one megaton warheads raises the possibility that the 300 Soviet urban centers might be attacked with such warheads. The results of this hypothetical attack are shown in Graph 2. As it turns out, a saturation attack against Soviet cities does not require anywhere near 1,500 one megaton warheads. In fact, slightly less than 700 air-bursts would be sufficient to cause approximately 100 million prompt deaths in these Soviet cities. To understand this, it is necessary only to consider the relatively small area (and high population density) of Soviet cities, which indicates that the urban population of the USSR is so densely packed that they are extremely vulnerable to nuclear attack. Given the systemic (though unavoidable) distortions that occur when one attempts to project urban casualties, this finding is even more striking when it is compared with the number of one megaton warheads that would have to be used against US urban areas.

There is an inherent disadvantage to using one megaton warheads against the full panoply of Soviet urban centers. It is that most of the Soviet cities are much smaller than the area of damage of a one megaton air-burst, which means that some theoretical portion of the lethal radii of the weapons is wasted when the overpressure ring extends substantially beyond the city limits. Conversely, this means that the population of the city is compressed into the more lethal (and correspondingly higher) regions of overpressure, which in the end causes a greater number of fatalities. For a typical Soviet city, which has a population between 100,000 and 250,000 and an area of 30–50 square miles, a one megaton warhead has considerably more destructive power than necessary. A city that covers 50 square miles would have a radius of 4.0 nautical miles, whereas a one megaton air-burst has a lethal radius of 8.5 nautical miles. Even if one is willing to accept the instantaneous death of the entire city as a measure of an efficient targeting criterion, there still is an unavoidable waste of destructive power when an individual weapon affects an area that is much larger than the city itself.

Almost everyone accepts the possibility that US Poseidon SLBMs might be used against urban-industrial targets in the Soviet Union, particularly after a Soviet preemptive attack against the United States. What is less obvious is that US ICBMs or bombers might be used in this way. It is conceivable, for instance, that surviving Minuteman II ICBMs (after a Soviet countersilo attack) might be one element of an attacking force against Soviet cities. Rather than targeting residual Soviet missiles before they are launched, MMII ICBMs could be used in concert with Poseidon SLBMs to annihilate urban areas in the USSR. One positive effect of this scenario is that the United States could retain its SLBM force for a longer time after the war as a secure reserve force for intra-war bargaining and termination. Unlike ICBMs, which can be destroyed in short order by the USSR, the US SLBM force could remain at large for a protracted time, presenting the constant threat of retaliation. In one sense, using MMII ICBMs, or B-52 and FB-111 bombers in attacks against Soviet urban areas simply keeps the level of US reserve forces higher than it would be with purely Poseidon strikes.

In summary, less than half of the 1,500 one megaton warheads in the US nuclear arsenal are sufficient for the complete destruction of the immediate Soviet urban population on a prompt basis, which means 100 million deaths and the loss of one-half to two-thirds of the industrial capacity of the Soviet Union. In strategic terms, this concentration of Soviet population represents an enormous vulnerability to countervalue exchanges at any level. Perhaps it was in recognition of the vulnerability of a highly-concentrated population that led the leadership of the USSR to pursue a civil defense program. Without rendering any judgments as to the effectiveness of the Soviet civil defense program, it is at least clear that the vulnerability of the USSR's urban population is so pronounced that some form of protection probably would seem to be essential. In any event, we see no reason to question the assured destruction capability of US strategic forces at this time.

US Countervalue Targeting Capability

In the last chapter, we examined the case of a hypothetical attack by the Soviet Union on 300 urban targets in the United States. Given the large area of this US countervalue target set, it was found that even the large Soviet nuclear arsenal would have difficulties covering all US cities with sufficient overpressure to kill all of the US civilians. In the limited example of an all-out Soviet attack on the 300 largest urban areas in the United States, surprisingly large numbers of people would not die in the first wave of explosions. Many would be wounded, although a variable number, somewhere between 50 and 60 percent, would be expected to die eventually. While we did not intend to confront the admittedly difficult problem of nuclear overkill, these tentative results indicated that, in terms of prompt effects alone, the Soviet arsenal was not large enough to kill all Americans in the first wave. The possibility of a nuclear winter and long-term biological and ecological consequences aside, an all-out attack would leave many tens of millions wounded in the cities, not to mention the 80 million or so who, not living in the 300 largest metropolitan areas, would escape unscathed. At first glance, the general effect is that not all Americans would die in a Soviet countervalue attack.

In this section, the issue is the effect of a US countervalue attack on the 300 largest urban centers in the Soviet Union. To recapitulate the vital Soviet demographic statistics, there are 108 million people in 306 cities covering roughly 23,000 square miles for an average population density of 4,713 persons per square mile. (See Table 13.) Two general cases are addressed here: the exclusive air-burst and surface-burst attacks. In the case of the exclusively air-burst attack, the total US nuclear arsenal can cover more than 1.1 million square miles with at least 2–3 psi overpressure. Since, however, this ideal value excludes the degradation of the attacking force by the launch and detonation attrition rates, a more realistic value for the deliverable area of damage is 466,000 square miles. For the surface-burst attack, the US arsenal can cover 440,000 square miles in an idealized attack, while in reality a deliverable attack falls in the range of 175,000 square miles. To be explicit, the assumption here is that the entire nuclear arsenal would be used in an attack on 306 urban centers in the Soviet Union. The result, for either an air-burst or surface-burst attack, is the death of the 108 million people in these cities. This applies regardless of whether the attack is based on an idealized or an attrition-added nuclear attack.

The figure of 108 million prompt deaths excludes those Soviet civilians, some 170 million, who do not reside in the 300 primary urban centers in the USSR. Yet, the United States has sufficient residual forces if it sought to expand the countervalue attack to include the hundreds of small cities and towns that have populations of less than 25,000. Predictably, this would increase the number of prompt civilian casualties. The point of this analysis remains the effect on the 300 large urban areas. On that score, the United States could annihilate the urban population of the Soviet Union with relative ease, as long as we exclude any possibility of large-scale counterforce attacks. In sum, the high population density of Soviet cities creates a condition of vulnerability to nuclear attacks that is comparatively greater than the vulnerability of US urban centers. The effect of this demographic situation is to make the USSR significantly more vulnerable to city-busting nuclear attacks, particularly because even a limited strike will destroy a significant fraction of the Soviet Union's industries and critical resources.

COUNTERVALUE RETALIATION: US SSBNs

In the two preceding sections, we addressed the effects of nuclear attacks on Moscow with weapons of varying yields, and the consequences of large-scale US nuclear attacks on hundreds of Soviet cities. Properly speaking, one could view these options as the extreme ends of a spectrum of countervalue nuclear war: from the destruction of one major metropolitan area to massive attacks on several hundred urban centers. If we were to plot this violence as a series of curves (as we did for alternative scenarios based on weapon yield), it is apparent that the effects range from one million to one hundred million dead. It is easy to defend the plausibility of these two scenarios. In the first case, in an attack on Moscow, the United States objective could be to demonstrate its resolve and willingness to run the risks of escalation beyond the destruction of one urban center.

On a parenthetical note, this brings to mind the somewhat apocryphal anecdote of Secretary of State Alexander Haig's testimony before the Congress in 1981 when he admitted that the United States (whether it was with or without the sanction of the NATO allies) would consider demonstration attacks in the case of a war in Europe. We do not really believe that demonstration attacks would, in signalling one's political resolve, allow the antagonists to forfend further nuclear escalation, especially in the case of the "recipient" of the demonstrative attack. Thus, this is presented as a purely suggestive example of the etiology of an attack against one major urban area, rather than being a serious policy option. While a smaller city is more suitable for such demonstration attacks, the destruction of Moscow surely would send a clear message to the Soviet leadership on how urgent the crisis had become. (In reality, it probably would prompt the USSR to destroy New York or Washington in retaliation, and thus increase the incentives for both nations to escalate to still larger countervalue attacks.) In the second case, what we have is an enlarged assured destruction attack that, while perhaps beyond the norm for urban exchanges, carries the logic of urban targeting to the extreme. Neither is more or less plausible than the other, but each represents a clear, if foreboding, option that the United States might execute in a nuclear crisis.

There is a third option. It is the consequences of a retaliatory strike by the US SSBN force on patrol that happens to survive a Soviet counterforce attack. Such a force in theory could attack a number of different targets, both counterforce and countervalue, but there might be a tendency in a time of a severely constrained arsenal to see counterforce attacks as too costly in terms of the number of RVs that would be necessary for targeting the secondary military centers in the USSR and Eastern Europe. Thus, there is the inevitable option of destroying Soviet cities in an assured destruction attack. Here, we examine this option as it relates to expected Soviet losses. As in the earlier sections of this chapter, this scenario is addressed independently of the others.

Distributed Countervalue Retaliation

It is important to re-examine the outcome of the Soviet counterforce attack (in Chapter 4), in terms of the fate of the US SLBM force. In this analysis, the dominant assumption was that the vast majority of the US submarines on patrol would survive a preemptive attack by the Soviet Union, whereas the US SSBNs in port would be assumed to have been destroyed. If it is assumed that 60 percent of the 31 US SSBNs are on patrol, then 19 submarines would be available for retaliatory strikes against, in this case, 300 Soviet urban-industrial targets. Given the uncertainties that surround estimates of the number of SSBNs that might survive a Soviet attack, we will examine the consequences of two hypothetical cases. In the first case, we consider the countervalue capabilities of 19 SSBNs, and in the second case, the effects of retaliation based on the survival of 9 SSBNs.

As shown in Table 16, the first case concerns the estimated urban losses from an attack by 11 Poseidon and 8 Trident SSBNs. These projections are based on the number of deliverable weapons after we take into account the launch and detonation attrition rates of the SLBMs. While there are more than 3,000 surviving RVs after the Soviet attack, attrition rates could reduce the force to some 1,500 warheads: 844 Poseidon RVs and 652 Trident RVs. In the case of air-bursts, this reserve force would be expected to kill nearly 70 million people in the 300 urban targets in the USSR and wound more than 40 million. This attack is equivalent to a 60 percent level of fatalities in these Soviet cities. If the attack were based on surface-bursts, the number of dead would decline to 34 million and the number of wounded would increase to 64 million. In effect, the surface-burst attack results in a 30 percent level of fatalities. From this analysis of the retaliatory potential of 19 SSBNs at sea, we may conclude that the United States has a clear and unimpeded ability to execute an assured destruction mission against Soviet cities. This optimistic assumption about the survivability of US SSBNs, i.e., that most of the submarines at sea will be able to retaliate, reinforces the time-worn equation of deterrence, which is based on the US ability to attack Soviet urban centers. It is safe to reason that, in the event of a US SSBN attack on Soviet cities after a Soviet first-strike attack, the USSR could lose a substantial fraction of its critical urban population and industry. On a large scale, we

Table 16

US Countervalue Retaliatory Attack

	US SSBNs At Sea		Total RVs	Area of Damage		Attrition Rate		
SLBM	SSBN	MIRVs		AB*	SB**	Delivered	AB	SB
POSEIDON	11	10	1,760	44,000	17,000	.48	21,120	8,448
TRIDENT	8	10	1,360	61,200	23,120	.48	23,616	9,178
Total	19		3,120	105,200	40,120		54,736	17,626
POSEIDON	6	10	960	24,000	9,600	.48	11,520	4,608
TRIDENT	3	10	560	25,200	9,520	.48	12,096	4,570
Total	9		1,520	49,200	19,120		23,616	9,178

* AB = Air-burst
** SB = Surface-burst

could reasonably infer from this study that the US capability for counter-value retaliation is secure, and that it will grow with the addition of Trident SLBMs to the arsenal. In a word, the US retaliatory countervalue capability is as secure today as it was in the past.

The second case that will be examined is the countervalue capability of 9 US SSBNs: 6 Poseidon SSBNs and 3 Trident SSBNs. In this attack, the surviving 728 Poseidon and Trident SLBM RVs would be targeted against the 300 largest urban centers in the USSR. As shown in Table 16, this attack could be based on either air-bursts or surface-bursts. In the case of the air-burst attack, the available Poseidon and Trident RVs could kill approximately 65 million people and wound an additional 42 million on a prompt basis. This number of fatalities represents 61 percent of the USSR's urban population. If the attack was executed with surface-burst detonations, the prompt casualties will fall to 32 million dead, 60 million wounded, and the remaining 15 million, who probably would be unharmed. By contrast, the level of damage in this scenario is 30 percent fatalities. Even in this highly pessimistic example, in which the Soviet Union's nuclear and naval forces destroyed roughly half of the American SSBN force, the retaliatory power of US SLBMs is more than sufficient for killing between 30–60 percent of the USSR's urban population, and presumably an equal or greater portion of its industrial capacity. Although this study excludes from attack the 170 million Soviet civilians who reside in largely rural areas, we believe that the loss of the USSR's primary urban population will be more disastrous to the Soviet society than the annihilation of the small, and typically remote, rural towns that are scattered throughout the USSR.

In Chapter 5, we examined the possibility that Soviet countervalue retaliation might, given the limited number of residual RVs on the SSBNs, be targeted against selected large cities in the United States. The rationale was that the effect of annihilating the dominant American urban areas (Boston, New York, and Washington to name but a few) might be more compelling than a distribution of warheads over many large and small cities alike. Perhaps the driving force behind this option would be that the Soviet reserve force was limited to a maximum of 100 or so deliverable warheads. In the case of US retaliation after a Soviet counterforce attack, US SSBNs have thousands of warheads in reserve for urban targeting, a point that removes any incentive to allocate scarce RVs against the most important cities. Given that the United States can attack virtually all major cities in the Soviet Union with surviving submarine-launched missiles, we do not think it is necessary to concentrate on a handful of Soviet cities unless the policy objective were to terminate the war. It should be noted, moreover, that US retaliation could follow the direction that is implied in Table 12, which is from the largest to the smallest cities. Not being constrained by the number of warheads, the point is that the United States simply makes it farther down the list of potential Soviet cities—at least, farther down the list than the Soviets could achieve in an attack against US urban centers.

SUMMARY

Perhaps the best way of looking at nuclear forces is in terms of *asymmetries*. By asymmetries, we mean those differences, sometimes significant but often trivial, in the American and Soviet arsenals that affect how we calculate the nuclear balance. It is clear that the USSR has achieved a large, and possibly significant, edge in countersilo capabilities in its land-based missiles. At the limit, this asymmetry results in a lessened residual capability against American cities, at least if we assume that the war begins with a counterforce strike. Whether this will prove to be a prudent or rational choice remains indeterminate at this time.

In the case of the United States, there is evidence that it has achieved a massive countervalue capability, particularly on a retaliatory basis, at the expense of a counterforce capability. At the limit, we can infer from this asymmetry that the United States has lesser countersilo capabilities than the Soviet Union. Yet, in the event of the need to retaliate against Soviet cities, US capabilities are awesome even under the worst of conditions for the submarine force. At the most general level, the United States can launch such an effective retaliatory attack against cities in the USSR that the USSR cannot reasonably weaken this capability even in a successful first-strike attack. In the logic of countervalue retaliation, we find no evidence to suggest that the United States cannot retain a sufficient nuclear force after Soviet preemption that is adequate for the annihilation of almost all Soviet cities. Quite simply, the US submarine force poses such a credible threat to the USSR that not even the most successful Soviet preemptive attack (see Chapter 4) could erase this capability.

In theoretical terms, a logical scheme must be internally consistent and sound. If the logic of deterrence is the ability to retaliate against urban-industrial targets, and the capability for doing so is intact, then we may say that the logic of assured destruction, or retaliation if you like, is sound. Yet, we wonder if the initial premise of assured destruction, which was examined in this study and the preceding chapters, is sound. Does it make sense ultimately to kill people in the event of a nuclear war? Since the death of millions of civilians will have no direct effect on the adversary's military power, and moreover is likely to cause him to retaliate against one's own cities, the logic of countervalue retaliation may be entirely outdated in an age when the technology allows us to destroy military targets. The sad truth is that the United States still has a nuclear arsenal that is limited, by and large, to countervalue missions on a retaliatory basis. Almost from the start, U.S. declaratory policy has centered on the countervalue mission for the

SSBN force. It should be noted, however, that the submarine force is quite capable of attacks against some elements of Soviet strategic forces—bomber and submarine bases, soft C3 targets, other military targets (OMT), as well as war supporting industries (WSI). That point notwithstanding, the overwhelming countervalue potential of US submarines is but one indication of the possible US intention to slaughter Soviet people in the event that deterrence should collapse in the face of a global or regional crisis.

7

Reflections and Recommendations

There is a tendency in many studies on nuclear war to start with the conclusion that the research points to a litany of serious, and quite possibly catastrophic, strategic errors and miscalculations. With the theme of the study entrenched so firmly in the reader's mind, subsequent chapters would proceed to embellish the details of the travesty. By the time we reached the concluding chapter of the study, it would be easy to see how the reader had been drawn from the opening premise to the final conclusion along what would seem like an obvious, if not unavoidable, path. In this study we might have exercised this literary option. It would have run as follows.

From the very beginnings of the nuclear age, there have been clear signs that the United States not only mismanaged nuclear policy but also the deployment of strategic forces on which we probably have spent in excess of one *trillion* dollars. In terms of nuclear policy, the United States pursued a set of doctrines that, in what became a perversion of traditional military thought, opted for the intentional slaughter of millions of Soviet civilians on the somewhat questionable premise that this would deter any sane Soviet leader. In both historical and strategic terms, this represented perhaps the single greatest military blunder in the modern world, principally because it signified that the evolution of strategy never matched the revolution in technology. Indeed, one could say that there has been a retrogression in US nuclear policy. In any event this would be but the opening salvo in what would become a large-scale assault on the nuclear establishment, including possibly a few *ad hominem* attacks on the principal authors of the policy. Yet, this approach would not be complete without a characterization of the adversary who, inevitably, never seems to commit the same cardinal sins.

To contrast the failure in American strategic thought, we need only look at the evolution of what can be discerned as nuclear policy in the Soviet Union. From the beginning the Soviet Union was hindered by inferior technology—at least in comparison with the United States. Yet, it is apparent now that the USSR developed a nuclear policy that stressed the destruction of counterforce targets as the *sine qua non* of military (nuclear or non-nuclear) strategy, at least as evidenced by the development of their ICBM program since the early 1970s. What was for the Americans the foundation of nuclear policy (retaliation against Soviet cities) was the antithesis of the counterforce nuclear policy that evolved in military circles within the Soviet Union. Out of Soviet strategic thought there emerged a clear emphasis on the destruction of US counterforce targets: ICBMs, SSBNs and SLBMs, and bombers on a preemptive basis if possible. On one scale, this approach caused a (precursive) tremor—the effects of which we are only now beginning to feel—in American policy because it signified that what might deter the Americans (i.e., the loss of their cities) might not necessarily deter the Soviets. In effect, Soviet nuclear policy threatened to negate the foundation of nuclear deterrence that the Americans had accepted as a universal constant in nuclear "politics." On a larger scale one could interpret this state of affairs as the worst type of cultural centrism wherein the United States assumed that the Soviets are moved or deterred by the same things. While, in fact, the Soviets may be just like the Americans in these suicidal matters, there is no firm evidence to allow this premise to be the unchallenged cornerstone of policy. In a word, Soviet nuclear policy evolved in directions that threatened to undermine the nuclear balance, global stability, and national security.

In recent years the large-scale deployment of Soviet ICBMs, which reportedly are capable of destroying American land-based forces, caused a further shock to the system of nuclear deterrence in what some analysts have interpreted as the demise of an environment that had been heralded as evidence of a US-Soviet consensus on the rules of the game. During the nascent years of this shift, the United States failed to match the Soviet deployments that continued to be politically destabilizing for the Americans.

Thus, from this general tenor one could discern that the purpose of the study was to examine the implications of what apparently were erroneous assumptions by the United States. This, at least, was one framework which we could have used to write this book. In its simplicity, this approach would allow us to cast the details of the nuclear balance as growing evidence of a failure within both the political and military establishments to grasp the essential elements of contemporary military thinking and technology. It would make excellent journalistic prose. Yet, we chose not to pursue this approach because we believe that a more detached, non-partisan, and scientific analysis of the nuclear balance and the operational implications of policy and nuclear deployments would allow readers to judge the merits of our analysis and thereby draw their own conclusions. A clear exposition of the assumptions and methods that were used in this study will allow the reader to understand what we have done.

There is no doubt that an indictment of the general evolution of US nuclear strategy would be a compelling, not to mention satisfying, work on national defense. It would allow us to build "bridges" from the theories of nuclear deterrence to the policies of the present in what would appear as a never-ending saga of strategic perfidy. Bureaucracies, services, and policymakers would be convenient targets in a condemnation that would reach to the deepest levels of a democratic political system, particularly insofar as the system works to produce defense policies. We might ask if the consensus that coalesced on the decision to make Soviet populations the target of American retaliation really represented the type of national security policy that a pluralistic society should embrace, or is that policy something we ought to expect from a totalitarian society wherein the bridges between policy and ethics, not to say sobriety, are more muted than in democratic societies. An even more profound question is whether the United States, which at heart is based on a fractious and deeply divisive political structure of shared power, has the ability to formulate defense policies that do not reflect more than a fleeting consensus which is based principally on idiosyncratic political personalities and bureaucratic infighting. (On a personal note, our suspicions are aroused that, in fact, the answer is no.)

For reasons that should be clear, we decided instead to examine the implications of US and Soviet nuclear policies using the only decisive method: to project their general capabilities in broad scenarios of nuclear war. Our aim was to be as fair-minded as possible, to present the case for each side without first drawing inferences as to the quality of the decisions that underlay the capabilities. Only after we had drawn a comparison between the nuclear capabilities of the United States and Soviet Union did it seem appropriate to characterize the soundness of the respective policies. Yet another reason for this approach was our belief that too many "studies" on nuclear war, which is perhaps the most sensitive issue of our time, are based on either a defense of or assault on the status quo: Too many analysts derive their power and acceptability from the assertion, typically at the beginning, that the defense establishment is to be anointed or vilified for its actions. Surely, as we and others have noted, it is easy to indict the establishment—it is they who make the decisions that guide policy. Who else, after all, can one blame? Another shortcoming that plagues many analyses of nuclear war is the use of static models of interaction. In our case, we have employed dynamic models of nuclear war scenarios in order to provide more robust and illustrative conclusions as to the interactions between literally millions of events that would occur in a real nuclear war. In any event, we did not seek to write just one more in a never-ending series of spirited critiques. Instead, the purpose was to understand nuclear capabilities and therefore the policies that could emerge as plausible options from those forces. While in theory a policy ought to be the starting point for options, the persistent reality is that options typically define the policy. All in all, this was not to be another condemnation of nuclear defense policies. Still, we wonder whether to observe that egregious errors have been committed in the name of nuclear deterrence is to become "radicals" of one ideological or political ilk. We fervently hope that this is not the case.

With this overview in mind, we will address three related issues in this chapter. In the first section there is a summary of our findings on the counterforce and countervalue capabilities of the United States and the Soviet Union. This summation will provide some indication of the realistic options that are available to each side in a nuclear war. The second section will be a reflection on nuclear policy, in particular the targeting, weapons, and basing elements of a nuclear policy. And, in the third section, we will propose a series of recommendations for the United States (and ostensibly the Soviet Union) that will contribute to a more secure nuclear balance and stable political climate.

OVERVIEW

This will not be a detailed recapitulation of the preceding four chapters. Instead, the purpose of this summary is to provide a brief overview of the analysis of US and Soviet capabilities in the areas of counterforce and countervalue scenarios. Inasmuch as this concluding chapter focuses on general observations about the relationship between forces and policy, the trend here will be to look at the policy-relevant dimensions of nuclear forces rather than the genre of operational details as we did in earlier chapters.

American Counterforce Capability

It certainly was not difficult to infer from the analysis in Chapter 3 that the counterforce capabilities of the United States are constrained somewhat by the paucity of hard-target kill warheads for the destruction of Soviet nuclear forces. With the exception of the 900 Minuteman IIIA RVs, which pose a credible (if limited) threat to Soviet silos, the remainder of the US nuclear arsenal is not prepared credibly for counterforce exchanges under first-strike conditions. The dimensions of this constraint are clear when one considers that *effective*, high-confidence counterforce strikes against hard targets in the USSR required, in some cases, up to four RVs per target. In any sense of the word, this capability does not accord with the dictates of military rationality and efficiency, if for instance, it requires four Poseidon SLBM warheads to kill each silo in a Soviet ICBM field. It was necessary, as we pointed out earlier, to use SLBMs in this attack, principally because the United States could not destroy Soviet targets before its ICBM RVs were depleted. On a theoretical level, this scenario is evidence of a clear shortage of hard-target kill warheads. We wonder whether the United States has any plans in the SIOP for using Poseidon or Trident warheads against Soviet ICBM silos. But even if this were true the United States still would threaten to disarm itself in the process of attempting to disarm the Soviet Union. And if the definition of a *credible* counterforce attack is one that requires substantially less than the total US arsenal to destroy most Soviet counterforce targets, then it follows that the United States does not have such a capability.

On a broader level, the limited counterforce potential of the United States can be traced to deployment decisions, and hence policies (however ambiguous or ill-conceived they might have been) that eschewed hard-target kill as an active dimension of the retinue of options in a nuclear war. At the Congressional level, to cite but one example, there has been a clear and persistent affirmation that US nuclear policy will not be allowed to shift in the direction of hard-target kill, for a number of complex political and ideological reasons. By far the most recurrent theme behind this trend has been the argument that to move in this direction is to run the risk of destabilizing the nuclear balance and thereby increase the incentive on both sides to launch a first-strike attack. The effect of the near unanimous consensus in the Congress on the undesirability of counterforce options during the early 1970s was to delay the entry of the United States into the field of active counterforce capabilities. It was not until the mid 1970s, when the United States deployed the NS-20 guidance system and the MK12A warhead on the Minuteman III ICBM, that the Americans could be said to have acquired a plausible counterforce capability. In any conceivable case, a counterforce attack on the Soviet Union would deplete American nuclear forces in short order. Beyond the realm of purely theoretical scenarios of nuclear exchanges, we see that a counterforce policy is neither a realistic nor credible option for the United States at this time, and that this shortcoming effectively pushes the US toward the countervalue option. In our judgment, the possession of a counterforce option that is credible, or if you will, equal to that of the Soviets, is an essential element of stable nuclear deterrence. On a more caustic note, the failure to have more than a nominal counterforce capability is to reinforce the decidedly unacceptable option of retaliation against urban-industrial centers in the USSR. This is a case of a collapse in strategic thinking that is characteristic of both Republican and Democratic administrations.

Soviet Counterforce Capability

It should come as no surprise, after detailed and persistent reports of Soviet ICBM deployments, to find that the USSR has the ability to destroy hard counterforce targets in a nuclear war. The SS-17, SS-18, and SS-19 ICBMs provide the foundation for a credible hard-target kill capability which, in theory, can destroy at least two legs of the American nuclear triad—and do so with roughly half of its land-based missiles. While some relatively (and numerically) insignificant elements of the US triad, such as a few bomber bases and command centers, may survive a Soviet preemptive attack, the bulk of American nuclear targets are at risk to a Soviet attack. (This is not to say that such a counterforce attack would erase the ability of the American SSBNs to annihilate Soviet urban centers, for it surely would not. Nor is it to say that, if the United States were to possess a counterforce capability similar to that of the Soviet Union, US nuclear forces would not be at risk today.) This capability evolved out of a Soviet decision to concentrate its modernization efforts on the ICBM force, and in particular on the creation of a force of MIRVed, highly-accurate warheads that in theory could destroy American hard-targets. In recent years, this has been the dominant theme in Soviet nuclear policy, at least insofar as we may infer from the writings of prominent Soviet military and political strategists. This is hardly a path that ought to be vilified for in real terms it signified the decline of countervalue options as the mainstay of Soviet nuclear deterrence. In no small sense we may attribute the recent revolution in US nuclear policy (toward counterforce) to the Soviet Union, for it is the Americans who now appear to ape the Soviets in their commitment to hard-target kill.

As one compares the results of the Soviet counterforce attack on the United States with the American attack on the USSR, it is striking to observe that the Soviet attack is a paradigm of simplicity and order. In essence, what the Soviets could accomplish through attacks with ICBMs and a limited number of SLBMs the United States must do with virtually all of its nuclear forces. From this fact we may infer that the explicit function of Soviet land-based forces is the destruction of American counterforce nuclear targets.

American Countervalue Capability

It is clear that, if US nuclear forces are not capable of credible counterforce options, then the primary mission for the forces must be countervalue retaliation. Enough resources have been invested in the ability to wage countervalue operations to give the United States an enormous destructive potential against the Soviet Union. Even after the worst possible Soviet counterforce attack, the United States still would retain sufficient forces for the utter annihilation of the 300 largest urban centers in the USSR. Indeed, the survival of only a fraction of American SSBNs still translates into the ability to deliver an awesome attack on Soviet cities. By any definition, the countervalue option is such a dominant part of US nuclear capabilities that it unfortunately threatens to become the driving force in the minds of American policymakers. Indeed, it is this feature of American nuclear capabilities that is the most dangerous, for it threatens to make urban-industrial targeting an inevitable, if not immediate, and spontaneous characteristic of a nuclear war. Yet, despite the danger of urban-industrial targeting, in particular that it will magnify the costs of a nuclear exchange, countervalue options are such a well-entrenched aspect of US nuclear policy that there may be a reticence, if not an outright recalcitrance, on the part of the defense establishment to alter the policy.

On a strategic level, the dominance of countervalue options in American plans for nuclear war is evidence that the United States still is committed to the policies of the 1950s and 1960s, when there was little else the superpowers could do but to target urban areas. While the United States now has a limited repertoire of counterforce options, the balance has not shifted to a position where counterforce, as opposed to countervalue, options are the central reference point in nuclear strategy. Until such time as the United States deploys enough systems to *match* (preferably not exceed, in deference to stability) Soviet capabilities, the United States will be forced to rely on countervalue retaliation as the backbone of nuclear deterrence—in full recognition of the fact that the Soviet Union will retaliate against American urban centers, in what will become the large-scale and frenzied annihilation of western civilization.

In 1983, the urban population of the USSR was 110 million people in 300 urban areas. In terms of the assured destruction criterion the United States ought to be able to kill somewhere between one-third and one-half of the Soviet urban population in a retaliatory strike. It is interesting to see, as shown in Table 16, that the United States retains roughly that level of destructive power on its SSBN force. On the assumption that 18 of the 31 submarines on patrol are available for urban-industrial targeting with a 2:1 mix of Poseidon and Trident SLBMs, the US can kill 56 million Soviets on a prompt basis. This represents roughly fifty percent of the USSR's urban population and 20 percent of its total population. In this case, the fatalities are based on the assumption that the number of deliverable SLBMs are constrained only by their reliability rates. In effect, the SSBNs on patrol provide the United States with a credible countervalue retaliatory force, if it is accepted that urban-industrial targeting is a credible option given the likelihood that the Soviet Union will do the same in retaliation. What is not in doubt, insofar as we can infer, is that the countervalue option is firmly entrenched in American nuclear policy. For those who may argue that urban targeting is not part of American plans, we wonder what those plans really are in view of the real capabilities of the triad. Moreover, from what can be learned about US nuclear policy there simply is no evidence to suggest that the United States would not retaliate against Soviet cities. An SSBN force that is equipped with thousands of nuclear warheads, which have no credible counterforce potential, points to an implicit countervalue nuclear policy. In other words, the rhetoric of counterforce options is not reflected in policy.

Accordingly, the annihilation of Soviet cities is and will remain for some time the primary option, unless the United States chooses to launch a first-strike attack using all of its nuclear forces. If, however, the first strike is not a politically acceptable option and urban targeting raises the specter of a reciprocal Soviet response, then we may conclude that neither option is particularly palatable or credible. The unavoidable conclusion is that American nuclear policy is the captive of systemic flaws and inconsistencies that appear to be related to the decision to use nuclear weapons against cities and towns in the Soviet homeland.

Soviet Countervalue Capabiity

It was observed that the USSR's nuclear forces appear to emphasize hard-target kill, a point that is reinforced by the fact that nearly 6,000 of the 8,000 nuclear warheads in the Soviet arsenal clearly are capable of counterforce attacks. The remainder of the Soviet nuclear arsenal is composed of relatively primitive bombers and submarines, whose primary missions are to attack countervalue centers in the United States, presumably after a counterforce attack. In comparison with the nuclear forces of the United States, the Soviets do not place the same level of emphasis on an assured destruction capability against urban areas. Hence, as we noted in Chapter 5, the countervalue option is not an essential (first-order) element of Soviet nuclear strategy, and to the extent that there is a countervalue component in Soviet policy it probably will be in response to an American attack on Soviet cities.

It is when we focus on the actual countervalue capabilities of the Soviet Union that the extent of the divergence between American and Soviet nuclear policies most evident. Here, in the case of the Soviets, the nuclear forces that are to be allocated against American cities are the remnants of the earlier and less capable generation of nuclear forces. Bombers and SLBMs, some which are so decrepit as to be paleoliths in comparison with their present force of highly-accurate MIRVed ICBMs, still constitute the mainstay of the Soviet Union's reserve force for use against American urban population centers. Indeed, many of the SLBMs are more likely to be used in attacks against U.S. command centers, bomber bases, and submarine bases than strict countervalue centers. In thinking about the structure of Soviet forces and the attendant policy behind the forces, it seems that the destruction of American cities is a secondary strand of thought in Soviet nuclear policy. Only in the event of an American response against Soviet cities, which is becoming an increasingly dubious proposition, does one sense that the Soviet Union would contemplate a nuclear exchange against urban areas. That exception aside, there is considerable evidence to support the conclusion that the foundation of Soviet nuclear policy is the counterforce option, and that the countervalue option has become an aberration in policy which the USSR, unlike the United States, has learned to repudiate.

Projected American Capabilities

Much of the rancorous debate about nuclear policy in the United States over the last few years, and in some ways coincident with the genesis (and now it appears, demise) of the nuclear freeze movement, has focused on the modernization of its nuclear arsenal. Weapons, such as the MX ICBM, B-1 Bomber, Trident SLBM, and cruise missiles launched from a variety of systems, have generated not only charges that the arms race is about to be fueled by the deployment of yet another series of (unnecessary) weapons, but also counter-charges that the United States must match in a rough way the deployments of the Soviet Union if there is to be stable deterrence. Here, we do not take issue with either charge directly, for in reality the crucial issue is the effect of the MX and Trident II (otherwise known as "D-5") on the counterforce and countervalue capabilities of the United States. For now, the B-1 bomber and the air-, sea-, and ground-launched cruise missiles will not be addressed in this analysis, since neither has the ability to destroy hard targets on a *time-urgent* basis.

Counterforce Projections The MX and Trident II missiles are quite similar: each is MIRVed with ten warheads and has a nominal CEP of 100 meters. The only real difference between the two missiles is in the yield of the warheads. The MX RV reportedly has a yield of 335 kilotons, while the Trident RV has a yield of 485 kilotons. In terms of hard-target kill, the MX and Trident II are roughly equivalent, for in a two-on-one attack each has a high confidence of destroying the target. Thus, we can project the effect of MX and Trident II on the counterforce potential of the US nuclear arsenal, as shown in Graph 3. If it is assumed that MX and Trident II have similar reliability rates and that the RVs are allocated on a 2:1 basis against hard targets such as silos, then the effect of each on hard-target kill will be roughly the same. Graph 3 shows the deployment of 100 MX ICBMs will translate into the ability to destroy roughly 400 silos or similar hard targets in the Soviet Union. Alternatively, if the present plan for the deployment of 15 MX missiles remains unchanged, the United States will gain the ability to destroy some 60 Soviet hard targets. However, if the United States sought the ability to destroy 1,400 or so silos and roughly 200 command centers in the USSR, it would be necessary to deploy more than 400 MX ICBMs. While this force would have a significant first-strike potential, the envisioned deployment of 15 MX can hardly be said to constitute a real increase in American counterforce capabilities, or concomitantly an expansion in the US first-strike potential.

In the case of the Trident II SLBM, the discrete effect on American counterforce capabilities is the same as the MX. The difference, however, lies in the fact that the United States will deploy more than 20 Ohio-class SSBNs with 24 Trident II SLBMs on each. A force of some 500 Trident II SLBMs would give the United States the ability to destroy more than 2,000 hard targets in the USSR. This force will have a pronounced effect on the counterforce capabilities of the United States.

Countervalue Projections While the counterforce potential of the MX and Trident missiles always has been a well-established fact, there remains the

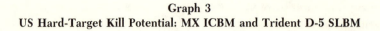

Graph 3
US Hard-Target Kill Potential: MX ICBM and Trident D-5 SLBM

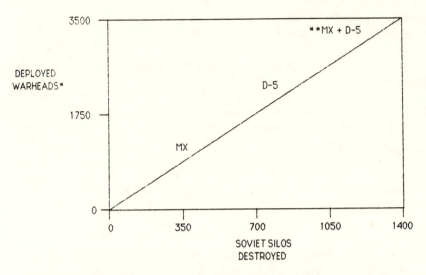

* This assumes that 1000 MX warheads or 2496 D-5 warheads are deployed, a two-on-one warhead allocation per silo, and an overall system reliability of 0.80.

** Obviously, a combined force of MX and D-5 of this magnitude would be sufficient to destroy the Soviet ICBM force of 1,398 silos.

possibility, however remote, that these weapons will be used against urban targets. As noted, the Trident II RV has a larger yield warhead, which translates into a larger area of destruction than an MX RV. As an air-burst, one Trident warhead has an area of destruction of 129 square miles, while for the MX it is 88 square miles—if we assume a 2 psi overpressure level. The effect, quite naturally, is that an equal number of Trident II warheads will cause more casualties than MX. In the case of an attack with 1,000 MX RVs, there would be a resultant 85 million prompt fatalities in the 300 largest urban centers in the Soviet Union. And in the case of 1,000 Trident II RVs there would be roughly 100 million prompt fatalities. It should be noted that 1,000 Trident RVs is the nominal deployment case of 100 SLBMs, while in reality, the United States plans to deploy on the order to 300–500 Trident II SLBMs during the next decade. There is no doubt that the countervalue option is a remote possibility for the MX and Trident missiles, as their design by itself is strong evidence that they would be used in counterforce strikes. Still, even the slightest chance that they might be used in a countervalue mission is sufficient justification for assessing the effect of MX and Trident on the countervalue balance of forces. In reality, each would have a significant effect on American countervalue capabilities, although we strongly doubt that either would be targeted against anything other than hard counterforce targets in the USSR.

REFLECTIONS ON NUCLEAR POLICY

In a democratic society, it so often seems that the easiest tasks are the hardest to achieve. Conversely, there seems to be evidence that the most difficult things are the simplest to accomplish. In the latter case, the election of a president is a difficult, quite often impossible, task for most political systems, yet in the United States we choose executives in a casual, almost self-deprecatory, style. We write this just days before the 1984 Presidential election, realizing that what is so extraordinarily hard for most political systems is so easy for the Americans. In the case of the former, those tasks which on the surface could be such simple affairs are, for a democracy, almost herculean in nature. Let us take, for example, the case of policy— independent of any specific type of policy. It seems that democratic systems quite often fail miserably in terms of the ability to articulate a consensus on the goals, scope, or means of policy. In democratic theory we can find the reason for this dilemma: It is that to resolve a policy is to signal a victory, however insignificant it may be, for one of the many coalitions that participate in the process. Moreover, when it becomes impossible to resolve the competing and contradictory goals of the interest groups, there are only two possible solutions in a democracy: compromise or conflict. As outright conflict rarely manifests itself in the United States, we must turn to the case of compromise. As a general rule, we may say that when the formulation of military policy falls prey to the vicissitudes of compromise in a consensus-based political system, the difficulties emerge.

In most spheres of policy, the inability to formulate what might be approximated as an optimal, even marginally workable, solution to policy disputes can create confusion and trouble for the political system. Yet, in the realm of nuclear policy these same systemic difficulties can lead to catastrophes of a magnitude that only a nuclear war can fully make clear. Here, the central question is the structure of nuclear policy, in particular the coherence of American nuclear policy in 1984 and thereafter. By inference, we must be concerned as well with what might be termed Soviet nuclear policy, for it is the dynamic relationship between the two that provides the foundation for deterrence and general political stability. To understand nuclear policy it is not necessary to recreate in excruciating detail the discrete evolutionary path along which US and Soviet military thinking coalesced from an observable body of knowledge and intentions into a policy. Instead, we will examine the constituent elements of nuclear policy on an abstract level. From that starting point, it is easy to see how the nuclear policies of the United States and the Soviet Union compare, and thereby to deduce where errors have been made and similarities exist. Once that task is completed, we will move on to examine a series of recommendations for American nuclear policy specifically, and nuclear policy in general.

Nuclear Strategy: What It Is and Is Not

As there is much to suggest that we often fail to distinguish between what is meant by policy and strategy, it is essential to differentiate between the two. In theory, a nuclear policy is that broad set of operational principles which represent how a nation will fight a nuclear war. A further distinction is in order. There is *declared* policy which symbolizes what the nation wants its adversary and its constituents to think it will do in a nuclear war. For obvious reasons, the declared policy may not reflect necessarily what the nation's policy actually is. By contrast (and exclusion), *real* policy is the plans for how the war actually will be fought. Again, it should be obvious that the real policy is a closely and jealously guarded secret of the state, usually classified as "code-word" information. For real policy to be effective, many argue that it should be kept as secret as possible, as an enemy's uncertainty about one's actual plans for war will foster a measure of security: The enemy never can know exactly what one will do or how effective such actions might be. This in encapsulated form is the traditional approach to nuclear policy. In recent years, at least since the advent of the nuclear age, a number of prominent civilian and military strategists have argued (correctly) that it is not entirely necessary to shroud nuclear policy in a cloud of absolute secrecy to deter a war. Some enemy knowledge about one's real policy, such as the intention of killing millions of civilians in retaliation for any nuclear attack, can have a healthy influence on stability and the potentially provocative and adventurous proclivities of the adversary. This, parenthetically, in abridged form is the case for assured destruction.

Thus, on a simplified level, nuclear policy, whether declared or real, signifies what one will do in a nuclear war. The much larger issue, which often is confused with policy, is nuclear strategy. Strategy is an explicit formulation of what, in this case, a nuclear war will do for the global interests of the state. This may sound paradoxical, for everyone knows (or should know) that a nuclear war can never be in the interests of any state at any time. The more manageable and practical way to express nuclear strategy is to ask how the *threat* of nuclear war can be used to further the interests of the state. The difficulty that is implicit in this thinking is at once clear for those who seek to define nuclear strategy in ways that are amenable to the disparate interest groups that populate a democracy. The paradox is that for many in a democratic society, the prospect of a nuclear war or even the specter of the threat, is not an acceptable basis for nuclear policy or strategy. And even for those civilian and military thinkers who can sidestep this emotional quandary, there remains an aversion to certain domains of nuclear

policy or strategy on the grounds that some "theories" lead to more thinka-
ble (i.e., plausible) scenarios of nuclear war, and thereby increase the probability of such an occurrence. When in the general populace there is such a
deep and irreversible revulsion against the formulation of nuclear policy and
strategy, and when in the intellectual circles there are deep fissures over the
structure that nuclear policy ought to take, we have a prescription for disas-
ter. The obvious and immediate result is that nuclear policy will not be a
firm structure that is reinforced by a broad and bipartisan political consensus. An even more likely result is that nuclear policy will become (and
remain) a vacillating and ephemeral structure, driven by the dictates of
technology, and therefore characterized by the institutionalization of inter-
mittent chaos, turbulence, and occasional reform.

For those who prefer to think in sociological terms, the gulf that separates
not only the disparate intellectual schools of thought on nuclear policy, but
also the public and establishment views on nuclear policy, could be the
decisive explanation for the apparent vacillation in American nuclear policy.
There are more than a few historical precedents for this friction. A notable
example was the French Revolution, when the alienation between the upper
and lower classes in French society over political and religious issues led to
the figurative desertion of the intellectual elements from the mainstream
body politic. This is the *trahiers des clercs,* that often is interpreted as a
signal that a fundamental tension or rift has deepened between the government and the intellectual elite. We do not think for a moment that there is
even the remotest chance of a fundamental realignment or revolution in
American politics along these lines, yet this difference over the role of
nuclear weapons in US foreign and national security policy may be a significant factor in an explanation of why the United States has failed to create a
coherent and broad-based consensus on nuclear policy. Indeed, if it is true
that there is alienation between the groups, and among the specialists within
the defense establishment over the proper structure of nuclear strategy,
then it would be the worst sort of naivete to expect that a coherent policy
could emerge out of the strife.

In order to establish a theoretical framework for looking at policy and
strategy, we quite deliberately have sidestepped what might be called the
classic example of strife over nuclear policy. On a contemporary scale, the
issue is whether nuclear deterrence ought to be based on annihilatory retaliation or protracted war-fighting. How one views this debate will go a long
way toward highlighting the ills of strategy formulation in the United States.
And since we cannot deduce a policy without first knowing what the strategy
is, this will serve to highlight the relationship between the two.

Fundamentally, US nuclear policy can be based either on the threat of
retaliation against the population centers of the enemy, or the destruction of
the military resources of the enemy. Each can contribute to stable deterrence as long as neither presents the threat of a credible first-strike ca-

pability. Yet, in terms of the debate over nuclear strategy the two positions never can be reconciled: The first sees deterrence as a function of certain civilian slaughter, while the second views deterrence as the ability to destroy nuclear forces. Aside from the simple observation that a policy based on civilian slaughter has serious practical and ethical dilemmas associated with it and that a counterforce policy always appears destabilizing because it is virtually indistinguishable from a preemptive capability, we will not proceed, for ours is not the task to become embroiled in this debate.

The central issue, however, remains that in the midst of this systemic dispute over the aim of strategy, the United States has not the slightest hope of establishing a coherent nuclear policy, one that has the broad-based support not only of the defense establishment, but also the public, the Democratic and Republican parties, and the numerous interest groups, religious organizations, and political factions that typically display intense interest in nuclear issues. Without such a consensus, what emerges as "policy" or "strategy" more often than not resembles the proverbial horse, which is the animal that was designed by a committee. Just as a coherent US foreign policy cannot emerge out of the Congress, a rational nuclear policy and all that is associated with it (weapons, organizations, and so forth) cannot flourish in such a fragmented environment. In a somewhat circular fashion, this brings us back to one of the opening themes in this book. We argued that, more often than not, American nuclear policy is driven by technological imperatives rather than conceptual themes. And if it is clear that this reliance on technology is a well-entrenched phenomenon in the United States, the systemic problem is that it may not be as dominant in the Soviet Union, at least that it may not occur as frequently or with the same magnitude. While we will return to this theme, at this stage it is essential to examine some of the dominant elements of nuclear policy as they relate to the evolution, whether progressive or regressive, of US nuclear policy.

Nuclear Targeting: The Execution of Policy

Perhaps the most explicit form of nuclear policy is the targeting doctrine, which specifies the types of targets that are to be attacked and the effects thereof on both policy and strategy. As one would expect, a targeting policy, therefore, is extremely sensitive to the structure of nuclear policy as well as to any flaws, inconsistencies, or ambiguities that may arise. To the extent that nuclear policy is operationalized, it occurs when it is expressed as an explicit targeting doctrine. Just as it is not possible for nuclear policy to evolve out of an incoherent strategy, a coherent targeting doctrine can not emerge de novo out of an ambiguous nuclear policy. In this "tree" of nuclear strategy, policy, and targeting, all of the errors will be magnified the farther one proceeds down the "branches" of the policy to the actual plans for war.

In the United States the ultimate targeting document is the SIOP (Single Integrated Operational Plan), which is a highly classified compendium of contingency plans for nuclear war.[1] Neither of the authors has ever seen the SIOP, and all information pertaining to the SIOP has been obtained from unclassified sources. On a simplified scale, the SIOP is composed of a variety of general options or "packages" for targeting in a nuclear war that encompass the spectrum of all conceivable options from counterforce to countervalue scenarios. Each targeting package, however, consists of hundreds of potential targets, that are designated to be attacked with specific weapons in the US arsenal. Perhaps the best way to conceptualize such a target plan is to picture a large matrix with thousands of cells, wherein each cell represents one discrete targeting option. If large numbers of cells are clustered into one package, one generates a set of targeting possibilities. So that the inherent flexibility of the SIOP is retained, each nuclear weapon on the launchers can be programmed to hit a variety of targets, and while a particular weapon will hit only one target, before launch the target can be selected from among a number of targets (perhaps as many as 99) stored as "target constants" in the memory of the launch center's targeting computer. Thus, the SIOP is a list of thousands of potential targets and a smaller number of target packages. In a nuclear war, the National Command Authorities (NCA) can select a particular option or package of options from the SIOP to suit the circumstances of the war.

All of this is, more or less, how it ought to be. The problem, however, arises in the types of targets that are incorporated in the American targeting plan. To understand how the confusion in policy affects targeting, let us return briefly to the distinction between counterforce and countervalue targets. Ideally, one should select targets on the basis of their potential lethality. Counterforce sites such as silos, for instance, would be a logical choice because of the lethality of the ICBMs contained therein. Yet, in a constrained (i.e., realistic) environment of finite nuclear arsenals, the targets that are chosen must be within the targeting capabilities of the nuclear forces. In the case of the United States, the failure to shift from countervalue to counterforce capabilities translates into a SIOP that to this day appears to be dominated by urban-industrial targets. Simultaneously, however, the pressure to move in the direction of counterforce options has resulted in the illusion that much of the US ICBM force and segments of the SLBM and bomber forces are targeted against Soviet counterforce sites, despite the inherently self-disarming nature of the exercise (see Chapter 3). While the countervalue option on a retaliatory level may be the most realistic option for the United States, there are signs that the arsenal is pointed in the direction of a counterforce first-strike attack in the event that a Soviet first-strike attack appears imminent. We should recall, first, that the United States consistently has disavowed a first-strike doctrine (just as have the Soviets), and second, that a counterforce first strike is an illusory option given that even under the most favorable of circumstances it would strain the American arsenal to its operational limit.

We can trace this revolution in US targeting to the tension between counterforce and countervalue options, and on a larger scale to the confusion in nuclear policy. In our view, this confusion is related to the tendency for nuclear policy to evolve in the direction of counterforce options. With considerable justification, many have opposed just this change for the simple and compelling reason that it destabilizes the nuclear balance. As true as that assertion may be, and frankly, we think that the charge, which is that of counterforce being destabilizing, is correct, the concern is that there is a greater danger in a targeting policy that imagines counterforce to be a *realistic* option. In fact, such thinking pushes the United States in the direction of a first-strike doctrine that, worse yet, cannot be supported by the capabilities of the arsenal.

If we confine ourselves to the operational desiderata of the first strike, there are enormous difficulties for the United States. As we saw in Chapter 3, a first-strike attack against the USSR's counterforce targets would disarm the United States without the expectation that the Soviet Union would find all of its arsenal destroyed. Looking beyond the operational to the political issues of a first strike, this trend, at least in the United States, can create immense political problems. If, as the result of the untenable assumptions about the countervalue nature of nuclear war, the United States finds itself without adequate counterforce capabilities (relative to the Soviet target complex), and the possibility of a first-strike doctrine, it is not surprising if the political consensus on nuclear policy continues to evaporate. Perhaps it is the failure to differentiate between a counterforce and a first-strike policy (for the two are quite distinct) that accounts for the turbulence in American nuclear policy.

In any event, we find that the first element of a nuclear policy is how one plans to use nuclear weapons against specific targets. In our view, the United States now finds itself in the position of possessing a dominantly countervalue posture with only limited counterforce capabilities, that is governed by an incoherent policy. However, to the extent that there are some evolutionary forces at play in policy, it appears to be in the direction of a first-strike doctrine, for reasons that are clear. First, the countervalue option is seen as incredible because it guarantees a similar response by the Soviets. Second, the existing Soviet arsenal threatens the US nuclear arsenal with nearly complete destruction in a preemptive attack. And, it is as unacceptable to lose US nuclear forces by riding out the attack as it is to depend on an essentially countervalue response. In effect, the vulnerability of American forces is as unacceptable as urban-industrial targeting. Third, the only solution to this dilemma is the adoption of a *crisis* first-strike doctrine that may be either preemptive or responsive (moments after one detects a Soviet launch). Thus, we believe that the disintegration of nuclear policy and the resultant instability in deterrence are attributable to the inability of the United States to coordinate advances in weaponry with the evolution of policy, as well as to the rapid development of Soviet counterforce capabilities. While there are different causes for this turmoil, the effect is the same.

Deployment of Nuclear Weapons

The second significant dimension of nuclear policy is the weapons that are deployed. More than words or innuendos, weapons provide the clearest indication of what one's policy is, and what it must be. Just as a counterforce policy makes no sense if the arsenal has predominantly countervalue capabilities, a countervalue policy makes no sense if one has the weapons to support a counterforce policy. What we learned in this study rests entirely on this relatively simple point. Beyond this quite obvious, although often forgotten, dictum of military policy, it remains to be seen how a nation, in this case the United States, structures its nuclear forces. Here, we will focus on three critical elements of deployment that affect the viability and coherence of nuclear policy: the weapons, how the weapons are based, and the command and control system.

Weapons Fundamentally, a nuclear policy involves either counterforce or countervalue options, and operates on a preemptive or a retaliatory basis. In our view, the nuclear policy of the United States has shifted during the last decade to predominantly counterforce options (despite the paucity of true counterforce-capable weapons), and simultaneously from a retaliatory to a preemptive doctrine. In the latter case, this is the result of the vulnerability of US land-based forces and the shift to a counterforce capability that creates pressures to use the force against Soviet targets before the Soviets have the chance to do the same. We emphasize that none of this applies in day-to-day affairs, but only in a full-blown political or military crisis, wherein the use of nuclear weapons might become a realistic option. If we consider how radical this shift is, particularly in view of the political significance of the emergence of a first-strike doctrine in a polity that tacitly forswears such a policy, then it is necessary to reflect on the factors that influenced this gradual evolution. In earlier sections, it was suggested that the force of technology and the incessant influence of the Soviet Union, in conjunction with a policy that was losing political and intellectual support among specialists and non-specialists alike, were the twin vectors of strategic decay.

On a different level, the deployment of the new weapons such as MX, Trident, Midgetman, B-1, and cruise missiles, which are being or will be introduced into the American nuclear arsenal, clearly do not have the broad-based consensus that a coherent and credible policy requires. Again, despite the clear symptoms of dissent that manifest themselves within the groups that define nuclear policy, the United States is forging ahead with weapons that do not have a firmly established place in American policy or strategy. Rather than having a conceptual framework, we have deferred to our technological infrastructure for a solution to the problem of "where do we go in nuclear policy." One example is the bomber force: Aside from the perennial Air Force argument that the bomber force is the *sine qua non* of stable deterrence because it complicates Soviet first-strike attack calculations, the driving question really is whether it still makes sense to spend billions of dollars on the (questionable) ability of bombers to penetrate Soviet airspace. Is this still practical in the age of ballistic missiles?

An entirely different issue concerns the deployment of weapons that have a hard-target kill capability. Is it sensible to deploy a handful of MX or Midgetman ICBMs in light of the fact that the Trident SLBM will be as effective as the ICBMs in terms of hard-target kill, as well as more survivable than the ICBMs? An even more important question is the structure of American targeting policy, for only after resolving what it is that we seek to do can we properly acquire weapons. Thus, there is no acceptable answer as to whether the United States ought to deploy Trident, with or without MX, until we have settled what US nuclear policy ought to be. And if that does not happen, the United States will continue to deploy an arsenal that does not have a clear and rational foundation in nuclear policy.

Basing The function of basing in nuclear policy is to provide the most survivable and enduring weapons possible. If this objective can be achieved, the United States thereby gains the assurance that it can follow its targeting plans without the fear of losing its forces in a preemptive attack. To date, we believe that the United States has failed completely in the selection of *ICBM, bomber, and command post* basing options that will preserve the force against most (but clearly not all) *reasonable* threats. For many, a rational basing mode is one that protects the force, or a component of the force, against all conceivable nuclear or conventional attacks. In the narrow sense of ensuring that the largest possible number of forces will survive an attack, this definition of an acceptable basing mode is as appropriate as it is logical, for basing certainly must address the survivability of the missile in the silo or the bomber at the base. But once we step beyond this rather simplistic requirement for basing, we suggest that the basing mode for strategic forces has an equal, if not larger, function in nuclear policy. We propose a more comprehensive definition of basing that includes the concept, which is hardly novel, of "national vulnerability." It is the vulnerability of the nation, in particular its people, industry, and resources to the direct and indirect effects of a nuclear attack that should be a dominant factor in the selection of basing modes.

It certainly is important that a basing system protect nuclear forces, so that the forces may survive to threaten retaliation against the attacker. Suppose, however, that some basing modes increased the vulnerability of the urban population to damage as a function of their proximity to the base. Earlier we addressed the civilian losses that are expected to occur as the result of post-attack radioactive fallout, near misses, and outright guidance system failures. Such losses were measured in the *tens* of millions in "pure" counterforce attacks against both the United States and the Soviet Union. By far one of the larger concerns was that these unintentional, but nonetheless real losses might compel the victim(s) to escalate to assaults on urban targets in order to balance civilian losses, thus shifting a nuclear war from a limited exchange to unrestrained urban annihilation. All this could happen because of the decision to locate nuclear forces near or upwind of major urban centers. From the perspective of policy or strategy, basing decisions of this sort hardly could be said to exemplify foresight, rationality, or coherent strategic planning. Thus, what we must address are the elements of basing that properly constitute part of a rational and coherent nuclear policy. By definition, a nuclear policy that falls short in this most critical area must be dismissed as an abject failure and an utter negation of what a real policy is all about.

The first factor in basing is the location.[2] To determine where bases for strategic forces should be placed, we must think about the dynamics of meteorology and in particular the wind patterns that will influence the deposition of post-attack radioactive fallout. Prevailing seasonal winds in the United States flow from west to east, with the nominal variations one would expect from high and low pressure regions. This means that the fallout from a typical nuclear attack on counterforce targets will travel in an easterly direction. Depending on the distance between the warhead impact points and the city that happens to lie in the fallout vector, in a massive counterforce attack civilian fatalities can range between five and twenty percent of the US urban population. At present, most of the missile bases and bomber bases in the United States are upwind of, or proximate to, the major urban centers in what is called the "urban triangle": the cities that lie within the triangle that is formed by Boston, Atlanta, and St. Louis, which contains more than half of the population and economic resources of the United States. In theory, bases for strategic forces ought not to be within or upwind of this area, yet in reality US basing policy has violated this rule. Where, then, should we emplace ICBM, bomber, and command and control bases? The answer is as obvious as it is logical.

The optimum location for bases is the extreme eastern seaboard. In the case of bases for land-based ICBMs, the mountainous regions in the Northeast (Maine, New Hampshire, Vermont, and New York) would be ideal. If the silos are placed on the southwestern slopes of the mountains, then the targets will be located behind the mountain from the perspective of the RV, thus making it more difficult for the ICBM or SLBM RVs to hit the targets. More specifically, this approach to basing depends on the slope of the mountain and the trajectory of the RV. If the slope of the mountain is greater than the trajectory angle of the RV, then the RV will not be able to hit the target silo or base. For instance, in the case of bomber bases, we should use the same mountainous terrain, and employ the methods of the Swedes, Norwegians, and the Swiss who have constructed hardened bases in the mountains, or the Israelis who have constructed bases in the Negev Desert.

Before launch the aircraft are secure in the hardened underground bases. And even though the bomber bases would remain relatively close to the coast where Soviet SLBMs and SLCMs could reach them more quickly, the hardness of the bases would increase the difficulties for the attacker. Parenthetically, the difference in time that is available for the bombers to escape from their bases does not decrease significantly if the bases are near the coasts as opposed to 500–1000 miles inland. In any event, this eastern-seaboard, mountain-based deployment scheme for nuclear forces would be less vulnerable. And as important, the expected radioactive fallout would sweep, not over hundreds of American cities, but rather more or less harmlessly out over the Atlantic Ocean where it probably would decay to less lethal levels before it reached Europe.

One of the natural advantages of mountain basing for ICBMs and bombers is the hardness of the region. The hardness of the bases that are built in natural granite formations, whether south-slope silos or underground bomber bases, would increase an attacker's uncertainty about the outcome of the attack. This approach would reduce the attractiveness of the attack and thereby reinforce inhibitions against such an attack. Moreover, the minimal number of collateral civilian casualties would not compel the United States to attack Soviet cities just to balance the "civilian tally sheet." Both of these advantages are elements of a coherent nuclear policy to which we alluded earlier.

If we think on a longer timescale, there may be great merit in a deployment scheme that bases nuclear forces out to sea. SSBNs and SLBMs and SSNs with SLCMs, for instance, as well as surface ships with cruise missiles could increase the survivability of the US deterrent force. The American decision to move to the sea-based hard-target kill Trident II SLBM, which may replace the need for a land-based system, ought to be applauded. While this will threaten Soviet land-based forces, we might observe that it can do no greater harm to deterrent stability than did the Soviet deployment of SS-18 and SS-19 ICBMs during the last five to seven years. Moreover, this is a significant step in the shift of nuclear forces to the more survivable sea-based environment, a move that based on our present experience with SSBNs will strengthen deterrence because it remains certain that some American nuclear forces will survive even the best executed Soviet pre-emptive attack.

Signs of Convergence

In the 1960s two eminent political scientists raised the possibility that, despite the severe polarization of the American and Soviet ideological systems, the systemic and plausibly acultural forces of technology, economics, and bureaucracy could lead to a convergence of the two systems. More than a *rapprochement* or detente and less than outright reconciliation, Brzezinski and Huntington wondered whether the two deadly superpowers someday might find that infrastructural forces had led to a convergence.[3] Here many of their significant differences would be submerged beneath the necessities of existence in a world where technological, economic, and bureaucratic factors are more important than ideologies. While this theory spawned a new wave of hope for those who were deeply worried about the strident antagonism between the two nuclear-armed giants and the concomitant dangers of war thereof, many rejected the approach as too simplistic and naive for a complex world. Perhaps one reason why the idea did not become the cornerstone of US–Soviet relations was that it was seen as a metaphysical solution (i.e., one that, transcending ordinary human understanding and control, became a necessity in the philosophical sense of the word. A destiny with a metaphysical correlate that implies a better world in the future always has appeal to those who are most concerned about the present state of affairs. To the rest it seemed so counter-intuitive and counter-factual as to be absurd). It did not seem to matter that the theory of convergence could operate in one domain, such as technology, yet remain dormant in so many other fields, such as politics and ideology. In the domain of nuclear policy, it is our view that the United States and the Soviet Union in fact have converged at a startling rate. This trend, however, was preceded by an era which could be characterized by conceptual divergence.

Mere "convergence" of itself is not correlated historically with peace. Republics have battled republics, monarchies have fought monarchies, and nomads have slaughtered one another, yet nations that have fully "converged" culturally, linguistically, and economically still have collapsed into protracted civil war. The convergence theory resembles the old Kantian argument that it is the murderous ambitions of princes which drive an unwilling population to warfare. Hence, if all the world were republican in form, the "people" having only an interest in peace would constrain their governments from war and there would be "eternal peace." That this argument is false is evident even from a brief scan of history.

During this period of divergence, the United States discovered that many of the fundamental assumptions about nuclear policy were not necessarily shared by the Soviet Union. The ascendancy of counterforce capabilities, for one, signaled that the underlying premise of nuclear policy—the ability to measure deterrence roughly in terms of expected civilian losses—was no longer the doctrine of assured destruction. Gradually, the United States was forced to rethink its nuclear policy in the early 1970s, a time when nuclear policies had a half-life of only several years. Indeed, this was the era of counterforce options, limited nuclear options, strategic sufficiency, countervailing policies, war-fighting strategies, and a host of other variations on policy.[4] The cause of this revolution in policy was the realization that anything short of a predominantly counterforce doctrine no longer had the credibility or robustness that deterrence seemed to require in an age of rapid technological progress. The shift to hard-target kill mechanisms is perhaps the best example of that progress. What has been clear during the past fifteen years (1970–85) is that the United States has struggled to find a nuclear policy which could be sustained by the domestic coalition and remain equivalent to that expressed in Soviet thinking. Sadly, the United States still has not resolved this dilemma at the time of this writing and appears unlikely to do so in the foreseeable future. To make matters worse, the technological imperative now has introduced anew the perennial factor of ballistic-missile defense, which even in stable times is enough to upset the conceptual order of things. Thus, the conceptual decay which has symbolized the last fifteen years of nuclear policy has not come to an end. However, we can detect subtle signs of convergence in American and Soviet nuclear policy even though the fundamental form of US policy remains unclear to date.

Before we speak about the convergence in US–Soviet nuclear policies, let us compare the political cultures within which nuclear doctrines are being established. In the case of the American political system, the first factor is a decentralization of power and a pluralism that requires some level of consensus within the competing centers of power over the essential structure of nuclear policy. This pluralism effectively eliminates the possibility that an organization or, for that matter, a presidential administration could control fully the process of policy formulation. In essence, a nuclear policy that evolves out of a pluralistic and democratic system must pass through the "gates" of consensus: the Congress, interest groups, media, and intellectual centers of power and persuasion.[5]

The second dominant force in the American system is technology, whose influence we have mentioned before. In the ultimate technological society, weapons technology exercises a perhaps greater measure of influence on policy than conceptual and strategic factors. One should recall that a pluralistic system effectively negates the influence of conceptual factors because a particular conceptual framework signals a victory for one among a number of competing groups. In any event, from the technological factor we can explain much of American nuclear policy, and in particular the current chaos over the shape of policy in an age when technology is altering in fundamental ways how we think about nuclear capabilities and scenarios. Stated in another form, we confuse the technologically possible with the rational and the desirable.

The third factor that determines how nuclear policy is formulated in the United States is the institutional and personnel turmoil that pervades the centers of policymaking. On the one hand, there are the appointed officials who arabesque in and out of government positions on a massive scale that is regularized in synchrony with each and every administration. In an environment that is influenced by the rapid turnover of individuals who make policy, whatever policy emerges from the process perforce will be the product of many authors. It is, therefore, diluted and distorted from the original form and intent of its progenitors. On the other hand, the permanent core of civil servants, who might otherwise be able to exert a stabilizing influence on the institutionalized turbulence of the policy making centers at the National Security Council, State Department, and Defense Department, are unable to counteract the power of their typically transient (appointed) superiors or peers. When we couple these chaotic trends to the ambiguous, but none-theless pervasive, policy aspirations of the President and his Cabinet secre-taries, the expected result is a nuclear policy that encompasses everything and nothing. It vitiates the aspirations of all the dominant players in the policymaking game, yet solves nothing because it does not lead to the cre-ation of a rational and workable policy. Thus, it creates a consensus but not a rational, coherent, and sustainable nuclear policy.

The environment within which nuclear policy is made in the Soviet Union is entirely different, although we can use the same factors for comparing it with American policymaking. For a start, the Soviet policymaking system is characterized by a centrism that is quite unlike the pluralism in the United States. Soviet policy appears to be the result of protracted, yet often well-disguised disputes within the military, party, and government bureau-cracies. While there is no analogue in the USSR for the fractitious media and public interest groups in the West, it can hardly be said that Soviet pol-icymaking is not a contentious process. Indeed, the recent removal of Marshal Ogarkov and the ascendancy of Marshal Akhromeyev signal just how tough the internal policy disputes may be in the USSR. The essential difference is that the dominant influence in Soviet policy debates is the absence of the need to reconcile internal political views with external public demands. This means that those who formulate Soviet policy by definition are in agreement as to the *essential* rules of the game. Dissent, of course, can and does occur, but what is known in the West about the process suggests that the boundaries of dispute are not nearly so wide as they are in the United States. We neither imply nor accept that Soviet policymaking is a monolithic or excessively byzantine arrangement; rather, what we seek to stress is the broader consensual base upon which nuclear policy evolves in the USSR.

There is evidence to suggest that technology is a driving force in the Soviet Union when it comes to nuclear policy. Perhaps the central difference is that the USSR, which lacks the extremely sophisticated technological infrastructure of the United States, such as in the case of computers, has not been able to harness technological innovation as the impetus behind its nuclear policy. To date, we think there is a fundamental Soviet fear of the western predilection for rapid and unexpected technological change, and a not so subtle contempt for the apparent absence of long-range strategic thinking in the US. By contrast, it appears that if the leadership in the Kremlin has been able, as we suspect, to grapple with nuclear policy devoid of the forces of public pressure and technological change, then the Soviets have succeeded in defining nuclear policy in ways that are in agreement with the fundamental national interests of the USSR, without saying just what those interests in fact are.

Finally, there is the matter of the institutional and personality milieu. In the Soviet Union, access to the high positions of power in the military, party, or political bureaucracies is jealously guarded by those who sit at the top. The obvious result is the exclusion of the young and inexperienced from positions of leadership, and an emphasis on a decision-making style which is marked by conservatism and incrementalism. None of the institutionalized turbulence that typifies American leadership appears to be present in the Soviet Union, with the exception of occasional purges by the party. Instead, the Soviet leadership has institutionalized personalities in its policymaking centers, yet it appears to have avoided many of the dangers that emerge from charismatic, cult-of-personality figures. The Soviets stress long-term commitment from their career officials and civil servants who, much like the British do in their foreign and domestic bureaucracies, remain in policymaking positions for decades, such as Andrei Gromyko who was Foreign Minister from 1957 to 1985. Nuclear policy, therefore, is the product of a decades-long evolution that has acquired broad-based support among the dominant actors in the national security domain. If we remove the western proclivity for institutionalized turbulence (which prevents the accumulation of power, just as Madison and other framers of the American Constitution sought), then the result can be a nuclear policy that represents a coherent expression of a long-range refinement in the thinking of essentially the same individuals in the Soviet government. Whatever Soviet nuclear policy may be, the central point is that it manifests a degree of coherence and institutional support that has no analogue in the United States. Soviet nuclear policy could be described as the single-minded expression of the Soviet leadership on the role and use of nuclear forces in the international system.

We began by noting that there are signs that the United States and the Soviet Union are converging in several critical areas of nuclear policy. This in itself is not remarkable. What is extraordinary is the degree to which the nuclear policies of two such divergent political and ideological systems could evolve in the same direction. How then are the nuclear policies of the superpowers converging?

At the outset we believe that this policy convergence is happening on three levels. The first such level is on the utility of the *first-strike attack* in the event that a nuclear war appears to be an imminent or unavoidable event. The rationale for the first-strike policy will be the unacceptable consequences of riding out an attack launched by the other side, and in particular having to face the unpalatable choices of a limited counterforce attack, a countervalue response, or surrender. Each option for the United States in particular carries with it the alternatives of either an inadequate counterforce attack, a suicidal plunge into the abyss of city-busting exchanges, or capitulation. The most plausible way out of the dilemma will be to strike first against the primary counterforce targets of the other side in the hope of minimizing the retaliatory options of the victim, and thereby putting him into the aforementioned quandary, assuming of course that the surviving counterforce resources of the opponent are inadequate for a credible counterforce second strike. As the counterforce potential of the superpowers grows, albeit unequally, their options in a nuclear crisis over time will be narrowed to the first strike. Clearly, the superpowers aver that they neither have nor will have a first-strike policy. Any other declaration in the West would have disastrous political consequences. Perhaps the same cannot be said of the political dynamics in the East. At any rate, their nuclear capabilities now signal that the United States and the Soviet Union probably have first-strike policies in a nuclear crisis. We shall not attempt to generalize about the moral or normative implications of this transition in nuclear policy. Nevertheless, it appears to be the case today.

The second point of convergence in the nuclear policy matrix is the *counterforce* option. In contrast to the nascent decades of the nuclear age when the options for nuclear war were confined to urban-industrial annihilation, the trend today is toward the destruction of the counterforce targets of the other side. This was the motivation behind the USSR's deployment of the SS-18 and SS-19 ICBMs, and the US's deployment of the Minuteman III A ICBM. Each, in a similar fashion, evinced the desirability of destroying the sources of the other's nuclear power. And, somewhat serendipitously, this represented the decline of countervalue options as the foundation of policy. On the positive side, this revolution in nuclear policy signaled that the central issue of a nuclear war will be the attempt to destroy nuclear forces first, rather than launching an assault on cities as punishment for the original nuclear attack. To be fair, the negative side of the transition to counterforce policies has been to put the United States and the Soviet Union in the precarious and less stable position of possibly having to launch a first-strike attack to avert the consequences of the other side's doing so. While this has not quite put the arsenals on the "hair triggers" that some have claimed, it certainly does portend much more cautious crisis management in the future.

The third point of convergence in the nuclear policy matrix concerns the value of *decapitation* in the initial round of the war. It is relatively easy to discover that the United States and the Soviet Union concur on the immense tactical value of nuclear decapitation (i.e., destruction of command centers). While there is some danger that the destruction of command centers will bring about an unrestrained war, decapitation always will present the tantalizing prospect of delaying enemy retaliation just long enough to give the aggressor time to execute a successful preemptive attack. The American deployment of the Pershing II IRBM (intermediate-range ballistic missile) in the European theater and the USSR's deployment of the SS-19M2,

SS-18M3, and SS-17M2 ICBMs, as well as the SS-20 IRBMs, are firm evidence of the intention to destroy hard command posts. As a corollary of a first-strike attack, the decapitation strike is seen as having great military utility because it lessens (somewhat) the probability that the victim's response will be as effective or threatening. That is, once the premises behind a first-strike doctrine are accepted by the two defense establishments, the road to a doctrine of decapitation is both easy and short to traverse.

On the broadest level the United States and the Soviet Union, who are implacable and ideologically hostile adversaries, are moving in increasingly parallel directions in the realm of nuclear policy. This is no less than surprising, for one would expect two such divergent political systems to find unique solutions to the dilemma of nuclear deterrence, even more so given the similarity of the superficially strident rhetoric that has been emanating from Washington and Moscow during the last several years. While the content of the rhetoric is not significant, representing material aimed for consumption by domestic and international audiences, it does suggest that at least on a public level superpower relations are nowhere near the cooperative level that is necessary for arms control. Still, the point remains that the degree of convergence in US and Soviet nuclear policies, even though it focuses on the least stabilizing dimensions of deterrence, represents an opportunity for a consensus on nuclear arms that may transcend the period of detente in the 1970s. It is debatable whether SALT signified that the superpowers ever held compatible views of nuclear deterrence, for at the same time they may simply have perceived that it would be mutually advantageous to have a temporary cessation in the modernization of their nuclear arsenals. If, as we suggest, the superpowers have shifted to essentially, symmetrical, and therefore reciprocal, forms of nuclear policy, then it may be possible to use this alignment to mutual benefit. It still may be too early to tell whether the chief executives in the United States and the Soviet Union will recognize that the similarity of their views provides the conceptual foundation for a period of strategic stability and restraint. We see this condition as only the "ghost" of the foundation of a possibly sustainable rapprochement that can last more than a decade. And curiously, this may emerge out of a convergence in nuclear policy, on such things as the value of a first-strike attack that is limited to counterforce options that, by all accounts, are superior to being locked into a policy of city-busting. But, as many commentators have noted, the essence of perceptive policymaking is the ability to see opportunities where others see only obstacles. We hope that those in power will see this as the truly significant opportunity that it is.

RECOMMENDATIONS FOR NUCLEAR POLICY

The time comes when it is necessary for us to put away the long knives of criticism, however blunt or sharp they may be. What we must do now is to look at nuclear policy with an eye toward making constructive suggestions and recommendations so that American (and peripherally, Soviet) policy and nuclear deterrence may be more secure and coherent. We labor under no illusion that these recommendations will alter the world one way or another for, as Henry Kissinger remarked plaintively, those who do not have immediate and unobstructed access to policymakers seem condemned to make policy recommendations that are either too general to be of use or so specific as to engender the distrust of the "insiders."[6] They rightly suspect that outsiders simply cannot make workable suggestions without a degree of direct participation in daily policymaking. Bearing these remarks in mind, we still will make recommendations on the structure of nuclear policy on three levels. The first level concerns nuclear policy itself, on both the declared and real levels, where we will examine the policymaking process as well as doctrinal and arms control issues. In the second area, we will address the admittedly sensitive domain of nuclear targeting and the SIOP. And finally, in the third section the issue will be nuclear forces and the triad. Again, this is not meant to be an exercise in grand strategy and policymaking, but rather an expression of our views on the future based on a detailed study of nuclear war which, we believe, highlighted some of the serious problems in nuclear policy, targeting, and forces. And since experience can be of no use for glimpsing a dim future that none of us has ever seen or is likely to remember, our prescriptions by exclusion will have to be based firmly on introspection and analysis.

Nuclear Policy

1. Disavow the First-Strike Attack. To be precise, we should distinguish between nuclear first strike and "first use." A disavowal of the first-strike option implies that a nation will not use strategic offensive forces first in a crisis. This is not the same as a "first use" policy, which in contemporary terms implies the use of nuclear weapons by NATO in response to a Warsaw Pact conventional invasion of Europe. A disavowal of first use would have disastrous political consequences for the Western alliance, and therefore should not be adopted by the United States or NATO. But a first-strike attack, wherein one side attempts to disarm the other with a massive counterforce attack, or the *threat* of such an attack, has no utility by itself as long as we recall that the nuclear balance of terror has been predicated on the threat of nuclear retaliation. If the United States can posit that a disavowal of the first-strike option in no way implies that it will not retaliate against a Soviet conventional or first-strike attack, then the essential axiom of deterrence remains unaffected. All of this explication, of course, is easy enough to propose, which is why such a policy must be accompanied by specific (and observable) actions in the deployment of nuclear forces. Thus, it is clear that such a disavowal means absolutely nothing, either to the Americans or the

Soviets unless it is accompanied by changes in real policy that are apparent to both sides. Changes of this magnitude, however, cannot be done *de ipse* but must be part of an overall framework for nuclear policy that includes reforms in targeting and weapons. For instance, a disavowal of the first strike would be credible if American counterforce capabilities were moved out to sea instead of being poised in vulnerable ICBM silos. Since the first strike typically is related to the threat of losing one's retaliatory forces, it is plain that there is a synergy between policy and forces: Changes in one are neither possible nor meaningful unless accompanied by changes in the other.

2. *Establish a Strategic Planning Staff.* Neither the Joint Chiefs of Staff (JCS) nor the Joint Strategic Target Planning Staff (JSTPS at Offutt Air Force Base in Omaha, Nebraska) are able to resist or circumvent interservice rivalries. Officers who serve on the JCS or JSTPS still retain loyalty to their respective services which results in a "fiefdom" mentality that effectively diffuses authority and thus makes the process of rational policy planning more difficult.[7] For evidence of the neutralization of rational planning, it is important to note that the representatives of each service are selected to balance military ranking, so that tri-service equality reigns supreme. At one extreme, there are indications that the rivalry between the Air Force and Navy extends to the realm of nuclear policy and targeting where such differences ought to be reconciled in less than pernicious ("pie-slicing") ways, such that the Air Force is responsible for hard-target kill—even if it does not have the wherewithal for the mission—while the Navy carefully guards its urban-industrial mission. In short, the existing planning structure cannot produce the type of coherent nuclear policy that is so singularly necessary in the United States. To reverse this condition, we need to create a system wherein policy is the product of long-term, independent political and military professionals.

Such a Strategic Planning Staff (SPS) should be composed of representatives from the military, the executive branch and Congress, and the civilian sectors. The Director of SPS, who will be a cabinet level official, also will have the rank of a Chief of Staff on the JCS and will report directly to the Secretary of Defense and the President. This streamlined planning system will avoid many of the paralyzing features of the present system of multiple and diffused authority, and thereby will centralize and rationalize the planning system for nuclear policy. Preferably, the core of the SPS should be composed of military professionals, permanently detached from their services, who will serve as career-level members, with other members being solicited every four years. This core of career members will stabilize the otherwise turbulent structure that one expects to find in a democratic system that purges its leadership at least once every four years.

3. *Create a Bipartisan Commission on Nuclear Policy.* There is no doubt that bipartisan commissions are quite in vogue today. Nevertheless, a bipartisan commission on nuclear policy would have the difficult, yet supremely

essential, task of formulating a nuclear policy that has broad-based political and public support. Individuals from the military, Congress, executive branch of government, and academia would be responsible for the formulation of a nuclear policy that reflects a consensus among the important participants of defense policymaking. As with the Strategic Planning Staff, the commission would report directly to the President and the Secretary of Defense. The selection of members ought to balance both political and ideological viewpoints, for if the commission is "stacked," then it will find itself unable to create the consensus on nuclear policy for which it was designed in the first place.

Such a commission would have to address the most difficult issues of nuclear policy: counterforce versus countervalue targeting, preemption versus retaliation, the utility of decapitation, and the role of defense in nuclear policy. We do not expect that a truly effective commission would serve sporadically for a year or so, but it should be a permanent arm of the American defense policymaking establishment. It might be chaired by a Cabinet level official so that its recommendations do not become the "fodder" of the usual "guns" in Washington.

One of the corollary functions of the commission should be to define how arms control fits into the overall framework of nuclear policy. If it is true that there has been a convergence of their nuclear policies, the United States and the Soviet Union may have a *modus vivendi* that is sustainable for the foreseeable, but not indefinite, future. Should this chance for arms control be missed, the next window of opportunity will emerge in the next ten years or so when the Americans and Soviets reach the time for the deployment of ballistic-missile and space defenses. At that time, their nuclear policies will converge again when the implications of defense against nuclear attack are understood more fully. Nevertheless, in terms of an agreement on offensive arms, for both strategic and theater forces, we should act within the next two to three years.

4. *Study How To Terminate an Accidental Nuclear War.* Once a nuclear war begins, whether by accident or miscalculation, it is clear today that the only logical terminus will be when the American and Soviet nuclear arsenals are empty or nearly so. In this study, we explored the consequences of such a war: there would be on the order to 50–100 million prompt deaths in the United States *and* in the Soviet Union. Based on that information, the next question is how to terminate a nuclear war as quickly as possible. If the question is easy to ask, the answers surely are as elusive as they are difficult. So, while it is absolutely necessary to do all that we can to avoid such a war, logically it is imperative to think about how to stop one. And while there may be some danger (minimal, we think) that such thinking may make a nuclear war slightly more palatable, the greater danger is not knowing how to stop such madness if it happens.

One logical place for beginning such a study is the (proposed) Commission

on Nuclear Policy. A host of other institutions, such as government organizations, "think tanks," and universities are well suited to address the problem.
Nevertheless, the driving force behind this recommendation remains the
fact that there are no coherent and compellingly realistic plans in nuclear
policy for the termination of a nuclear war. It is not enough to posit that the
war will stop at the behest of the antagonists: nuclear decapitation, EMP,
and a nearly infinite list of unknowns could prevent, for instance, the communication between the nations that is believed to be necessary to stop the
war. In any event, termination ought to become a clearly defined corollary in
US (and hopefully Soviet) nuclear policy.

Targeting

1. *Exclude All Soviet Cities from the SIOP.* Even under the appellation of
"urban-industrial" or "economic" targets, the United States should not have
Soviet cities on its SIOP target lists. As to whether the United States in fact
does plan to attack Soviet cities in a nuclear war, we leave it to the reader to
discern what the 31 American SSBNs will do if they cannot destroy hard
targets. The reason for this proposed change in targeting is that the destruction of urban centers in the USSR will neither limit damage to the United
States nor compel the Soviets to forfend similar attacks on American cities.
Simply, the existence of such targets in the SIOP, whether or not they are
vital economic centers, *guarantees*, if the option is used, the death of 100
million Americans. This just makes no sense whatsoever. National capitols,
even with their abundance of primary command centers, should not be
attacked. In short, no urban target—that is, any target that has a civilian
population in or near it—should be a target in a nuclear war. To be frank, we
can think of no compelling reason for the annihilation of civilian populations,
nor any justification for the threat of doing so. This prohibition should apply
for both real and declaratory nuclear policy. We attribute the "MAD"ness of
earlier nuclear policies to the ill-conceived thinking that accompanied the
nuclear revolution, with the view that such times are more often driven by
frenetic rather than cogent thought.

2. *Restrict the SIOP to Strategic Counterforce Targets.* By exclusion, the
SIOP should be structured to include only ICBM fields, bomber and submarine bases, SSBNs on patrol, and (possibly) command and control centers.
Collateral damage to civilian populations is "acceptable" inasmuch as it is an
unavoidable facet of countersilo attacks. However perverse and callous that
wording may seem, collateral damage from counterforce strikes is far prefer-
able to the damage that a countervalue nuclear war would produce. We
emphasized the word "strategic" in this recommendation. While there is no
compelling reason to avoid general purpose force targets (army, navy, and
air force bases), one should be forewarned that attacks of this sort will be
difficult to distinguish from a countervalue attack. Is it even necessary to add

the admonishment that the United States would not hesitate to target Soviet urban-industrial centers if the Soviets were to deploy strategic offensive or defensive weapons in their cities? Obviously, US nuclear policy must be responsive to the nature and dimension of Soviet actions if it is to be credible both as a deterrent to Soviet actions and as a basis for a coherent foreign and national security policy. Thus, in proposing that the United States restrict the SIOP to strategic counterforce targets, we are advocating a general philosophical approach to targeting policy; inasmuch as the rigid application of any philosophical system leads inevitably to catastrophe, a certain element of flexibility is implicit in this (and the other) recommendations.

3. *Make the SIOP Simpler and Less Unwieldy.* From what little is known publicly about the SIOP (principally on the basis of what others have written, which inevitably means that some distortion will occur given the "code-word" classification of the SIOP), one element always seems to come through. It is that the SIOP, and even the discrete options therein, is an extraordinarily complex and unwieldy plan. One way to conceptualize this complexity is to imagine a two-dimensional matrix: the vertical axis contains every nuclear weapon in the US arsenal, and the horizontal axis every possible target in the Soviet Union. This means more than 30,000 entries for US weapons and, as some have suggested, perhaps as many as 40,000 potential targets in the USSR.[8] This SIOP matrix theoretically would have more than a *billion* cells in it, each cell representing a potential targeting option. In reality, however, the number of cells would be substantially less than that because most Soviet targets would be assigned several warheads. This factor, in turn, would reduce the size of the matrix to perhaps several thousands or tens of thousands of options. From here, it is easy to collapse the SIOP into general options: COUNTERSILO, URBAN-INDUSTRIAL, COMMAND AND CONTROL, and so forth.[9] What is of concern with respect to the usability of the SIOP is that the multiplicity of potential targets and weapons, and the resulting calculations for the optimal allocation of warheads, particularly as the composition of the matrix changes during a nuclear war, may be so large as to confuse a political decision-maker. The answer is a SIOP that is as simple as possible—even if that simplicity excludes the more remote contingencies from the plan. In present form, the danger is that the proliferation of targets (which always seem to grow and change) and weapons (as new systems are added and old ones deleted from the arsenal) may make a SIOP that has so many options that the permutations may make it difficult to manage. One can imagine how difficult it might be to select a simple, limited option, such as hitting a bomber base with an SLBM, in the heat of war when all the weapons are tied to larger, discrete target packages.

4. *Do Not Target Command and Control Centers.* It would appear that decapitation is an increasingly popular option in nuclear policy today, at least so one would think given its level of attention in the literature. This tactic, however, will prove to be the undoing of both sides as it will prevent the

communication between the United States and the Soviet Union that is necessary for the cessation of the war.[10] Accordingly, the United States should not destroy Soviet command centers—unless so attacked first. To do otherwise is to commit both sides to a nuclear war that may escalate either gradually or suddenly to an all-out exchange. The existence of the SS-19M2, SS-18M3, and SS-17M2 ICBMs on the Soviet side, and the Pershing II on the American/NATO side, suggests that even changes in declaratory policy will not convince the US and USSR that decapitation is not an option for the other. In the absence of confidence in the other's declaratory policy, each will be tempted to launch a preemptive attack against the other in order to avoid the pernicious effects of decapitation. Thus, an effective "no decapitation" policy will involve operational alterations in the arsenals, probably under the aegis of an arms control agreement. No matter how difficult it may be for the superpowers to assure each other that decapitation is not a first-order policy option, the consequences of decapitation are so stark as to make the case for no decapitation quite compelling indeed.

Nuclear Forces

1. *Exchange the Nuclear Triad for a Dyad of SLBMs and Bombers.* We see no compelling reason for keeping the ICBM leg of the triad, particularly in view of the vulnerability of ICBMs in fixed silos and the political difficulties of deploying ICBMs on mobile launchers, which will require dispersal on public roads and highways. Since the ICBM does have hard-target kill capabilities, then we might amend this recommendation in favor of retaining a force of Minuteman III A and B ICBMs. Otherwise, the existing land-based force of ICBMs should be retained both as a symbol of power and because of their hard-target kill capabilities, although the older Minuteman II and Titan II should be retired, leaving a force of 550 Minuteman III A and B. The SLBM force should be limited to Trident C-4 and D-5 missiles so that the United States will retain a *survivable* counterforce capability against hard targets in the Soviet Union. Indeed, the deletion of the Minuteman II, Titan II, and Poseidon missiles would excise the exclusively countervalue component of the arsenal. In this scheme, the MX ICBM is an unnecessary weapon primarily because of the limited scale of the projected deployment (less than 500 RVs), and tangentially because of the vulnerability of the silos. In reality, because all land-based forces are vulnerable, American and Soviet alike, vulnerability *per se* is not a critical determinant of MX deployment.

The value of a bomber force should be measured in terms of its ability to destroy hard targets, and the ability to launch either all or part of the bomber force on receipt of strategic or tactical warning, and to do so under the positive control of the National Command Authorities. While non-alert bombers are inherently vulnerable at their bases on day-to-day (normal)

alert (up to 70 percent of the US force), the alert force could pose a significant threat against the relatively small number of high value hard targets
(leadership bunkers as well as command and control centers) in the Soviet
Union that survived an initial attack. Once on alert, the bomber force could
deliver a large number of weapons (relative to this target set) with a level of
reliability that is constrained only by the ability of the force to penetrate
Soviet airspace. Moreover, in an age of nascent ballistic-missile defenses
(BMD), bombers will offer an important hedge against Soviet defenses
against US ballistic missiles, and thereby give the United States some confidence in its ability to threaten the Soviet homeland with an aerodynamic
force. Thus, a US force of SLBMs and bombers, complemented by the
existing force of ICBMs, will give the United States confidence in its deterrent force against a range of technological threats, and force the Soviet Union
to defend against two very different nuclear delivery systems. From a Soviet
perspective, a force of SLBMs and bombers would pose enormous uncertainties for an attacker, and thereby raise the threshold of nuclear deterrence. It goes without saying that the economic burden that is imposed on
the Soviet Union in attempting to counter this American deterrent force
could be staggering.

2. *Concentrate Hard-Target Kill on the SLBM Force.* In view of the
projected lethality of the Trident II SLBMs against hard targets, the logical
place to deploy hard-target kill systems is on the SSBNs, which are relatively
secure from Soviet attack. In this mode, the United States can retain an
assured counterforce capability in almost any conceivable scenario, and be in
the enviable position of having more than a countervalue option for retaliation. In comparison with the land-based ICBM, the SLBM is the preferred
weapon if it is deemed to be important for the United States to have a
residual counterforce capability.

3. *Construct Deep Underground Command Posts.* The most secure command center in the United States is Cheyenne Mountain in Colorado. While
most estimates conclude that it can withstand several hundred psi of overpressure, it is agreed that this level of hardness is not sufficient to guarantee
its survival against nuclear attack. In fact, most high-yield nuclear warheads
in the Soviet ICBM arsenal probably could destroy the Cheyenne Mountain
complex quite easily. By contrast, the most secure command posts in the
USSR reportedly can withstand up to 10,000 psi—if numerous reports are
correct. (The Pershing II, however, could pose a significant threat to such
centers.) A RAND study in the late 1950s argued for placing the Cheyenne
Mountain complex under the mountain, where it would be able to withstand
10,000 psi of overpressure, instead of inside the mountain, as we did.[11] In
the future, any command centers should be buried very deep underground.
In any event, the construction of such deep underground command posts is
one, albeit expensive, option for ensuring that military and political elites
would survive the threat of decapitation.

CONCLUDING REMARKS

As we conclude, it is proper to note that, given the uncertainties of how a nuclear war could be fought and the consequences of such a calamity, the inexactitude of our mathematical and conceptual models is too readily apparent. No matter how systematic or rigorous we may be, from the collection of data to the construction of the algorithms that project the effects of a nuclear attack, it is inevitable that errors and biases will creep into the model. Although this is unavoidable, it may act as a stimulus for more comprehensive and detailed analyses. Indeed, on a methodological level, we should remember that inexactitude is necessary when using mathematics to project the shape of what is admittedly a highly uncertain future. By this standard, ours is a crude model of nuclear war. Accordingly, the reader ought to exercise caution in interpreting the "results" of this analysis, which can either underestimate or exaggerate the outcome of hypothetical counterforce and countervalue exchanges between the United States and the Soviet Union. Thus, perhaps we can derive some satisfaction and comfort from the prophetic words of Albert Einstein, who in lamenting the inexactitude and hence inadequacy of mathematics for understanding physical (particularly, quantum) reality, said: "Where mathematics is exact, it is unreal; Where mathematics is real, it is inexact." Unfortunately, the enormous destructive power of nuclear weapons may erase these inexactitudes and thus give us an understanding of nuclear war that is more realistic and exact than we should ever wish to know.

Appendix: Notes on Methodology

In this study on the effects of a nuclear war, we have utilized an unclassified model to project the outcome of counterforce and countervalue exchanges between the United States and the Soviet Union. In this model, there are two sets of databases: two counterforce databases for the strategic nuclear arsenals of the two superpowers, and two countervalue databases for the 300 largest urban areas in the US and USSR. And, of course, there are the appropriate algorithms that were used in these projections of nuclear exchanges. It is neither illuminating nor surprising to find that, in comparison with many of the classified models of nuclear war on the mainframe computers in Washington and elsewhere, this is but an austere and simplified model. It, after all, resides in an Apple microcomputer, which is by any standard a rather simple form of the extremely complex computers and supercomputers (such as the CRAY-2) that are on the market today. Nevertheless, we believe that this model of a nuclear war provides fairly reasonable estimates of the effects of counterforce and countervalue exchanges. In this Appendix, we will examine the methods that were used to develop the databases and assumptions that underlay the calculations about the effects of nuclear attacks. It is our intention to make these assumptions as transparent as possible.

STRATEGIC NUCLEAR FORCES

By any standard, it was a relatively easy task to assemble what we believe is an accurate representation of the strategic nuclear arsenals of the United States and the Soviet Union. A number of sources on this subject are readily available in the open literature. Perhaps the most important sources were:

195

John M. Collins, *U.S.-Soviet Military Balance: Concepts and Capabilities, 1960–1980*, 1980; James F. Dunnigan, *How To Make War: A Comprehensive Guide to Modern Warfare*, 1982; and *Military Balance* by the International Institute for Strategic Studies. An important new work on this subject is the *Nuclear Weapons Databook: U.S. Nuclear Forces and Capabilities*, 1984. From these sources, in particular the data in Collins and Dunnigan, it was possible to construct databases for the ICBMs, SLBMs, and bombers in the American and Soviet arsenals. The designated names of the weapons, as well as the number deployed, MIRVs, yield and CEP, reliability rates, and basing information were compiled. The location of each nuclear target was contained in the databases, as this would allow us to identify the primary collateral city for each counterforce target, and therefore rough estimates of the damage that fallout would cause to the American and Soviet civilian populations. In the case of Soviet ICBM fields, the location of the individual missile fields was found in the Department of Defense's *Soviet Military Power*, 1983. In the case of the Soviet bomber force, we had to estimate, based on the references in *Soviet Military Power* and the references cited above, where the Soviet bomber force was stationed, in what was admittedly an exercise in "rudimentary" estimation. Otherwise, with the exception of US and Soviet C3 targets, the sources listed and a host of others which may be found in the Bibliography, provided the foundation for this representation of the US and Soviet strategic nuclear arsenals in 1983.

The case of the C3 targets is a different matter. Frankly, very little is known about the American and Soviet C3 systems on an unclassified basis. Aside from the frequent (although unrevealing) references in the literature to the US C3 targets: Cheyenne Mountain, Fort Ritchie, Mount Weather, the National Military Command Center (NMCC) in the Pentagon, and the National Emergency Airborne Command Post (NEACP) and "Looking Glass," it is difficult to estimate where American command centers are located and how their destruction might affect C3 connectivity between the National Command Authorities (NCA) and nuclear forces. Several especially good sources on the US C3 system are: *Nuclear Strategy Issues of the 1980s: Strategic Vulnerabilities, Command, Control, Communication and Intelligence; Theater Nuclear Forces*, 1982, by the Carnegie Endowment for International Peace; and more recently, Ashton B. Carter, "The Command and Control of Nuclear War," *Scientific American*, January 1985. Other excellent references include: Daniel Ford, *The Button: The Pentagon's Strategic Command and Control System* (New York: Simon and Schuster, 1985); and Bruce G. Blair, *Strategic Command and Control: Redefining the Nuclear Threat* (Washington, D.C.: The Brookings Institution, 1985). As the most recent and certainly the most authoritative and comprehensive works on the subject of strategic command and control, Ford and Blair offer a fairly accurate analysis of US command systems. Still, these works really do not provide the detail that is necessary for connectivity studies in which we could have confidence.

As for the USSR's C3 system, nothing of substance can be inferred from the unclassified literature—indeed, there are some doubts about the ability of the US intelligence community to reliably locate Soviet command posts on a classified basis. Thus, in view of this veritable drought of information, the destruction of C3 centers has no effect on the connectivity of strategic forces in this model. However, the model does generate estimations of the collateral civilian casualties that would result from the destruction of the five arbitrarily designated C3 targets in the United States and the Soviet Union.

In general, our research culminated in the construction of counterforce databases for the United States and the Soviet Union that, to the best of our knowledge, represent a reasonably accurate portrayal of the existing strategic nuclear arsenals. As shown in Tables 1 and 2, this model is based on a portrait of the ICBMs, bombers, SSBNs (by type of SLBM carried), and C3 targets in the arsenals. We should note, however, that because the payload of Soviet bombers is highly uncertain, one megaton and ten megaton warheads were assigned somewhat arbitrarily to the bombers. In the next section, we will address the calculations that determined the effects of counterforce and countervalue nuclear attacks.

Nuclear Weapons: Effects and Calculations

In this model, we are concerned with two distinct types of nuclear explosions: surface-bursts (SB) and air-bursts (AB) at the optimum height of burst (HOB). For each warhead in the US and Soviet arsenals, the lethal radius of damage at a 2 psi overpressure level was computed for the optimum HOB. The reference for these data was Samuel Glasstone and Philip J. Dolan, *The Effects of Nuclear Weapons*, 1977, and in particular the "Nuclear Bomb Effects Computer" (the "wheel") therein. Based on this information, each warhead in the databases has a corresponding area of damage (or radius) for air-burst and surface-burst detonations, which would be essential information for the calculation of civilian casualties (addressed later).

Calculations of this sort will be useful when considering the effects of one or more nuclear detonations against soft, urban-industrial targets. Yet, a large number of counterforce targets in the database are extremely hard, meaning that they are resistant to the effects of overpressure (a crushing force) and dynamic pressure (wind). Since ICBM silos and command centers, for example, in theory can withstand several hundred to thousands of psi, it typically is assumed that a surface-burst detonation is required to ensure destruction. Thus, we derived a probability of kill (PK) for each reentry vehicle (RV) in the arsenals, and a warhead allocation scheme, each based on the yield and CEP of the warheads.

Probability of Kill. For each warhead yield, a potential crater radius was derived from an equation found in *Civil Defense: A Soviet View*, 1970, which provides an estimate of the radius of the crater that would result from a surface-burst detonation in a clay-sand soil. Knowing the yield and CEP of a particular warhead, it is relatively straightforward to calculate the probability of kill where the crater and CEP radii are in meters:

$$PK = \frac{\text{Crater}}{\text{CEP}} \qquad (1)$$

where "crater" equals the radius in meters of a crater that will be formed by a surface-burst explosion. The formula for the dimensions of a crater is $R = 19(y^3)$, where R equals the radius of the crater in meters and y is the yield of the warhead in kilotons. For instance, a one metagon warhead will produce a crater radius of 190 meters. The resulting value then is scaled to .5 on a standard z scale to produce the single-shot probability of kill (SSPK). If the PK for an RV has been derived from equation (1), and if a number of warheads has been assigned to that target, then the probability of kill equals:

$$PK = 1 - (1 - PK)^n \qquad (2)$$

where n equals the number of warheads assigned to the target.

A different case emerges when one must determine how many warheads, n, must be assigned to an individual hard target in order to ensure its destruction, such as an ICBM silo. A warhead lethality score (WLS), which is a dimensionless value, is equal to:

$$WLS = \frac{\log \text{Crater}}{\log \text{CEP}} \qquad (3)$$

where the crater and CEP values are in radii. For the weapons in the US and Soviet nuclear arsenals, the WLS typically falls between the value of 0.6 and 1.1, wherein values greater than 1.00 produce an OPk based on the detonation of one warhead, hence $n = 1$. For a WLS that is between 0.9 and 1.00, two warheads are assigned and $n = 2$; three warheads ($n = 3$) for a WLS between 0.8 and 0.9; and four warheads, $n = 4$, for a WLS that is between 0.7 and 0.8. Thus, for each warhead in the counterforce databases there is a corresponding WLS that indicates how many RVs with that yield and CEP are necessary for the destruction of *one* hard target.

It is possible to relate the probability of kill of a nuclear warhead to the crater radius, on the assumption that the minimum lethal radius of a warhead against a hard target is defined as the crater that would result for any given yield. Here, the primary lethal effect of cratering is ground-shock, which imparts the lateral shear forces to silos that are so lethal to silos. The cratering potential of a nuclear warhead may be said to provide the baseline, conservative estimate of the lethality of a nuclear warhead against a silo because, in the words of one Pentagon official, "Once the silo is within the diameter of the crater, it doesn't matter how hard the silo is." (Bill Keller, "Doubts Increase Over Future of U.S. Land-Based Missiles," *New York Times,* June 17, 1985, p. 1.) One problem, however, with basing a calculus of hard-target kill on crater potential, despite its apparent simplicity, is uncertainty over the dimensions of craters. In recent years, uncertainty about the cratering potential of a given yield nuclear warhead suggests that the more traditional methods for calculating the probability of kill for a nuclear warhead, which relies on the hardness of the silo, may be used. Roger Speed, in *Strategic Deterrence in the 1980s* (pp. 138–41), for one, presents the following as an example of such an approach.

An estimate of the distance at which a nuclear weapon can generate overpressure that is equal to a given hardness level is given by

$$r_k = (16 \ Y/H)^{1/3} \tag{1}$$

where r_k is in nautical miles, the yield Y is in megatons, and the silo hardness H is in pounds per square inch (psi). To calculate the probability of kill for a given re-entry vehicle (RV) against a target of hardness H, then

$$P_k = 1 - 0.5 \ k^{(r/CEP)^2} \tag{2}$$

And using the approximation for r_k then the P_k would be

$$P_k = 1 - 0.5^{\ (Y^{2/3}/CEP^2) \ (16/H)^{2/3}} \tag{3}$$

Thus, this approach provides an estimation of the probability of kill for a nuclear warhead that, based on the yield and CEP, relates directly the probability of kill to the hardness of the silo.

In the case of attacks against both hard and soft targets, the number of warheads that ultimately would reach the assigned targets is a function of the reliability of the missile or bomber. After the computation of the PK, the number of RVs that detonates is a function of the launch and detonation reliability rates. For each warhead there are launch and detonation reliability rates; the product of the two (the launch rate multiplied by the detonation rate) indicates the fraction of the RVs or warheads that will reach the assigned targets. This is straightforward enough in the case of a soft target, in which the effects of an attack are computed on the basis of the number of warheads that actually detonate. Alternatively, in the case of an attack against hard targets, the number that is destroyed is computed by dividing the number of detonations by the number or warheads that are necessary for the destruction of each target. Thus, the detonation of 100 warheads would destroy 50 silos if two such warheads are necessary for the destruction of each silo.

NOTES ON COUNTERFORCE METHODOLOGY

In this section on the methodology that was used to project the outcome of various counterforce exchanges, general methodological issues and specific examples will be addressed for each of the five types of counterforce targets: ICBM silos, bomber bases, submarine bases, command and control targets, and submarines on patrol.

Countersilo Attacks

As a hard target, which means that the silo is very resistant to the overpressure that results from a nuclear explosion, the ICBM silo is the most difficult counterforce target for an attacker to destroy. Indeed, a number of authors have noted that the destruction of missile silos is fraught with countless uncertainties and imponderables. In general, the destruction of a silo will depend on the hardness of the silo and the yield and CEP of the attacking warhead(s). Uncertainty usually is expressed in terms of warhead *bias*, which is the mean distance that a RV will land from its designated impact point as a result of random guidance system errors and systematic errors, and *fratricide*, which is the destruction of the second or later RVs by the detonation of the first RV. Perhaps one of the most comprehensive (and certainly one of the most contentious) analyses of the uncertainties of countersilo attacks is Matthew Bunn and Kosta Tsipis, *Ballistic Missile Guidance and Technical Uncertainties of Countersilo Attacks*, 1983. Although it is thought that fratricide can be avoided, it remains highly uncertain in the absence of real-world atmospheric tests. Beyond these operational uncertainties, Roger Speed, *Strategic Deterrence in the 1980s*, 1980, argues that silo hardness could be "the greatest source of uncertainty" in an assessment of the outcome of a countersilo attack.

Here, in this model we have predicated that ICBM silos will be destroyed if: first, at least one of the RVs detonates as a surface-burst and remaining warheads detonate as either air-bursts or surface-bursts; and second, the number of RVs allocated against each silo is sufficient in terms of the optimum allocation that is indicated by the WLS. After a wave of warheads (usually, but not always, ICBM RVs) are assigned to attack an ICBM field, the OPK and SSPK for the RVs are calculated. Next, the attrition process in the attack is considered. For instance, if 1,000 warheads are launched against a field of silos, and the launch and detonation reliability rates are 0.9 and 0.8, then 720 (1,000 × 0.9 × 0.8 = 720) warheads will reach the assigned silos. And if the WLS is 0.9, which indicates that two RVs of this type are necessary for the destruction of one silo, then a total of 360 (720 divided by 2) silos would be destroyed. In our analysis, we typically reversed this procedure to determine the minimum number of RVs that would have to be launched to ensure that the destruction of the targeted silos is accomplished with the minimum possible number of RVs. To account for the random errors that in reality might happen in an attack, each RV also is subjected to a random variable to account for the fact that RVs occasionally might fail for reasons that fall beyond the normal attrition processes.

In the research phase of this study, for each ICBM field in the United States and the Soviet Union, a primary collateral urban-industrial center was identified based on geography: the nearest large urban area *usually* was selected for inclusion in the countervalue database. For an attack against a specific ICBM field in either nation, the population of the collateral city is counted as a direct loss, meaning that half of the population will die and the remainder will be casualties. All of this was assumed to occur within a 30–60 day period. To be more realistic, we could have included all US and Soviet urban areas that happened to lie within the 45 degree fallout vector that extends from each surface-burst impact point to the east, depending on the prevailing winds. This approach certainly would have produced more realistic estimates of the collateral casualties from post-attack radioactive fallout, but this preferred option would have exceeded the capabilities of the available hardware (i.e., random-access memory and disk storage).

Counter-Bomber Attacks

The average bomber base in the United States or the Soviet Union is a soft, fairly widely dispersed target. As a prime target in a counterforce attack, the bases present an important issue, the vulnerability of the bombers at the bases, especially the difference in vulnerability between the alert and non-alert aircraft. In the United States, roughly 30 percent of the bomber force is on 10 minute alert—we have no idea as to the percentage of Soviet bombers that are on alert, although it seems likely that the figure is lower than 30 percent. The survivability of a bomber force depends, according to Bruce Bennett, *Assessing the Capabilities of Strategic Nuclear Forces: The Limits of Current Methods,* 1980, on several factors: the time it takes for bombers to take off; the "flyout curve," which is the relationship between the distance and time during takeoff and acceleration; and the time delay between escaping bombers. The "safe distance" from the base is defined as a function of the vulnerability of individual bombers; the yield of the attacking warheads; the number of warheads targeted against each base; and the pattern of warhead allocation and the bomber escape routes. In terms of the vulnerability of an individual bomber, it is estimated that a bomber can withstand overpressures of 2 psi. For a one megaton air-burst, the 2 psi overpressure gradient will be 9.5 miles from the explosion, for an effective area of roughly 285 square miles that is potentially lethal to escaping bombers.

A commonly cited scenario for an attack against bomber bases—at least for US bomber bases, which are rarely more than 1,000 nautical miles inland—

is executed with Soviet SLBMs. Here, the vulnerability of a bomber is a function of the flight-time of the SLBM, the distance between the SLBM launch-point and the base, and the trajectory of the SLBM. Bennett (1980a) provides an excellent analysis of bomber escape times on the assumption that US bombers can escape one every 15 seconds. Speed (1980), for one, suggests that if Soviet SSBNs launched their SLBMs from positions that are 100 nautical miles offshore, only the US bomber bases that are greater than 600 nautical miles inland will have a 50 percent probability of survival. An optimum attack against a bomber base, he concludes, would require four reliable RVs per base.

In the case of the Soviet Union's bomber bases, an attacking US force would encounter an air defense network of 6,000 radars, 2,600 fighter-interceptors, and 12,000 surface-to-air missile launchers. To overcome this defense, Speed (1980) estimates that the United States could destroy Soviet defenses with ICBMs, SLBMS, and SRAMs (short-range attack missiles, that are carried on bombers); use low-altitude penetration runs of less than 300 feet; degrade Soviet defenses with electronic countermeasures (ECM); and avoid defenses by sending, for instance, the bombers around the defenses.

In this model, the destruction of a bomber base—American or Soviet—is predicated on the detonation of at least two warheads. Either air-bursts or surface-bursts are sufficient, although the air-burst tactic increases the probability of kill against escaping bombers. As before, the destruction of a bomber base generates casualties in the primary collateral urban target. Any type of delivery vehicle is acceptable for an attack against bomber bases, but by far the ideal weapon is an SLBM, but as noted, it was not always possible to use SLBMs. Moreover, we often used the surface-burst tactic in order to preclude re-use of the base, recognizing at the same time that this tactic greatly increases collateral damage from fallout.

Counter-SSBN Attacks

The destruction of an SSBN on patrol depends on the ability to locate and engage the target. Bennett (1980a) suggests that the localization of an SSBN may take several forms: monitoring SSBN bases and repair facilities; trailing SSBNs as they leave port; searching from SSBNs with acoustic and non-acoustic search methods; and waiting for the SSBNs to reveal their position when they launch their SLBMs. While it may be plausible to target an SSBN with an ICBM if one knows the precise location of the SSBN, in general most analysts acknowledge that this "barrage" attack is not a realistic option based on existing American or Soviet technologies.

The actual destruction of an SSBN depends on the depth of the water and the lethal radius of the warhead. In deep water, in which a deep-underwater burst would be ideal, the greater distance between the burst and the sea-bed reduces the lethal effect of the reflected (incident) shock wave of the detonation. If the sea-bed is thousands of meters deep, then the intensity of the reflected blast wave will be less, which in effect lessens the vulnerability of the submarine. In shallow water, say along the American continental shelf, a shallow underwater burst would be ideal as this would subject the SSBN to greater overpressure from the impulse and the reflected shock waves.

No matter how one addresses the issue of killing an SSBN on patrol, a large number of uncertainties will arise. In recognition of these uncertainties, in this model the destruction of SSBNs is contingent on the detonation of at least ten surface-burst explosions. The value of ten warheads was selected as a purely arbitrary value to emphasize that such an attack probably would consume large numbers of warheads for the attacker, not to mention other ASW assets. Moreover, each counter-SSBN attack was given a 50 percent probability of kill even if this warhead allocation scheme is followed. While this method certainly addresses in generic terms the possibility of attacks against SSBNs, it probably is safe to assume that SSBN commanders are substantially more concerned about the threat of attacks with torpedos and a variety of other anti-submarine warfare techniques than they are with the possibility of ICBM barrage attacks.

Counter-C3 Attacks

It was noted in earlier sections that the structure of the American and Soviet C3 networks is highly uncertain, as one would expect in view of the sensitive nature of the subject. What is known is that C3 systems are based on large-scale redundancy and that an effective attack would have to involve attacks against different levels of the system. Bennett (1980a) argues that very high probabilities of kill are required against each node in the network if one is to cut completely all links in the system. In general, Bennett stresses that it is "difficult to construct a network model [of a C3 system] without a good understanding of each node and connection, since the survival of but a single link may make the postulated attack unsuccessful." In view of these imponderables, the destruction of a C3 target in this model is contingent on the detonation of at least ten surface-bursts. Again, ten RVs were selected for purely arbitrary reasons. As noted, the only effect of this attack is to generate civilian casualties in the designated collateral urban targets. Thus, we emphasize that there was no intention or effort to suggest that connectivity issues would be addressed in this analysis.

NOTES ON COUNTERVALUE METHODOLOGY

The compilation of a comprehensive countervalue (urban-industrial) database is at once easy and difficult: for the United States this was a relatively easy task because of the availability of data, while for the Soviet Union the task was exceedingly difficult because the data is, so to speak, sparse. For reasons of symmetry, we selected a countervalue target list that included the 300 largest urban areas in the United States and the Soviet Union. For the United States, the *Statistical Abstract of the United States,* 1982, provides a comprehensive list of the largest SMSAs (standard metropolitan statistical areas) with their population and area. This list of 300 urban-industrial areas represents roughly 150 million people or 65 percent of the US population that is distributed over 400,000 square miles. Hardly a Promethean task, the construction of the American countervalue database was a relatively straightforward and direct process.

In the case of the Soviet Union, the same could hardly be said. While it was easy to find lists of major Soviet urban areas, such as in the *Rand McNally Commercial Atlas and Marketing Guide, 114th edition,* 1983, or in the *Pergamon World Atlas,* 1968, it was difficult to locate these cities (for the purpose of collateral damage), for most unclassified maps of the USSR are less than up-to-date. But by far the greatest shortcoming was centered on finding references for the area of Soviet cities. It is rare to find even occasional references to the area of major urban areas, such as Moscow, in the *Britannica Atlas,* but there was no analogue for the lists and areas of Soviet SMSAs as for the United States in the *Statistical Abstract.* Through purely fortuitous research circumstances, we found what is perhaps the most authoritative and probably the most accurate source, *The Economics of Town Planning,* published in the Soviet Union in 1981, and written by Edward Bubis, a Soviet emigré who is a specialist in Soviet urban demography and planning. This study provided exhaustive data on the area of Soviet urban centers based on the population of the cities. Thus, the Soviet countervalue database of 300 SMSAs has a population of 110 million or 40 percent of the USSR's population, and it is distributed on roughly 24,000 square miles.

The central reason for our extreme interest in the area of urban zones is that it is absolutely essential to have this information to calculate the resultant casualties in a nuclear attack. In all cases, for both American and Soviet urban areas, it was assumed that the population was distributed evenly throughout the city, and that the city is in the shape of a circle. (We are aware that a uniform distribution of population violates the intuitive notion that people routinely exit cities during the day; nevertheless, this is one of the simplifying assumptions in this study.)

In an attack against an urban area, the total number of warheads that actually detonates over the target is summed to produce an aggregated area of damage—whether for air-bursts or surface-bursts. This area of damage is then superimposed mathematically on the urban target. There are three theoretical cases: The weapon's area of damage is equal to, less than, or greater than the area of the urban target. If the area of the weapon and the city are roughly equal, then the entire population is affected by the blast. If the weapon area of damage is less than the urban area, then that fraction of

Figure 1
Areas of Damage

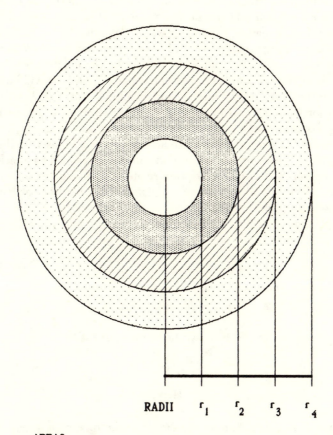

RADII r_1 r_2 r_3 r_4

AREAS

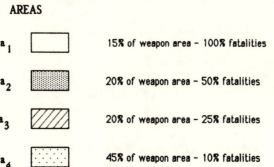

a_1 15% of weapon area – 100% fatalities

a_2 20% of weapon area – 50% fatalities

a_3 20% of weapon area – 25% fatalities

a_4 45% of weapon area – 10% fatalities

the population is affected by the explosion. And, if the weapon area is larger than the urban area, then the population is concentrated in higher over-pressure regions as one nears the center of the burst.

The weapon area of damage is composed arbitrarily of four discrete regions. In the inner ring, which accounts for 15 percent of the total area of damage for a nuclear weapon of any given yield, it is estimated that 100 percent of the population in that ring will be fatalities. In the second ring of damage, accounting for 20 percent of the area of damage, 50 percent of the population will be fatalities and 50 percent wil be wounded; in the third ring, which covers 20 percent of the area of damage, 25 percent will be fatalities and 75 percent will be wounded; and finally, in the fourth ring, which accounts for 45 percent of the area of damage, 10 percent will be fatalities and 90 percent will be wounded. Each of these rings of damage (see Figure 1) represents the overpressure gradients that form the basis for these estimates of the fatalities and casualties that will occur in a nuclear attack against an urban area. While this description relates levels of damage to the fractional area represented by each ring in comparison with the total area, it is proper to conceptualize these "rings" as radii of damage.

Prompt civilian casualties and fatalities were calculated using the following assumptions:

1. The radius of the kill area is a function of the weapon yield.
2. The population density is uniform throughout the target area.
3. The target area has unit area with a radius of k.

From assumption 3 we can derive the outermost radius:

$$pi(r_4)^2 = 1$$
$$r_4 = (1/pi)^{.5} = k$$

If the area of the outer ring is 45 percent of the total area, then

$$r_3 = [(1 - .45)/pi]^{.5} = (.55/pi)^{.5} = k(.55)^5$$

Similarly, for the two inner rings:

$$r_2 = [(.55 - .20)/pi]^{.5} = (.35/pi)^{.5} = k(.35)^{.5}$$
$$r_1 = [(.35 - .20)/pi]^{.5} = (.15/pi)^{.5} = k(.15)^{.5}$$

From assumption 2 we can determine the level of fatalities for each ring:

$$f_4 = .10 \ (.45n)^{.5} = (.07)n^{.5} \text{ for } k(.55)^{.5} <= r <= k$$

Table 17
Nuclear War Casualty Projections[1]

City Area[3]	40KT	100KT	170KT	200KT	335KT	500KT	600KT	750KT	900KT	1MT	9MT	10MT	20MT	24MT
10	65	84	100	100	100	100	100	100	100	100	100	100	100	100
	35	16	0	0	0	0	0	0	0	0	0	0	0	0
25	35	54	70	72	76	94	99	100	100	100	100	100	100	100
	65	46	30	28	24	6	1	0	0	0	0	0	0	0
50	17	31	44	45	53	72	75	77	82	84	100	100	100	100
	33	59	56	55	47	28	25	23	18	16	0	0	0	0
100	9	16	24	25	36	46	50	54	59	62	100	100	100	100
	16	30	45	47	58	56	50	46	41	38	0	0	0	0
250	4	6	10	10	12	20	23	25	29	31	79	81	100	100
	7	12	18	19	23	38	43	47	55	60	21	19	0	0
500	2	3	5	5	6	10	11	13	15	16	56	58	75	85
	3	6	9	9	12	19	22	24	28	30	44	42	25	15
750	1	2	3	3	4	7	8	8	10	10	41	44	62	73
	2	4	6	6	8	13	15	16	18	20	59	56	38	27
1000	1	2	2	3	3	5	6	6	7	8	33	35	51	62
	2	3	5	5	6	10	11	12	14	15	63	65	49	38
2500	1	1	1	1	1	2	2	3	3	3	13	14	23	32
	1	1	2	2	2	4	4	5	6	6	25	27	44	60
5000	1	1	1	1	1	1	1	1	1	2	7	7	12	16
	1	1	1	1	1	2	2	2	3	3	13	14	22	30

(Column group heading: Warhead Yield: Air-burst[2])

1. Numbers reflect percentage of dead and wounded; remainder are unharmed.
2. At optimum height-of-burst in clear weather, at 2 psi overpressure level.
3. In square miles for standard metropolitan statistical area (SMSA), with population distributed evenly in SMSA. Examples: New York City = 1400; Moscow = 1700; Boston = 1200.

$$f_3 = .25 \ (.20n)^{.5} = (.11)n^{.5} \text{ for } k(.35)^{.5} <= r <= k(.55)^{.5}$$

$$f_2 = .50 \ (.20n)^{.5} = (.22)n^{.5} \text{ for } k(.15)^{.5} <= r <= k(.35)^{.5}$$

$$f_1 = (.15n)^{.5} = (.39)n^{.5} \text{ for } r <= k(.15)^{.5}$$

Therefore, the total level of fatalities for the entire target area is:

$$f_T = f_1 + f_2 + f_3 + f_4$$

Obviously, where the population of the city is p and f is the number of fatalities, then w = p − f, where w is the number of wounded.

The algorithms, which are based on the assumption that there are varyingly lethal areas of damage for the weapon, simply project how many people will fall within the area of damage of the weapon, and compute the number of prompt dead and wounded. For instance, if an urban target with an area of 1,000 square miles and a population of 1 million is attacked with a 10 megaton air-burst (area of damage equals 1,029 square miles), then we would project 350,000 prompt dead and 650,000 wounded. For further reference, the *Nuclear War Casualty Projection Table,* as shown in Table 17, illustrates the relationship between the area of the urban target and the area of damage for various warhead yields in the American and Soviet nuclear arsenals, and generates estimates of the prompt casualties. For an illustrative example of the effects of a nuclear attack on a large metropolitan area, see Kevin N. Lewis, "The Prompt and Delayed Effects of Nuclear War," *Scientific American,* July 1979, which estimates the effects of a nuclear attack on New York City; and U.S. Office of Technology Assessment, *The Effects of Nuclear War,* for the consequences of a nuclear attack on Leningrad. As noted before, this estimation of nuclear effects does not include the long-range social, biological, or climatic consequences of a nuclear war.

Notes

CHAPTER 1

1. See Jonathan B. Stein, *From H-Bomb to Star Wars: The Politics of Strategic Decision-Making* (Lexington, Mass: Lexington Books, 1984). Stein argues that political and technological forces are constantly at play in US defense decision-making, with political forces more often than not circumventing, if not subverting altogether, the influence of technology.

2. The theory of convergence first became fashionable after it evolved from the work of Zbigniew Brzezinski and Samuel P. Huntington, *Political Power: USA/USSR* (New York: Viking Press, 1972), which proposed that "the Soviet Union and the United States are becoming more alike" (p. 9), but eventually concluded that the "evolution of the two systems, but not their convergence, seems to be the undramatic pattern for the future" (p. 436). Here, we seek to highlight the idea that the nuclear policies of the superpowers are seemingly converging on counterforce as the *sine qua non* of nuclear targeting in the modern age.

3. Freeman Dyson, *Weapons and Hope* (New York: Harper & Row, Publishers, 1984), p. 277. "American politicians perceive the Soviet doctrine of preemption as clear evidence of malign intent, while Soviet leaders feel threatened by our [American] tactical nuclear deployments close to their borders." Dyson wonders how we ever can "escape from this web of threats and misunderstandings?" (pp. 277–78).

4. See David Alan Rosenberg, "The Origins of Overkill: Nuclear Weapons and American Strategy, 1945–1960," *International Security* (Spring 1983): p. 12.

5. Ibid., p. 13.

6. See Carl von Clausewitz, *On War* (London, England: Penguin Books, 1968), p. 104.

7. Rosenberg, p. 15.

8. Ibid., pp. 15–16.

9. Ibid., p. 18.

10. Ibid., p. 34.

11. Ibid., p. 40.

12. Ibid., p. 57.

13. Ibid., p. 59.

14. Ibid., p. 62.

15. V. D. Sokolovskiy, *Soviet Military Strategy* (New York: Crane, Russak and Company, 1975), pp. 241–56.

16. Henry A. Trofimenko, "Counterforce: Illusion of a Panacea," *International Security* (Spring 1981): p. 35.

17. Sokolovskiy, pp. 61–62.

18. Ibid., p. 259.

19. Trofimenko, p. 33.

20. Ibid., p. 31.

21. Ibid., p. 30.

22. Ibid., p. 31.

23. Ibid., p. 46.

CHAPTER 2

1. It is evident, at least insofar as we can infer from the policy statements that emanate from successive American administrations, that US declaratory nuclear policy may change every four or so years. See, for instance, US Department of Defense, "The Potential Effects of Nuclear War on the Climate: A Report to the United States Congress," *Survival* (London: International Institute for Strategic Studies, May/June 1985), p. 132, for the statement that the United States does not have an "urban-industrial" targeting policy. "We believe that threatening civilian populations is neither a prudent nor a moral means of achieving deterrence, nor in light of Soviet views, is it effective. But our strategy consciously does not target population and, in fact, has provisions for reducing civilian casualties." The question remains whether the United States intends to target economic and "war-supporting industries" (wsi), rather than people per se. Yet, economic targets are located near urban areas, and such targeting will affect by necessity urban populations. This should be contrasted with the statement by former President Richard Nixon: ". . . the U.S. should alter its basic weapons strategy from targeting populations to a counterforce capability." (Roger Rosenblatt, "The Atomic Age," *Time,* July 29, 1985, p. 53.)

As Jeffrey Richelson in "Population Targeting and US Strategic Doctrine," *The Journal of Strategic Studies* (March 1985), p. 17 notes, "statements by US officials to the effect that 'we do not in our strategic planning target civilian population per se' can be taken only as a statement of targeting mechanics rather than a meaningful description of the effects (relative or absolute) of such a strategy."

2. For an excellent analysis of the ICBM vulnerability issue, see Matthew Bunn and Kosta Tsipis, *Ballistic Missile Guidance and Technical Uncertainties of Counter-silo Attacks* (Boston: Massachusetts Institute of Technology, August 1983), which presents the view that silo vulnerability is an overstated concern. Perhaps the most compelling analysis of silo vulnerability that intimates that American ICBMs may be vulnerable is Roger Speed, *Strategic Deterrence in the 1980s* (Palo Alto, California: Hoover Institution Press, 1980).

3. One of the underlying assumptions in this methodology is the use of the product of the launch and detonation reliability rates as the *predictor* of the number

of RVs that will reach the assigned targets. To be explicit, this approach probably overestimates, or at least provides a pessimistic assessment of, the fraction of warheads that will fail. Thus, we are on relatively firm ground when we say that this is a worst-case analysis of US and Soviet capabilities. It should be stressed that this approach was applied equally to both nuclear arsenals.

4. This point, which probably will be lost in the miasma of details in this study, should be noted carefully. The fact is that the US Minuteman IIIA ICBM is roughly as lethal as the vaunted Soviet SS18M4 ICBM in terms of hard-target kill potential. On a warhead for warhead basis, the two systems are equicapable, except that there are twice as many SS18M4 RVs as there are Minuteman IIIA RVs.

5. See John M. Collins, *U.S.–Soviet Military Balance: Concepts and Capabilities, 1960–1980* (New York: McGraw-Hill Publishing Company, 1980), *passim.*

6. See John D. Steinbruner, "Launch Under Attack," *Scientific American* (January 1984).

7. Speed, pp. 138–41.

8. See Peter Pringle and William Arkin, *SIOP: The Secret U.S. Plan for Nuclear War* (New York: W. W. Norton and Company, 1984), p. 158, for an estimate of the patrol areas for US SSBNs. The authors define the normal patrol areas for US SSBNs as the Mediterranean, the North and West Atlantic Oceans, whereas the Trident patrols are in the northern and western Pacific Ocean. Other patrol zones include: the North Sea off the coast of Norway, the Arctic Ocean, off the coasts of Japan and the Aleutians, the Kara Sea, and the Taimyr Peninsula.

9. See Collins, p. 141n.

10. The exact mix of Trident and Poseidon SLBMs remains classified, so this figure must be viewed as an *estimate.* There are 31 SSBNs in the US force, so a conservative estimate is that half of the force is now configured with Trident SLBMs.

11. Estimates range from eight to ten RVs on the Trident SLBM. Here, the latter figure of ten is used.

12. Conversation with an (anonymous) authoritative US Naval officer.

13. These bomber designations are arbitrary. To be frank, this bomber taxonomy simplified the classification of US (and Soviet) bombers, but in reality this taxonomy has no effect on the analysis.

14. For reference, see Speed, *Strategic Deterrence in the 1980s:* Bruce Bennett, *Assessing the Capabilities of Strategic Nuclear Forces: The Limits of Current Methods* (Santa Monica, California: The Rand Corporation, R-2577-FF, June 1980a); Archie L. Wood, "Modernizing the Strategic Bomber Force Without Really Trying: A Case Against the B-1 Bomber," *International Security* (Fall 1976); and U.S. Congressional Budget Office, *Retaliatory Issues for the U.S. Strategic Nuclear Forces* (Washington, D.C., June 1978).

15. See Speed, pp. 143–45, and Bennett, 1980a, pp. 19–24, for an estimation of the techniques involved in assessing the vulnerability of bombers.

16. See Stephen M. Myer, "Soviet Theatre Nuclear Forces, Part II: Capabilities and Implications," *Adelphi Papers,* No. 188 (London: International Institute for Strategic Studies, Winter 1983/4), pp. 32–35 for an analysis of Soviet command and control. An unstated, yet primary, Soviet concern with SSBNs is their inherent independence from the Soviet National Command Authority, at least in comparison with the control that is exercised over their land-based ICBMs.

17. A safe assumption is that an SSBN can fire its SLBMs at the rate of one every

30–60 seconds. As there is no firm data on this point, we still think that this probably provides an order-of-magnitude estimate.

CHAPTER 3

1. Oswald Spengler, *Decline of the West* (New York: A. A. Knopf, 1939).

2. See Robert Ardrey, *The Territorial Imperative* (New York: Atheneum, 1966); Konrad Lorenz, *On Aggression* (London: Methuen, 1966); and Lionel Tiger and Robin Fox, *The Imperial Animal* (New York: Holt, Rinehart and Winston, 1971).

3. Futurological analyses are the most difficult, yet least dangerous, of all. Those who accept the plausibility of the projections, which is distinct from their possibility, are not compelled to accept such views as either necessary or probable. And if they are not viewed in that light, then they become nothing more than intriguing epithets. In short, the ability to generate intriguing sketches of the future is hardly ever grounds for serious contempt or derision. This means that to offer futurological assessments is to engage in a not too terribly dangerous profession.

4. Since most scenarios of nuclear war are by definition limited to a particular sequence of events, and hence a specific sketch of the occurrence of military actions, we have structured this analysis to be as neutral as possible with respect to scenario-dependent events. On a positive note, this approach provides a comprehensive view of the events that will happen in a nuclear war, while the negative aspect is that some patterns of events may be distorted if there is no temporal reference. For instance, what is the effect of destroying command centers preemptively if the victim already has detected the launch of ICBMs? Despite the obvious potential difficulties of analyzing a nuclear war in a time vacuum, this approach still provides a dynamic understanding of the relative capabilities of the United States and the Soviet Union.

5. For an analysis of the implications of targeting conventional forces bases in Europe and the western Soviet Union, see Meyer.

6. This is the "ontological" error. In the realm of models, it means to assume that the model, rather than being a simplified construct of reality, is in fact a representation of reality itself. Needless to say, this is one of the more deleterious of the potential intellectual traps that are associated with the creation of models.

7. Quite often, analyses of nuclear war are seen as an affirmation of support for, or a subtle preference for, a particular nuclear strategy. To be explicit, this is not the case here. Indeed, our view is that *all* nuclear strategies to date have contained serious flaws, but this is another matter.

8. For an excellent analysis of decapitation, see John D. Steinbruner, "Decapitation," *Foreign Policy* (Winter 1981–82).

9. The implications of this possibility are addressed in William C. Martel, "Nuclear Decapitation: Some Preliminary Thoughts," *Military Operations Research Symposium,* June 1984.

10. We have employed a preferential offense: an attack against the most threatening Soviet ICBMs with the most lethal US ICBMs, and so forth down the list of US and Soviet ICBMs to the least lethal and least threatening missiles, respectively.

11. While this attack is structured around surface-bursts, it would be just as acceptable to use air-bursts against the silos, so long as the final RV was a surface-burst. This tactic would minimize fratricide.

12. See Speed, for a penetrating analysis of bomber vulnerability in a preemptive

attack. Although Speed's analysis was limited to the case of the vulnerability of US bombers, the same technique can be applied to the Soviet bomber force.

13. A more prudent assessment would be that such attacks really are beyond the present capabilities of the United States and the Soviet Union. In this context, such an analysis admittedly falls within the realm of the hypothetical.

14. The 50 percent probability was selected as a purely arbitrary value to denote a neutral view about the possibility of executing such an attack successfully.

15. For an analysis of Soviet civil defense, see John M. Weinstein, "Soviet Civil Defense: The Mine Shaft Gap Revisited," *Arms Control Today* (Washington, D.C.: Arms Control Association, July/August 1982), who concludes: "civil defense will not affect significantly the strategic balance or the perceptions of a superpower's leadership that such a capability could contribute to anything more than a Pyrrhic victory in a nuclear war. Neither will civil defense spare the victims of a nuclear attack from unprecedented horror and suffering nor will it permit the continued superpower status of the combatants." (pp. 9–10)

CHAPTER 4

1. Michael Howard, "On Fighting a Nuclear War," *International Security* (Spring 1981), offers his own view of the post-nuclear environment: "It is my own belief that the political, cultural and ideological distinctions that separate the West from the Soviet Union today would be seen, in comparison with the literally inconceivable contrasts between any pre-atomic and any post-atomic society, as almost insignificant" (p. 14).

2. Some analysts have intimated that American nuclear forces may be released through a pre-war delegation of authority to subordinate military commanders. See, for instance, Paul Bracken, *The Command and Control of Nuclear Forces* (New Haven, Connecticut: Yale University Press, 1983), pp. 196–200.

3. Bracken, *passim*.

4. Steinbruner, "Decapitation," estimates that 100 Soviet RVs could disrupt the US command system in a decapitation attack. See p. 18.

5. We might qualify this statement in view of the significance of the Strategic Defense Initiative (known somewhat figuratively as "Star Wars") and the projected effect of defenses on traditional concepts of deterrence.

6. Prominent among these critics is Kosta Tsipis, whose studies claim that the uncertainties in a countersilo attack are so many that they may overwhelm the attacker with catastrophic failures that, in effect, disarm the attacker at a rate equal to or greater than the victim of the attack. See, for instance, Bunn and Tsipis.

7. It is interesting to follow the evolution of assessments of the Soviet Union's counterforce capabilities against US ICBM silos. Compare, for instance, the projections of US ICBMs destroyed in Bernard T. Feld and Kosta Tsipis, "Land-Based Intercontinental Ballistic Missiles," *Scientific American* (November 1979); and Bunn and Tsipis, "The Uncertainties of Countersilo Attacks," *Scientific American*, August 1983. The primary difference between these analyses is the number of RVs that the Soviets are willing to expend in an attack, while in earlier estimates, the central issue seemed to be the theoretical possibility of silo vulnerability. See also John Steinbruner and Thomas M. Garwin, "Strategic Vulnerability: The Balance Between Prudence and Paranoia," *International Security* (Summer 1976). The central point,

however, remains that, if the attacker is willing to accept high attrition rates in his countersilo attack, then it is conceivable that such an attack could be executed successfully.

8. This is essentially a first-order projection of casualties, for in reality far more than 1.6 million Americans would be affected by a Soviet nuclear attack on US silos. In the case of a strike against the 300 Minuteman IIIA silos, certainly more than 100,000 civilians would be killed or wounded.

9. The number of 1.6 million casualties is relatively small in comparison with most contemporary estimates of American collateral casualties after a Soviet counter-silo attack. Since, however, we are counting only the populations in the primary collateral cities, it is safe to estimate that the eventual number of casualties will be one order of magnitude greater if we consider the areas downwind of the silos that will be exposed to post-attack radioactive fallout.

10. See Bennett, 1980a, and Speed, 1980, and the Appendix for analyses of the vulnerability of bombers and the method for attacking a bomber force.

11. Conversation with a former (anonymous) US Naval commander of an ASW destroyer.

CHAPTER 5

1. Whether a large-scale nuclear war will be followed by a "nuclear winter" is a subject that is fraught with innumerable uncertainties and incalculables. Carl Sagan, "Nuclear War and Climatic Catastrophe: Some Policy Implications," *Foreign Affairs* (Spring 1984), argues that "it is natural to assume . . . that the more or less simul-taneous explosion of ten thousand [nuclear] weapons all over the Northern Hemi-sphere *might* have unpredictable consequences" (emphasis added). The research indicates, Sagan avers, "that the long-term consequences of a nuclear war *could* constitute a global climatic catastrophe" (emphasis added). See also, R. P. Turco, O. B. Toon, T. P. Ackerman, J. B. Pollack and Carl Sagan, "The Climatic Effects of Nuclear War," *Scientific American* (August 1984). It is to be stressed that nuclear winter is still a largely theoretical postulate about the structure of the post-nuclear environment; there is, of course, considerable debate about this possibility.

2. An alternative view is that the complexity of a modern urban center is such that, in comparison with the relatively well-defined effects of a nuclear attack on a hard target, it is more difficult to calculate the precise consequences of a nuclear explosion in a city. Our view is that, if one is willing to accept rough estimates of casualties as sufficient, then it is more uncertain what will happen to a silo than to a metropolitan area.

3. See Samuel Glasstone and Philip J. Dolan, *The Effects of Nuclear Weapons* (Washington, D.C.: U.S. Department of Defense and Department of Labor, 1977), for data on the effects of nuclear explosions. Since most of the data and assumptions in this study were derived experimentally, it is by far the most authoritative source on the effects of nuclear explosions.

4. Since the blast effects of a nuclear explosion will affect the entire radius of damage, while selected effects, such as neutron radiation or thermal pulse, may affect only limited areas of the explosion, the standard approach is to compute casualties as a function of blast. We have followed this approach in this study.

5. An interesting, albeit fictional, account of what EMP could do to a modern electronic society is Whitley Streiber and James Kunetka, *War Day* (New York: Warner Books), 1984.

6. We have deliberately avoided the subject of recovery from a nuclear war. Nothing thus far really has been adequate, either in the form of models or studies, to give an idea as to what plausibly will happen in the post-nuclear environment. And if nothing compelling on this topic has been produced so far, it seems useless for us to engage in yet another theological polemic about what will or will not be the case for recovery.

7. U.S. Office of Technology Assessment, *The Day After Midnight: The Effects of Nuclear War* (Palo Alto, California: Cheshire Books, 1982).

8. There is, at present, an unfortunate shortage of studies and models on the ultimate number of casualties that will result on a long-term basis after a nuclear war. Rough estimates of long-term casualties range from two to five times the number of prompt casualties. Yet, in some sense the answers ultimately may be incalculable.

9. It is to be stressed that an attack with surface-bursts would create so much radioactive fallout that virtually the entire continental United States would be covered with fallout. In effect, the number of prompt casualties would be lower than in an air-burst attack, but the long-term effects might be far worse.

CHAPTER 6

1. See Adam Ulam, *Stalin: The Man and His Era* (New York: The Viking Press, 1973), and John Barron, *KGB* (New York: Bantam Books, 1974).

2. Perhaps one of the corollary issues that emerges from this analysis is the matter of "overkill." As a practical matter, large numbers of warheads would be necessary in a massive attack to produce large numbers of *prompt* casualties. This is not to say that a small number of warheads would not cause an unprecedented castastrophe for a society for it most certainly would.

3. This entire issue of shelters for Soviet elites is a bit murky. If there are such shelters, the United States probably can destroy them with Minuteman IIIA ICBMs or Pershing II IRBMs. As we can neither confirm nor deny that such shelters exist, reference here is intended only to suggest *why*, rather than if, Moscow might be attacked in a nuclear war.

4. The Arms Control and Disarmament Agency (ACDA) study, *An Analysis of Civil Defense in Nuclear War* (ACDA, 1978), provides an estimate of the distribution of population in US and Soviet urban areas, and finds that the USSR's urban population is substantially more densely concentrated than the US urban population (p. 3).

5. An illuminating finding was that the area of the average Soviet city is 50–70 square miles with a population of 100,000–250,000. See Edward Bubis, *The Economics of Town Planning* (Moscow: Moscow Publishing House, 1981), for data on the area of Soviet cities. To cover such urban areas would require between two and four warheads with areas of damage of 20–25 square miles. The Poseidon SLBM 40KT RV has an area of damage of 25 square miles for an air-burst. Thus, between two and four Poseidon RVs targeted against most Soviet urban areas would constitute an optimal attack.

CHAPTER 7

1. For all references to the SIOP, see Peter Pringle and William Arkin, *SIOP: The Secret U.S. Plan for Nuclear War* (New York: W. W. Norton and Company, 1984).

2. See William C. Martel and Michael Caruso, "MX Alternative: The White Mountain Plan," *National Review* (June 28, 1985).

3. See Brzezinski and Huntington, 1972.

4. One need only review the literature on strategic forces and policy in the 1970s to realize that US strategic policy, and the basic thinking behind it, were in a state of rapid flux. Essentially, the debate over policy focused on the transition from a countervalue to a counterforce policy.

5. See Henry A. Kissinger, *American Foreign Policy* (New York: W. W. Norton and Company, 1974), for an analysis of how foreign policy is formulated in a pluralistic society. Even more so than foreign policy, the formulation of nuclear policy is such a potentially difficult and divisive subject that few dare tackle it.

6. Henry A. Kissinger, *White House Years* (Boston, Massachusetts: Little, Brown and Company, 1979).

7. The JSTPS has 269 seats: 219 are designated for the Strategic Air Command (SAC), 10 each for the Navy and the Army, and 8 for the Air Force. Of the 34 key positions on JSTPS, 51 percent are reserved for SAC and Air Force officers. See Pringle and Arkin, 1984, p. 112.

8. Pringle and Arkin, 1984, write that there are "40,000 potential targets, and [that] the SIOP contains numerous options and suboptions for major and minor strikes" (p. 37).

9. See Rosenberg, and Pringle and Arkin.

10. See Steinbruner, "Decapitation."

11. This reference to NORAD at Cheyenne Mountain is from Paul Bracken, *The Command and Control of Nuclear Forces* (New Haven, Connecticut: Yale University Press, 1983). He reports that Rand Corporation analysts "argued that NORAD should be built deeply beneath, not inside, Cheyenne Mountain." While the "exact hardness of NORAD is probably somewhere between 500 and 1,000 psi . . . the Rand Corporation in 1959 argued for a deep, 10,000 psi structure." (pp. 187–88) In addition to Bracken's citations, other useful references include: H. L. Brode, *A Case for Survival Deep Underground* (Santa Monica, California: Rand Corporation, P-2263, 1961), especially page 4; *Proceedings of the Second Protective Construction Symposium* (Santa Monica, California: Rand Corporation, R-341, 1959); P. M. Dadant, *Why Go Deep Underground?* (Santa Monica, California: Rand Corporation, P-1675, 1959); and S. M. Genensky and R. L. Loofbourow, *Geological Covering Materials for Deep Underground Installations* (Santa Monica, California: Rand Corporation, RM-2617, 1960).

Afterword

The "War game," often conducted on computers, is to nuclear war what all of military history is to conventional war. During the thirty-five years of the nuclear age, nuclear strategists have built up a body of thought, untested by experience and untestable by it, that rivals the most rarefied and highly elaborated philosophical and theological systems. Although this body of thought is inaccessible to the ordinary person, everyone's survival depends on its soundness and reliability.

—*Jonathan Schell*

When William Martel and Paul Savage first invited me to write the afterword for this book, I wondered what a layman could possibly add to a discussion that appears to be so intrinsically technical and arcane. How could a computer illiterate contribute to the analysis of a subject rooted in calculations and abstruse mathematical predictions? The question led me to the passage written by Jonathan Schell and quoted above which, in turn, led me to realize that if the current nuclear balance of terror has any active reality it is not to be found in the motionless, hidden missiles themselves nor in the fitful diplomatic exchanges and treaties between the superpowers. The lifeblood of the nuclear world courses through the top secret American and Soviet military computers that are continuously engaged in revising and playing out every imaginable scenario, fighting dozens of theoretical world wars a day.

These computer war games, which lay the foundations of nuclear strategy and doctrine, form a branch of the military as important as any part of the American nuclear triad. The fact that they have remained "inaccessible to the ordinary person" until now has prevented fundamental information and, more critically, strategic technique from informing the public nuclear debate. With the advent of the Martel/Savage game, however, a significant act of demystification may well occur. The game's import will be measured on a broad scale, in college classrooms and suburban living rooms, by concerned laymen like myself rather than by the cognoscenti already familiar with most of what the game has to offer. The effect that is hoped for is not a nation of armchair generals so much as an end to the insular elitism of the nuclear strategists and an increased accessibility to the avenues of information for the ordinary person.

The Martel/Savage game was first played publicly at St. Anselm College, a small Catholic college in southern New Hampshire. A group of fourteen undergraduate political science students was divided into two teams, one representing the United States and the other the Soviet Union. Each student was assigned the role of a top-ranking official in his or her team's government. These positions included President, Vice President, Secretary of State, Chairman of the Joint Chiefs of Staff and Chairman of the Strategic Air Command on the American side, and General Secretary of the Communist Party, Minister of Foreign Affairs, Minister of Defense, Minister of the Navy and Chairman of the KGB on the Soviet side.

The two teams were closeted in adjoining "war rooms" which were each outfitted with world maps, Apple IIe computers and copies of the game program. No communication was permitted between the two rooms except for handwritten messages that were relayed by Martel and Savage who served jointly as Control. Each team was assigned a technical aide to operate the computer. I was invited to watch as an official observer.

10:30 A.M. The two teams, isolated in their respective rooms, are issued nearly identical intelligence summaries. The U.S. copy reads as follows:

DURING THE PAST WEEK VIOLENT INCIDENTS BETWEEN ALLIED AND SOVIET FORCES HAVE OCCURRED IN EUROPE AND THE MIDDLE EAST AND INCREASED IN FREQUENCY. US FORCES COMMITTED TO THE STRAITS OF HORMUZ HAVE ADVANCED INTO THE PASSES OF THE ZAGROS. FORWARD ELEMENTS OF THE 101 AIRBORNE AND 82 AIRBORNE HAVE ENCOUNTERED ATTACKING SOVIET COLUMNS. THE SOVIET ARMY ENTERED IRAN AT IRANIAN REQUEST WHEN THE US RESPONDED TO THE IRANIAN BLOCKADE OF THE STRAITS BY OCCUPYING THE SOUTHWEST COAST OF IRAN ON THE STRAITS TEN DAYS AGO. SO FAR SOVIET FORCES HAVE BEEN HELD IN THE FOUR PASSES OF THE ZAGROS BUT ATTRITION IS REDUCING US RESISTANCE DUE TO INABILITY TO REINFORCE HEAVILY WITH TROOPS AND SUPPLIES.

WITHIN THE PAST 24 HOURS WARSAW PACT (WP) FORCES PLACED IN ATTACK POSITION SOME DAYS PAST AND IN RESPONSE TO THE US IN-

TERVENTION IN IRAN HAVE CROSSED THE WEST GERMAN BORDER AT HOF, FULDA, AND INTO THE LUENEBERGER HEIDE SOUTH OF HAMBURG. SUBSTANTIAL PENETRATIONS BY SOVIET FORCES HAVE BEEN MADE AT ALL POINTS. US SEVENTH ARMY HAS BEEN DRIVEN BACK OVER 50 KILOMETERS AND LOST ONE THIRD OF ITS FIGHTING VEHICLES AND TWENTY PERCENT OF PERSONNEL. AT THIS TIME PRESIDENTIAL AUTHORITY HAS BEEN GIVEN FOR TACTICAL NUCLEAR RELEASE AND FIFTEEN LOW YIELD (20 KT OR LESS) WEAPONS HAVE BEEN EMPLOYED AGAINST WP FORWARD AND REAR ELEMENTS CONCENTRATED AS NOTED ABOVE. SOVIET NUCLEAR RESPONSE HAS TAKEN PLACE WITHIN THE LAST TWO HOURS ASSAULTING NATO FORWARD AND REAR AREAS BUT PRINCIPALLY AIR AND PORT FACILITIES IN WEST GERMANY ESSENTIAL FOR US RESUPPLY. FURTHER THREE SOVIET SLBMS HAVE BEEN DETONATED OVER NAVAL BASES ON THE EAST COAST: NORFOLK, HAMPTON ROADS AND PORTSMOUTH. ADDITIONAL HIGH YIELD WEAPONS HAVE STRUCK SAN DIEGO AND BREMERTON ON THE WEST COAST. FURTHER ATTACKS ARE ANTICIPATED AGAINST SAC AIRBASES VERY SOON.

WE BELIEVE THAT SOVIET ESCALATION WILL ACCELERATE. SATELLITE INTELLIGENCE DATA SHOWS THAT SOVIET ICBM FIELDS ARE AT FULL READY OR WILL BE VERY SOON. ADDITIONAL SOVIET SLBMS ARE MOVING RAPIDLY TO SEA FROM PETROPAVLOVSK, MURMANSK AND KAMCHATSKII.

ALL US STRATEGIC FORCES ARE ON FULL ALERT. FIFTY PERCENT OF US SLBMS ARE AT SEA.

One by one, the Soviet team members raised their heads after reading the Soviet intelligence summary. Their boisterous enthusiasm for the day's game lessened dramatically as they realized the severity of the political situation with which they were confronted. They drew their chairs into a tight circle and, after a few deep breaths and some shocked head-shaking, the General Secretary opened the discussion by outlining the two possible responses to the most recent US actions as either action or threat. The Minister of Defense suggested a third possibility, a synthesis of the first two alternatives. "This is already a war," he said with deliberate emphasis, gazing at each team member in turn. "We should send a communiqué saying we would like to negotiate while we actually prepare a surprise attack."

But the rest of the Soviets quickly voted this proposal down as too extreme for so early in the game. (The General Secretary did add, however, "We will file that idea in the back of our minds for later.") Instead, it was decided that the best immediate option was to open a backchannel to the White House Situation Room and establish the Soviet negotiating position. Accordingly, the following message was composed and transmitted:

10:37 A.M.   THE SOVIET UNION DEMANDS THAT THE US IMMEDIATELY
WITHDRAW ALL FORCES FROM IRAN. IN TURN WE WILL
WITHDRAW FROM WEST GERMANY.

At the bottom of the Soviet communique the Soviets added:

NOTE: THIS IS AN ALTERNATIVE TO FULL-SCALE CONFLICT BETWEEN
OUR TWO COUNTRIES.

Receipt of the Soviet team's opening message caused a quiver of panic in
the American team, which was seated in a loose semi-circle in the next room.
Prior to receiving the Soviets' demand, the American team had been calmly
discussing various options, but none of the alternatives had seemed very
attractive. Now that the Soviets had stepped up the pressure to choose a
course of action, a frustrated silence gripped the room.

"We're the ones that are up against the wall," said the Secretary of State
grimly. "Their message is really a thinly veiled threat."

"We have to decide on *something*," insisted the President, his eyes
searching his teammates' faces. "But what?" he asked softly. No one seemed
capable of answering.

10:48 A.M. A second Soviet message arrives, repeating the original demand. This only increases the Americans' strategic vertigo. Several team
members got up and began pacing outside the ring of chairs. Every few
minutes, one of them made a suggestion that was quickly argued away. Most
of the time, a tense silence reigned.

"Can't the game help us in some way?" the National Security Advisor
finally asked, his voice laced with desperation.

The Secretary of State glanced over at the Apple computer which waited
patiently in one corner of the room. "No, the game is really just a data
base . . . *we* have to come up with the moves . . . *we* are the game," he
said. His frown showed that he had already thought this through and it
worried him.

The President, feeling the responsibility to plot a response the most acute-
ly, finally suggested a limited retaliatory strike against a small number of
Soviet targets. "We have to let them know that strikes against the US are
totally unacceptable—we have to make it *cost* them," he stated with a
resolve that appeared somewhat false.

His proposal was put to a vote and it narrowly passed. The President
walked over to the technical assistant manning the computer to give him the
strike order. When the aide replied that it was first necessary to select a
target and a weapon, the President appeared surprised. The rest of the
Americans gathered around to debate the possibilities. A few minutes later,
the team had huddled even closer to watch the progress of four American
Polaris missiles heading towards a small submarine base outside of Mur-

mansk. The computer hummed for a moment before the first results flashed
on the screen:

Submarine Base: Murmansk	
Submarines in base:	10
Submarines killed:	10
Weapon launched:	Polaris
No. launched:	4
No. warheads:	4
Detonations:	1
Yield:	600 KT
Collateral city:	Murmansk

"We got them all," reported the technical assistant, but he seemed to be
the only one smiling.

"There was only one detonation," exclaimed the National Security Advisor, reading the screen in disbelief. "Only one warhead went off . . . and
it wiped out all ten submarines!"

In a moment, the results from a second strike flashed on the computer
screen, lighting each team member's eyes with an eerie green neon.

Pervouralsk		Population 129,000
Dead:	106,066	82%
Wounded:	22,933	18%
Unharmed:	0	0%

"Oh my God."

"We did it . . . we really did it."

"Not one person escaped unharmed."

"We just killed one hundred and six *thousand* Russians."

After the first shocked exclamations, a numbed silence swallowed the
room. It was quite apparent that each student was mulling over the same
questions. When I talked to some of the participants later I learned what
some of those questions were: Where the hell is Pervouralsk? What did it
look like and what does it look like now? How many is 106,066? Did they
hear the missiles before they hit—did they know for thirty seconds or even
for ten what was about to happen? Is it really like that—safe in the ignorance
of everyday activity one minute and the target of military strategists halfway
around the world the next? Does the fate of a city lie entirely in population
statistics, industrial production figures and proximity to military bases?

What is the relationship between numbers and people? Did we have to destroy Pervouralsk or was there another way? Did we save American lives or put them in even greater danger? Did we do the right thing?

There are very few people who are ever confronted with even the vicarious responsibility for mass murder such as the destruction of an entire large city. It was this five minute period, steeped in a dazed stillness, that was probably the most successful point in the game.

"Well," began the President, after what seemed a very long time, "we can't just hit them without explaining why we did it."

"We need to write a message," agreed the Vice President. "And we need to propose a cease-fire."

When Dr. Savage entered the Soviet war room, all heads snapped his way. He held two pieces of paper.

"Oh Christ, they've hit us!" shouted the General Secretary. He read the strike results aloud first. Then he turned to the American communiqué, which read:

IN RESPONSE TO SOVIET NUCLEAR STRIKES AGAINST THE CONTINENTAL USA TWO SOVIET TARGETS HAVE BEEN DESTROYED. ALSO USING *TACTICAL* NUCLEAR WEAPONS IN WEST GERMANY. DIPLOMATIC SOLUTION URGED. RESPOND IN FIVE MINUTES.

As so often happens, all the feeling and regret of the American team had been removed from the communication by the clipped language of international diplomacy the Americans felt they must use. The Soviet team's reaction was untempered by any understanding of the thoughts spinning through the minds of the Americans in the next room.

The General Secretary immediately dictated an outraged note that read:

TO USA. A CEASE-FIRE PROPOSAL SENT SIMULTANEOUSLY WITH A STRIKE IS *NOT* ACCEPTABLE!

"Look," commanded the General Secretary, "it is all going to happen, and happen soon. We might as well be on the better end of it. Let's send this and start targeting a comprehensive preemptive strike." He spoke forcefully and glared at the others, daring them to defy his reasoning. The Soviet team had become a study in group dynamics. In a crisis situation, its natural leader had emerged. Several Ministers nodded in assent.

But the rest of the team still was resistant to a full-scale escalation. Several, including the Foreign Minister, the Chairman of the KGB, and the Chairman of the Council of Ministers rallied around each other, raising objections and collectively opposing the General Secretary's bellicosity. The Commander-in-Chief of Strategic Rocket Forces pointed out that even if a large-scale strike was desirable, it would take time to coordinate an effective attack. Gradually, the General Secretary's hostility was subdued by the concerted effort of a more moderate faction of the Politburo.

By the time the Soviets set about writing their next communiqué, they had reached a consensus on accepting the cease-fire. "But we have to word it as an ultimatum," insisted the General Secretary. "Otherwise we'll lose our image of strength." The others agreed. As was the case with the last American message, the note that the Soviet team finally sent gave little indication of the turbulence that had preceded its composition. It read as follows:

WE AGREE TO A CEASE-FIRE. ANY VIOLATION BY THE UNITED STATES WILL BE MET WITH A STRATEGIC RESPONSE. IMMEDIATE REPLY REQUESTED.

Meanwhile, most of the US crisis team members had gotten to their feet and were milling around anxiously as they waited for a response from the other side of the wall. They knew that they had run a large risk in sending the Soviets such a contradictory pair of communications. The Soviets would have to react to either the strike or the cease-fire (and ignore the other). The Americans realized their immediate fate was entirely outside their control.

As the delay stretched on, the Secretary of State theorized that the wait, as agonizing as it seemed, was actually a good sign. "If they could move in West Germany and Iran, they would," he reasoned out loud. "Their hesitation proves that we're in a stronger position than we think we are. They must be either confused or incapable . . . or both."

Others disagreed, pointing out that the Soviets might actually be using the extra time to launch a large strike. But even as they spoke, the Americans recognized that they were indulging in rather nebulous speculation. There was only one thing that counted and that was the next communication carried through the door. The National Security Advisor, lost in his own train of thought, suddenly shook his head and muttered, "The whole idea is to avoid getting into a vengeance thing."

When Dr. Martel walked into the room holding the Soviet communiqué, all eyes scanned his face for an indication of the Soviet response. True to the spirit of the game, however, he remained impassive. He handed the message to the American President at precisely 11:05 A.M.

The initial reaction to the Soviet acceptance of the cease-fire was one of unrestrained jubilation, hand-shaking and congratulatory back-slapping all around. The Americans felt that a great deal of pressure had been removed, and there was a renewed sense of confidence floating through the air.

Within minutes, however, the Secretary of State voiced second thoughts about the cease-fire. Buoyed by the good news, he was soon carried away by his own revitalized logic. "If they had any strength, they wouldn't have accepted a cease-fire. And they certainly wouldn't have taken so long in doing it. Therefore, I don't think we should be satisfied with the *status quo*. . . . I think we should press for some concessions."

The Secretary of State was not alone in misinterpreting the Soviet message. Machiavellian ideas began seeping into the conversations of several Cabinet members. They took the Soviets' ultimate willingness to negotiate an agreement (a willingness the Americans had been fervently praying for only minutes before) as an indication of military weakness. Suggestions for the next American move became increasingly belligerent.

As the minute hand of the wall clock crawled inexorably forward, the President reminded his team that the Soviets had requested an immediate reply. Accordingly, the Americans dashed off the following confirmation of the cease-fire (the more ambitious options would have to wait):

11:10 A.M.   WE ACCEPT AGREEMENT ON BOTH NUCLEAR AND CONVENTIONAL LEVELS. WE PROPOSE TO BEGIN NEGOTIATION ON SITUATIONS IN IRAN AND WESTERN EUROPE. WE TAKE THIS TO BE AN AGREEMENT—NO FURTHER USE OF NUCLEAR WEAPONS WILL OCCUR. PLEASE CONFIRM.

Ironically, what was intended as a peaceable message caused a renewed agitation in the Soviet team. Several Ministers who had remained chairbound until now began to examine the world map that was taped to the blackboard in the front of the room. "I know the people across that wall," said one, pointing toward the American war room, "and I don't trust them." His mistrust, combined with the doubts of his fellow Ministers, snowballed dramatically.

The Soviets' new sense of unease had been caused by a communiqué that the Americans thought was moderate and even somewhat inconsequential, more a formality than a substantive communication. Once again, the team receiving the message had been unable to correctly interpret the thoughts of the team sending it.

The Soviet war room was quickly filled with an almost feverish anxiety. "What are they thinking?" and "What are they planning *right now?*" were questions the Soviets asked repeatedly while staring vainly at the wall that divided the two teams. The paranoia was almost palpable.

"You *know* they're planning something," said the General Secretary with a sudden decisiveness. "I say we confirm this cease-fire and hit them with everything we have. We simply can't afford not to. It comes down to a matter of first-strike policy and we've already agreed that we would rather hit first than be hit first."

This time, the General Secretary's aggression struck the rest of the Politburo in precisely the right frame of mind—fearful, distrusting and touched with something akin to "cabin fever." The vote on the General Secretary's proposal was almost unanimous. Several Ministers had already begun selecting weapons and targeting American military bases when the following message was transmitted:

11:16 A.M.   WE CONFIRM NEGOTIATIONS. FURTHER NEGOTIATIONS
WILL FOLLOW.

The Americans were pleased with this message. "We're not out of the woods yet," warned the American President, but he was smiling even as he spoke. The team surrounded their world map and became engrossed in discussions of possible diplomatic solutions to the military confrontations in Iran and West Germany. "We must come up with a fruitful proposal that encompasses both these regions," stated the President, sounding as if he were giving an election speech. His statement was met with approving nods and a burst of creative suggestions. At that very moment, the Soviet Commander-in-Chief of Strategic Rocket Forces and his technical aide were aiming 50 SS18M4 missiles armed with 10,500-kilo ton warheads apiece at the ICBM field in Grand Forks, North Dakota.

For the opening half-hour of the game, the Americans had been able to conduct their foreign policy discussions in an orderly, methodical manner. As the pressure mounted and the Americans became increasingly conscious that they were losing control of the geopolitical crisis, procedural method deteriorated into instinctive panic. Now that the American team had regained their security (and even began to feel that the decisions they had made were correct), they were determined to reassert their original deliberate but steady process. Accordingly, after several minutes of random discussion, the President called a policy meeting and his Cabinet resumed their seats.

"First, we must make a value judgment so that we can concentrate our efforts on one problem," stated the President, who tended to wax authoritative at such moments. "As I see it, we have a choice between our commitment to a NATO ally and our dependence on Middle Eastern oil. I think we must value West Germany above Iran," he concluded, taking the high ground. This was met with general agreement.

"Therefore," continued the Vice President, picking up where the President had left off, "we must word a message that communicates this priority *without trading away Iran*." Again, the speaker carried the majority.

As the American team continued examining their situation, they grew increasingly confident. Not only were they convinced that they were developing a coherent policy through the most thorough and logical process possible, they also took a great deal of pride in their careful maintenance of a fair and democratic system. At one point one of the students turned to another with a broad grin and remarked, "We're doing this just like Americans!"

When the Americans finally set about transforming their grandiose global policies into a concrete proposal, it contained quite a bit more bluff than substance. Yet, to those gathered in the American war room, it seemed entirely reasonable. It read:

11:25 A.M.   SITUATION IN WEST GERMANY UNACCEPTABLE. US DE-
             MANDS IMMEDIATE HALT AND WITHDRAWAL OF SOVIET
             FORCES TO PRE-HOSTILITY BORDERS.

             WE ARE WILLING TO NEGOTIATE WITH IRAN. RESOLUTION
             OF SITUATION IN WEST GERMANY IS PRECONDITION OF
             NEGOTIATIONS OVER THE IRANIAN SITUATION.

Despite the bluster in the American communiqué, it was undoubtedly
written in the spirit of negotiation. Many of the Soviets, however, had
already moved beyond this point. Upon receiving the latest American communication, the Soviets drew their chairs into an even tighter circle and
began speaking rapidly.
    "They're still talking about negotiations . . ."
    ". . . so we should be busy targeting!"
    "I say we trade West Germany for Iran."
    "If we make a commitment to negotiation we'll get hit first."
    "We could come up with a good settlement."
    "Negotiation is just a piece of paper."
    "Whatever we decide, we shouldn't respond for a while—let them sweat
it out."
    "Maybe we could force them to swallow an advantageous agreement. I
think they're running scared."
    "How long are we going to wait before we strike? After the next message?
Or the one after that? They could walk in the door at any minute and deliver
strikes that would wipe out half our forces. Any advantage we have now
could disappear in a second."
    As the Soviets jockeyed for position within the Politburo, the Americans
were succumbing to a wave of fatigue that might have been inevitable given
the strain of negotiating from what is perceived as the weaker position (the
Soviets seemed fresher and more lively at this point). The ashtrays that were
scattered throughout the White House Situation Room were overcrowded
with cigarette butts, and half-filled coffee cups decorated the desktops. "This
is what it's like," mumbled one weary American. "This is what Kennedy
did . . . all you can do is wait and worry and wait some more."
    Meanwhile, the Soviets had decided to maintain at least the pretense of
flexibility. They transmitted the following:

11:31 A.M.   IN RESPONSE TO THE DEMANDS OF THE UNITED STATES
             THE SOVIET UNION WILL WITHDRAW TO PRE-HOSTILITY
             BORDERS IN WEST GERMANY *ONLY* IF THE US AGREES TO
             THE WITHDRAWAL OF THEIR FORCES FROM IRAN. THE SO-
             VIET UNION WILL GUARANTEE TO KEEP OPEN THE STRAITS
             OF HORMUZ.

The Soviet offer was greeted with a collective "No!" when it was read out loud in the American war room.

"Just send them that message," suggested the Chairman of the Joint Chiefs of Staff. "No way!"

The American response was somewhat difficult to understand, especially in light of the even-handedness of the Soviet proposal. I did note, however, that the anxiety of waiting for the other side's reaction to a communiqué always seemed to cause a hardening of attitudes, perhaps as a confidence-building measure. The most extreme exclamations and off-the-cuff belligerence seemed to come immediately after receiving a communication. These observations applied to both sides.

The Americans set about debating the Soviet offer in a calm, almost sedate tone, speaking in turn and voting carefully after each motion. Their next message was rewritten several times, and refined until it struck just the right balance between firmness and diplomacy:

11:43 A.M.   WE COMMEND SOVIET REASONABLENESS IN WESTERN EU-
             ROPE. WITH REGARD TO IRAN, WE AGREE IN PRINCIPLE TO
             SOVIET PROPOSAL TO KEEP THE STRAITS OPEN. HOWEVER,
             A UN FORCE TO ENSURE FREE PASSAGE TO ALL NATIONS
             ALONG OIL LINES IS MORE ACCEPTABLE. BI-LATERAL
             WITHDRAWAL OF FORCES FROM IRAN IS IMPERATIVE.

The Soviets had settled into a frame of mind that was almost entirely negative. The latest American offer was unanimously sneered at and the delicacy of its language went unrecognized.

"How could they possibly expect us to acquiesce to this? They should be accepting what we're giving them instead of trying to wrangle more concessions out of us," said the Defense Minister.

The General Secretary did not even feel moved to respond. He was more concerned with how the military targeting was progressing. He called out to the technical aide for an up-to-the-minute status report. Before the aide could reply, the screen in front of him flashed to black and the printer abruptly quit tapping out American targets. Reality had intruded on the day's game in the form of a blown fuse. Within five minutes, in what might have been the most unusual development of the day, a Benedictine monk in full robes was bent over the computer terminal in an effort to resurrect it.

In the meantime, the Soviet team became panicky. They realized that if the Americans were engaged in the same targeting process, this technical malfunction could be critical. The Soviets immediately appealed to Control to suspend operation of the American computer until the Soviet fuse was replaced. Dr. Savage smiled and said that it was "all part of the game."

The Soviet team concluded that they had to act quickly to prevent the

Americans from gaining an advantage. They decided to send a quick coun-
terproposal in order to keep American attentions focused on negotiation.
Hastily, they put together the following:

11:55 A.M.   A UN FORCE IN IRAN IS UNACCEPTABLE AT ANY TIME. THE
             WITHDRAWAL OF SOVIET FORCES AT THIS TIME IS UNAC-
             CEPTABLE.

             THE SOVIET UNION IS IN IRAN AT THE REQUEST OF THE
             IRANIAN GOVERNMENT.

             THE SOVIET UNION PROPOSES A JOINT NATO/WARSAW PACT
             OCCUPATION TO ENSURE THE SECURITY OF THE STRAITS
             OF HORMUZ.

American opinion was split by this last suggestion. Several Cabinet members responded enthusiastically but others quickly disagreed.

"This is *not* acceptable," grumbled the Secretary of State. "Those guys
will be fighting like cats and dogs in no time. This is not a long-range
solution."

"It's like giving them a knife to hold against our throats later on," agreed
the Vice President.

The Americans were dissatisfied with the Soviet proposal but they felt
frustrated by what they perceived as an inherently weaker bargaining position. Their conventional inferiority left them nothing to use as leverage in
negotiations except nuclear weapons. Until now, they had resisted resorting
to the nuclear threat but the disgust with their own weakness was finally
approaching a breaking point.

"In a matter of hours, the situation in Iran will be a matter of history," said
the President urgently. "Their forces are simply too strong there. We have
to issue some sort of ultimatum—establish a bottom line—or we might as
well kiss Iran goodbye."

"We've been playing defensively and losing," said the Secretary of State,
summing up the team's growing discontent. "I think we should fire a warning shot."

This bold suggestion triggered an explosion of objections and discussions.
While some voiced stern warnings against such a move, several Cabinet
members began looking for a possible target, which they agreed must be a
relatively small Soviet city. The American team finally split into factions with
the Secretary of State leading a couple of disciples towards a more hawkish
approach. Into this storm came a flash bulletin written by Control, which
had reasoned that the conventional battle in Iran had never been stopped
and needed to be updated:

12:02 A.M.   . . . FLASH MESSAGE. US FORCES IN ZAGROS IN PROCESS OF
             BEING OVERRUN . . .

The Soviets, who received the same intelligence, were understandably pleased (although the unexpected good news did little to soften their aggression—they continued their targeting preparations in deadly earnest). The Americans, in contrast, were seething. This cable was the embodiment of their inadequacy. Their collective mood began to swing toward the Secretary of State's position. Although the news flash strengthened his resolve, it pulled most of the team into an inconclusive middle ground between moderation and the new hard line. Reaching a consensus was out of the question. It was all the US team could do to agree on the following stopgap note:

12:15 P.M.   US RESPONSE TO ANY SOVIET LAUNCH WILL BE ASSURED. MISSILES ARE IN HIGH CONFIDENCE CONDITION. IN THE CASE OF YOUR LAUNCH, WE LAUNCH. DO NOT FORCE OUR HAND. (PLEASE) RETURN TO NEGOTIATIONS.

The Americans' warning tone was belied by the word "Please," printed and crossed out (though still visible) before the penultimate sentence.

The message, when it was delivered to the Soviets, was all but ignored. They have already committed themselves to a large strike.

After a break for lunch (during which the two teams remained separated), the Americans plunged back into discussions on the fate of the Straits of Hormuz. In the spirit of freer communication (and in order to accommodate the varying attitudes of its internal factions), the US team sent the longest message of the game:

1:31 P.M.   THE CONTINUED PRESENCE OF SOVIET TROOPS IN IRAN UNDER THE PRESENT CIRCUMSTANCES IS UNACCEPTABLE. AS YOU KNOW THE STRAITS ARE VITAL TO THE INTERESTS OF THE UNITED STATES. WE CONTINUE OUR OFFER TO SETTLE THE SITUATION DIPLOMATICALLY, BUT IF NECESSARY THE FULL MILITARY FORCE OF THE UNITED STATES WILL BE USED TO RECTIFY THE SITUATION. TROOPS HAVE ORDERS ONLY TO FIRE WHEN FIRED UPON. WE ARE MAINTAINING STATUS AND AWAIT YOUR REPLY.

The Soviets quickly perceived that the latest U.S. missive contained nothing new (although they were amused by the phrase, "The full military force of the United States" which, by this time, meant little to them). Still, they felt a continuing need to stall the negotiations in order to gain more time for targeting. They sent a repetition of their proposal to install a joint NATO/Warsaw Pact occupation force in Iran.

The American team, still struggling mightily with a situation that was obviously beyond their ability to reason through, were upset by what they saw as Soviet intractability over Iran. "Who the hell is over there anyway?" demanded the President irritatedly. When he was handed a quickly assembled list of Soviet Politburo members, he began puzzling out how many of them might be "hawks." After a few more minutes, the President's frustration found its expression in a terse rejection of the Soviet plan:

1:40 P.M.   NUTS!

WARSAW PACT PRESENCE UNACCEPTABLE IN THE AREA.

The Soviets, with their computer in the corner busily matching Soviet weapons to American targets, were getting increasingly itchy. The General Secretary's immediate reaction to the American rebuff was "Let's do it!" As the American President had guessed, the General Secretary was the most hard-line of the Soviets, but the President would have been suprised at how many of the others agreed with him. Still, the more moderate members of the Politburo were able to postpone the attack once again.

Suddenly, both sides received the following dispatch, written by Control:

TEL-AVIV—HAIFA—JERUSALEM—ALL HIT BY SYRIAN NUCLEAR WARHEADS. ISRAELI RETALIATORY STRIKE—SOVIET FORCES IN IRAN HIT BY NUCLEAR WEAPONS. MORE DETAILS UNAVAILABLE.

Control, which had decided to plug in the possible actions of other involved countries, watched as this bulletin (which, although drastic, should not have had any direct effect on the two superpowers playing the game) proved to be the catalyst for the next, irreversible decisions.

"I think this will do it," announced the General Secretary. "The US will figure that this will push us into a strike. They are probably preparing a preemptive strike right now. We have to move first." The Soviet team unified behind its General Secretary. The vote was unanimous. The technical aide was already organizing the attack printouts.

The US response was one of extreme concern although it was not as dramatic as the General Secretary predicted. Indeed, while the Soviet team was united by the news flash, the US team began to splinter. The Secretary of Defense paced in wide circles. "Look," he said, "the Russians are bound to think we used the Israelis as surrogates. Hell, I would." Others reasoned that the Soviets might launch a strike against Israel alone. On both sides, the prevalent reaction once again proved to be a desperate effort to anticipate the other side's thinking (and, once again, the guesses proved almost entirely inaccurate).

Suddenly, the Americans froze as Dr. Savage walked into their room carrying a stack of computer printouts.

"Jesus Christ," exclaimed the Vice President.

"Oh my God, they did it," whispered the President.

"One bomber base," said the Secretary of Defense as he started to read the top page. "Two bomber bases, three, four . . . they've taken out all our bomber bases . . . Cheyenne Mountain . . . Grand Forks . . ." his voice trailed off.

After a few minutes of trying to gauge the size of the Soviet first strike (it was massive), a consensus was rapidly reached on the next move: retaliation. The Americans felt they had no other choice even though they knew such a strike might prove suicidal. The President gave the strike command to his technical aide. The Secretary of Defense began tallying American losses on the blackboard.

Meanwhile, the Soviets were busy wording an ultimatum. "We may be cutthroats but we have to be polite; we have to give them a way to save some face," warned one Politburo member. The effort to write a final chapter to the war continued until one Minister thought to ask who controlled Iran.

"Iran is gone," said the Chairman of the KGB. "What we were fighting for fifteen minutes ago doesn't exist."

"I want to go on record right now," said the Chief of Staff of the Armed Forces in a very determined voice, "as being opposed to just about every one of our actions."

The USSR finally sent the following:

2:00 P.M.   A SECOND STRIKE WILL BE FORTHCOMING UNLESS THE UNITED STATES AGREES TO A COMPLETE NUCLEAR CEASE-FIRE. WITH ONE STRIKE WE HAVE DESTROYED THE MAJOR-ITY OF YOUR MINUTEMEN, THUS CREATING A SITUATION BY WHICH YOU ARE GRAVELY WEAKENED. WE DO NOT WISH TO INCUR ANY MORE SUFFERING ON YOUR COUNTRY. AGREE TO A CEASE-FIRE.

The American team had counted their collateral dead at between ten and thirty million. They had decided on a countervalue retaliatory strike. "We don't have enough left to attack counterforce or we would," said the Secretary of State. "Now it's just a matter of retaliation . . . pride."

The Soviets had already begun planning a second strike, anticipating a military response from the US (this was the first and only time one side correctly predicted the other's intentions). But the American attack sheets arrived before the Soviets could decide on launching again.

"They were countervalue," announced the General Secretary grimly as he began reading through the American strike. "Moscow . . . Kiev . . . Leningrad . . . O.K., that's it, let's hit New York." The Soviet dead came to over two million, a fraction of the American losses.

The American team was shaken and anxious. They understood the Soviet superiority in warheads and they knew the entire country's fate was in the hands of its arch enemy.

"Should we negotiate or escalate?" asked the thoroughly depressed President. Everyone agreed on negotiation.

"Cease-fire," he continued, "or surrender?"

The General Secretary asked the same question in trying to formulate the demand he would force the US to accept. But while the Americans found a sorrowful solidarity in defeat, the Soviets were divisive in victory.

"We have gone too far not to get everything we wanted," said the Minister of Defense.

"We've done enough," argued the Armed Forces Chief of Staff, "more than enough."

The Soviet team eventually agreed with the Chief of Staff:

2:52 P.M.   ARE YOU WILLING TO NEGOTIATE A CEASE-FIRE OR NOT? WE HAVE MANY WARHEADS REMAINING, AND YOUR ACTIONS WILL DECIDE IF THEY WILL BE SENT. IN ESSENCE, YOU WILL DETERMINE YOUR OWN FATE. WE ARE READY TO NE-GOTIATE A CEASE-FIRE, BUT ARE JUST AS READY TO USE OUR REMAINING POWER TO ANNIHILATE THE UNITED STATES.

PLEASE REPLY IMMEDIATELY.

The American team responded quickly. No one had any heart left for fighting or for the game itself:

2:53 P.M.   WE ARE WILLING TO NEGOTIATE WHAT'S LEFT. FROM THIS POINT ON NO MORE MISSILES WILL BE FIRED. IN VIEW OF THE MASSIVE DEVASTATION, CEASE-FIRE WILL BE OB-SERVED.

And on this exhasuted note, World War III was ended. Much of America lay in smoking ruins. The Soviet Union's major cities were clogged with corpses and fatally wounded civilians. The nineteen-year olds responsible for the war filed out of their respective war rooms silently to meet each other face-to-face for the first time since that morning. "Thank God it's over," said students from both sides.

The second exercise was conducted at the John F. Kennedy School of Government at Harvard University. Two teams of seven undergraduate students were sequestered in adjoining rooms of the School's Institute of Politics. At 10:25 A.M. the American team was handed the following intel-ligence summary:

SENSITIVE (Close Hold) US INTELLIGENCE SUMMARY
National Security Council, 10:00 A.M. 29 September 1984

On 25 September 1984 a Soviet Whiskey-class submarine was detected in Swedish territorial waters near sensitive naval installation. This "intrusion" (UPI) is latest in series of similar incidents over past several years.

After detection of the submarine, Swedish naval units are placed on high readiness. Concurrently, Swedish authorities dispatched ambassadors to Baltic and European nations to warn that Sweden will react strongly to this "provocation."

US satellites confirm that Soviet fleet left ports of Murmansk and Vladivostok. Abnormally high levels of communication are detected between Soviet Defense Ministry and the naval task force. Soviet Foreign Minister Andrei Gromyko denied Swedish "allegation" that submarine in Swedish waters is Soviet, and urged "all parties to act with caution and restraint." Soviet fleet operations are "simply in response to Swedish actions."

On 26 September 1984 Swedish naval forces attacked submarine with *conventional* depth charges. Reports are that submarine was not destroyed. Meanwhile, US intelligence has detected large-scale naval operations in North Atlantic and Baltic regions. To counter this presence, US National Security Advisor reported that US Naval Forces are on alert, and there is an increased number of allied surface ships and submarines in area.

Later, on 26 September 1984 Swedish Navy detects movement of submarine, and attacks with depth charges. The submarine fired a *nuclear torpedo,* sinking eight Swedish ships. Casualties: 2,000 dead.

US and NATO leaders express "collective outrage" at this now confirmed Soviet action. All US and NATO forces are placed on high readiness level. West Germany recalls its reserve units.

During the past two days violent incidents between US/NATO and Soviet/Warsaw Pact forces have occurred in the Persian Gulf and Iran. US forces were committed to the Straits of Hormuz and advanced into the passes of the Zagros Mountains. Forward elements of 101 Airborne and 82 Airborne have encountered attacking Soviet columns. The Soviet Army entered Iran at Iranian request when the US responded to the Iranian blockade of the Straits by occupying the southwest coast of Iran on the Straits. So far Soviet forces have been held in the four passes of the Zagros, but attrition is reducing US resistance due to inability to reinforce with troops and supplies.

On 28 September 1984, US intelligence confirms an incident between British and Soviet naval forces. British destroyed Soviet reconnaisance aircraft as it approached British carrier task force. Soviet naval forces retaliated by destroying several British aircraft and damaging a destroyer.

US and Soviet governments urge "all parties to act with care" to "avoid actions that will precipitate further reprisals." These statements are *not* issued jointly.

Within the past 24 hours Warsaw Pact (WP) forces placed in attack position. US intelligence sources report convergence of large US and Soviet naval task forces in North Atlantic. US hunter-killer (attack) submarines have established "positive trails" on Soviet ballistic-missile submarines. US Navy reports similar, but lesser, Soviet efforts.

On 29 September 1984 at 10:00 A.M. GMT (5:00 A.M. EST), reported that US Franklin-class Poseidon submarine was destroyed by Soviet attack submarine. US nuclear forces are placed at readiness level DEFCON 2. NATO forces increase readiness level of forces as there are signs that Warsaw Pact forces have increased readiness levels also.

At 12:00 P.M. GMT (7:00 A.M. EST), Warsaw Pact forces crossed the West German border at Hof, Fulda, and Lueneberger Heide south of Hamburg. Substantial penetrations by Soviet forces have been made at all points. US Seventh Army has been driven back over 50 kilometers, and lost one-third of its fighting vehicles and 20 percent of its personnel. At this time presidential and NATO authority has been given for tactical nuclear release. Fifteen low yield, 20 KT or less, weapons have been employed against Warsaw Pact forward and rear elements.

US intelligence detects that Soviet nuclear forces are now on high readiness level. All US satellite and radar sensors are instructed to maintain high readiness in the event of (unlikely) preemptive attack.

At 12:20 P.M. GMT (7:20 A.M. EST), US naval task force was destroyed by several nuclear explosions. US VELA satellites confirm detection of nuclear explosions. Casualties: 30,000 dead. Shortly thereafter, US attack submarine destroyed Soviet carrier Kiev and support ships with nuclear ASROC. Soviet casualties: 25,000 dead.

At 12:50 P.M. GMT (7:50 A.M. EST), Soviet nuclear response was released against forward NATO positions and rear supply areas. Air bases and ports in West Germany are destroyed by SS-20 and SCUD nuclear missiles. US and Soviet nuclear forces are placed on highest readiness level (DEFCON 1).

At 1:40 P.M. GMT (8:40 A.M. EST), three Soviet SLBMs have been detonated over US naval bases on the east coast: Norfolk, Hampton Roads, and Portsmouth. Additional high-yield weapons have struck San Diego and Bremerton, Washington, on the west coast. The US retaliates immediately against Soviet ports of Murmansk and Vladivostok. Heavy loss of life on both sides.

US intelligence indicates:

—Soviet nuclear bombers have been scrambled

—US SAC bombers have been launched as a precautionary measure against preemption

—There are reports that large numbers of Soviet leaders are seen leaving Kremlin

—US Presidential 747 (National Emergency Airborne Command Post) at Andrews AFB is on ten-minute alert.

Soviet nuclear attack against the US is anticipated. Satellite intelligence data show that Soviet ICBM fields are at full readiness. Additional Soviet SSBNs are moving rapidly to probable launch points along the east and west coasts.

All US nuclear forces are on full alert. Fifty percent of US SSBNs are at sea.

The Soviet team was handed an intelligence summary that was identical except for point of view and the following differences: the Soviet Whisky-class submarine detected in Swedish waters was reported to have been on "routine manuevers"; the submarine commander who fired the nuclear torpedo sinking eight Swedish ships did so on his own initiative and for reasons that remain unknown although it is believed he was "not mentally competent"; the reason for crossing the West German border was that "indigenous political groups in West Germany requested Soviet intervention to assist in removing US nuclear forces from their soil"; Soviet intelligence believed that the carrier Kiev and its support ships were destroyed *before* the US naval task force and that US SLBMs were detonated over Murmansk and Vladivostok *before* the Soviet SLBM attack on Norfolk, Hampton Roads and Portsmouth, making the US the aggressor in both instances.

Both teams immediately expressed shock over the advanced state of the crisis. It was apparent that the students generally expected a milder and more easily manageable scenario. Their early morning confidence evaporated as they read through the intelligence summaries and, by the time they had all finished reading, many were already wearing lost, anxious expressions.

Despite the severity of the situation and an early atmosphere of fatalism, the Harvard students worked hard to avert military escalation. The first communication between the two teams came at 10:54 A.M. when the Soviet team requested an immediate cease-fire. After a spirited debate in the American war room—an explosion of democracy that threatened to degenerate into filibuster—the cease-fire was accepted and it held through the following six hours of complex negotiations in the face of several minor crises. The blind exchanges were capped by a face-to-face summit meeting convened at 4 P.M. where the terms of an extended cease-fire were hammered out. The teams also agreed to investigate long-range proposals for a bilateral arms freeze and the possible eventual removal of tactical weapons from the European theatre.

Although the Martel/Savage computer program never actually entered the course of action, its presence was constantly felt. The Chairman of Gosplan complained of being driven toward the computer "because we know it is much more sophisticated than we are." His observation was met with general agreement—the students' early depression was largely a result of feeling helpless in the face of what they perceived to be an overwhelming technological imperative.

The stress the participants felt led them through stages of frustration, anxiety, anger and fatigue, but it also inspired bursts of creative thinking. The most notable of these came from the Chairman of the KGB who made a quantum leap in logic in an effort to escape the grim attraction of the computer program. "The current crisis is largely a problem of communication and perception," he said, looking at the wall that separated the two rooms. "Therefore, it would be a great step toward mutual understanding if we could exchange intelligence summaries. This would reduce suspicion and increase understanding of the opposite country's point of view."

Several Soviet team members objected that this was not advisable and others wondered if it was feasible. Control ruled that it could not allow an exchange of the actual intelligence summaries because these were obviously genuine and, therefore, unrealistically reliable. However, if the teams were to copy the summaries in longhand, thus allowing for the possibility of misinformation, the exchange would be permissable. This exchange was subsequently agreed to by the American team and it ultimately took place. Surprisingly enough, very little consideration was given to falsifying information and the handwritten summaries exchanged were accurate and, once received, trusted.

As in the first exercise, the participants had to overcome an early feeling that the computer program would be part of the solution (rather than representing most of the problem). Once the students realized that *they* were really the game, the value of the exercise gradually became apparent. "Now I understand more of the degree of self-centeredness that is necessary in international negotiations," the American Vice-President commented later. "It is a lot less easy than it seems before you are actually immersed in the situation. Listen, I'm a biochem major, I don't think about this very much."

Michael Caruso

Bibliography

Aldridge, Robert C. *First Strike: The Pentagon's Strategy for Nuclear War* (Boston, Massachusetts: South End Press, 1983).

Ardrey, Robert. *The Territorial Imperative* (New York: Atheneum, 1966).

Ball, Desmond. "Targeting for Strategic Deterrence," *Adelphi Papers*, No. 185 (London: International Institute for Strategic Studies, Summer 1983).

Barron, John. *KGB* (New York: Bantam Books, 1974).

Bennett, Bruce W. *Assessing the Capabilities of Strategic Nuclear Forces: The Limits of Current Methods* (Santa Monica, California: The Rand Corporation, N-1441-NA, June 1980a).

———. *How To Assess the Survivability of U.S. ICBMs* (Santa Monica, California: The Rand Corporation, R-2577-FF, June 1980b).

Blair, Bruce G. *Strategic Command and Control: Redefining the Nuclear Threat* (Washington, D.C.: The Brookings Institution, 1985).

Bracken, Paul. *The Command and Control of Nuclear Forces* (New Haven, Connecticut: Yale University Press, 1983).

Brode, H. L. *A Case for Survival Deep Underground* (Santa Monica, California: Rand Corporation, P-2263, 1961).

Brown, Thomas A. "Number Mysticism, Rationality and the Strategic Balance," *Orbis* (Fall 1977).

Brzezinski, Zbigniew, and Samuel P. Huntington. *Political Power: USA/USSR* (New York: The Viking Press, 1972).

Bubis, Edward. *The Economics of Town Planning* (Moscow: Moscow Publishing House, 1981).

Bunn, Matthew, and Kosta Tsipis. *Ballistic Missile Guidance and Technical Uncertainties of Countersilo Attacks* (Boston, Mass.: Massachusetts Institute of Technology, August 1983).

Carter, Ashton B. "The Command and Control of Nuclear War," *Scientific American* (January 1985).

———, and David N. Schwartz. *Ballistic Missile Defense* (Washington, D.C.: The Brookings Institution, 1984).

Challenges for U.S. National Security. Nuclear Strategy Issues of the 1980s: Strategic Vulnerabilities; Command, Control, Communications, and Intelligence; Theater Nuclear Forces (Washington, D.C.: Carnegie Endowment for International Peace, 1982).

Chester, Conrad V., and Eugene P. Wigner. "Population Vulnerability," *Orbis* (Fall 1974).

Civil Defense: A Soviet View, U.S. Air Force, 1970.

Cochran, Thomas B., William M. Arkin and Milton M. Hoenig. *Nuclear Weapons Databook: U.S. Nuclear Forces and Capabilities* (Cambridge, Massachusetts: Ballinger Publishing Company, 1984).

Cockburn, Andrew. *The Threat: Inside the Soviet Military Machine* (New York: Random House, 1983).

Collins, John M. *U.S.-Soviet Military Balance: Concepts and Capabilities, 1960–1980* (New York: McGraw-Hill Publications Company, 1980).

Dadant, P. M. "Why Go Deep Underground?" (Santa Monica, California: Rand Corporation, P-1675, 1959).

Dunnigan, James F. *How To Make War: A Comprehensive Guide to Modern Warfare* (New York: William Morrow and Company, 1982).

Dyson, Freeman. *Weapons and Hope* (New York: Harper & Row, Publishers, 1984).

Fallows, James. *National Defense* (New York: Random House, 1981).

Feld, Bernard T. "The Consequences of Nuclear War," *The Bulletin of Atomic Scientists* (June 1976).

Feld, Bernard T., and Kosta Tsipis, "Land-Based Intercontinental Ballistic Missiles," *Scientific American* (November 1979).

Ford, Daniel. *The Button: The Pentagon's Strategic Command and Control System* (New York: Simon and Schuster, 1985).

Garwin, Richard L. "Will Strategic Submarines Be Vulnerable?", *International Security* (Fall 1983).

Genensky, S. M., and R. L. Loofbourow. "Geological Covering Materials for Deep Underground Installations" (Santa Monica, California: Rand Corporation, RM-2617, 1960).

Glasstone, Samuel, and Philip J. Dolan (eds.). *The Effects of Nuclear Weapons* (Washington, D.C.: U.S. Department of Defense and Department of Energy, 1977).

Ground Zero. *Nuclear War: What's In It For You?* (New York: Pocket Books, 1982).

Howard, Michael E. "On Fighting a Nuclear War," *International Security* (Spring 1981).

Jervis, Robert. *The Illogic of American Nuclear Strategy* (Ithaca, New York: Cornell University Press, 1984).

———. "Why Nuclear Superiority Doesn't Matter," *Political Science Quarterly* (Winter 1979–80).

Joyce, John M. "The Old Russian Legacy," *Foreign Policy* (Summer 1984).

Kaplan, Fred M. *Dubious Specter: A Skeptical Look at the Soviet Nuclear Threat* (Washington, D.C.: Institute for Policy Studies, 1980).

Kemp, Geoffrey. "Nuclear Forces for Medium Powers," *Adelphi Paper* No. 107 (London: International Institute for Strategic Studies, 1974).

Kissinger, Henry A. *American Foreign Policy* (New York: W. W. Norton and Company, 1974).

———. *White House Years* (Boston: Massachusetts: Little, Brown and Company, 1979).

———. *Years of Upheaval* (Boston: Massachusetts: Little, Brown and Company, 1982).

Lewis, Kevin N. "The Prompt and Delayed Effects of Nuclear War," *Scientific American* (July 1979).

Lorenz, Konrad. *On Aggression* (London: Methuen, 1966).

Martel, William C., and Michael Caruso, "MX Alternative: The White Mountain Plan," *National Review* (June 28, 1985).

Meyer, Stephen M. "Soviet Theatre Nuclear Forces," *Adelphi Papers*, No. 188 (London: International Institute for Strategic Studies, Winter 1983/4).

Military Balance, 1980–1981 (London: International Institute for Strategic Studies, 1980).

Miller, Steven E. (ed.). *The Nuclear Weapons Freeze and Arms Control* (Boston, Massachusetts: Ballinger Publishing Company, 1984).

National Academy of Sciences. *Long-Term Effects of Multiple Nuclear Explosions Worldwide* (Washington, D.C., 1975).

National Research Council. *Effects on the Atmosphere of a Major Nuclear Exchange* (Washington, D.C.: National Academy Press, 1985).

The New Encyclopaedia Britannica, Volume 12, 1974.

Pergammon Press. *Pergammon World Atlas*, 1968.

Pringle, Peter, and William Arkin. *SIOP: The Secret U.S. Plan for Nuclear War* (New York: W. W. Norton and Company, 1984).

"Proceedings of the Second Protective Construction Symposium" (Santa Monica, California: Rand Corporation, R-341, 1959).

Rand McNally. *1983 Commercial Atlas and Marketing Guide*, 1983.

Richelson, Jeffrey. "Population Targeting and US Strategic Doctrine," *The Journal of Strategic Studies* (March 1985), pp. 5–21.

Rosenberg, David Alan. "The Origins of Overkill: Nuclear Weapons and American Strategy, 1945–1960," *International Security* (Spring 1983).

———. "'A Smoking Radiating Ruin at the End of Two Hours': Documents on American Plans for Nuclear War with the Soviet Union, 1954–55," *International Security* (Winter 1981/1982).

Rosenblatt, Roger, "The Atomic Age," Time, July 29, 1985, pp. 32–59.

Russell, J. W., and E. N. York. *Expedient Industrial Protection Against Nuclear Attack* (Seattle, Washington: The Boeing Company, March 1980).

Sagan, Carl. "Nuclear War and Climatic Catastrophe: Some Policy Implications," *Foreign Affairs* (Spring 1984).

Scheer, Robert. *With Enough Shovels: Reagan, Bush and Nuclear War* (New York: Random House, 1982).

Sokolovskiy, V. D. *Soviet Military Strategy* (New York: Crane, Russak and Company, 1974).

Speed, Roger D. *Strategic Deterrence in the 1980s* (Palo Alto, California: Hoover Institution Press, 1980).

Spengler, Oswald. *The Decline of the West* (New York: A. A. Knopf, 1939).

Statistical Abstract of the United States, 1982.

Stein, Jonathan B. *From H-Bomb to Star Wars: The Politics of Strategic Decision-Making* (Lexington, Massachusetts: Lexington Books, 1984).

Steinbruner, John D. "Launch Under Attack," *Scientific American* (January 1984).

———. "Nuclear Decapitation," *Foreign Policy* (Winter 1981–82).

Steinbruner, John D., and Thomas M. Garwin. "Strategic Vulnerability: The Balance Between Prudence and Paranoia," *International Security* (Summer, 1976).

Steinlieb, George, and James W. Hughes. "The Changing Demography of the Central City," *Scientific American* (August 1980).

Streiber, Whitley, and James Kunetka. *War Day: The Journey Onward* (New York: Warner Books, 1984).

Sun Tzu. *The Art of War.* (London: Oxford University Press, 1973).

Tiger, Lionel, and Robin Fox. *The Imperial Animal* (New York: Holt, Rinehart and Winston, 1971).

Trofimenko, Henry A. "Counterforce: Illusion of a Panacea," *International Security* (Spring 1981).

Turco, Richard P., Owen B. Toon, Thomas P. Ackerman, James B. Pollack, and Carl Sagan. "The Climatic Effects of Nuclear War," *Scientific American* (August 1984).

Ulam, Adam B. *Stalin: The Man and His Era* (New York: The Viking Press, 1973).

U.S. Arms Control and Disarmament Agency. *Worldwide Effects of Nuclear War: . . . Some Perspectives* (Washington, D.C.: 1975).

———. *An Analysis of Civil Defense in Nuclear War* (Washington, D.C.: December 1978).

U.S. Congressional Budget Office. *Modernizing U.S. Strategic Offensive Forces*, Washington, D.C., May 1983.

———. *Retaliatory Issues for the U.S. Strategic Nuclear Forces*, Washington, D.C., June 1978.

U.S. Department of Defense. *The Potential Effects of Nuclear War on the Climate: A Report to the United States Congress* (excerpts) (London: International Institute for Strategic Studies, May/June 1985), pp. 130–34.

U.S. Government General Accounting Office. *Civil Defense: Are Federal, State, and Local Governments Prepared for Nuclear Attack?*, Washington, D.C., August 1977.

———. *Models, Data, and War: A Critique of the Foundation for Defense Analyses*, Washington, D.C., 1980.

U.S. Office of Technology Assessment. *MX Missile Basing*, Washington, D.C., 1981.

———. *The Day After Midnight: The Effects of Nuclear War* (Cheshire Books, 1982).

von Clausewitz, Carl. *On War* (Penguin Books, 1968).

Vining, Daniel R., Jr. "Migration Between the Core and the Periphery," *Scientific American*, December, 1982.

Weinstein, John M. "Soviet Civil Defense: The Mine Shaft Gap Revisited," *Arms Control Today*, Arms Control Association, July/August 1982.

Wells, H. G. *The Outline of History* (New York: Garden City Books, 1961).

Wood, Archie L. "Modernizing the Strategic Bomber Force Without Really Trying—A Case Against the B-1 Bomber," *International Security*, Fall 1976.

Index

MIRV. *See* Multiple independently targetable re-entry vehicle
Missile gap, 90
Missouri, 27, 94–95, 106
MK12A warheads, 165
MM. *See* Minuteman
Monarchy, 181
Mongol Empire, 7, 137–38
Montana, 27, 94–95, 106
Morality, 10
Moscow, 29, 56, 59–60, 89, 113, 139–46, 149, 186, 204
Mount Weather, 38, 196. *See also* Decapitation
Multiple independently targetable re-entry vehicle (MIRV), 14, 17, 19, 25–26, 61
Murmansk, 43
Mutual assured destruction, 11, 13–14. *See also* Assured destruction
MX ICBM, 40, 52, 169–70, 177–78

Nagasaki, 7
Napoleon, 83
National Command Authority (NCA), 9, 28, 46, 86, 175, 192, 196
National Defense (Fallows), 4
National Defense Council, 45, 56–57
National Emergency Airborne Command Post (NEACP), 88, 196
National Military Command Center (NMCC), 87
National Security Council, 183
NATO, 43, 60, 99, 155, 187, 192
Navy, Soviet, 2; U.S., 2, 22, 188
NCA. *See* National Command Authority
NEACP. *See* National Emergency Airborne Command Post
Nebraska, 188
Negev Desert, 179
Negotiations, 15. *See also* Bargaining
Neutron bomb. *See* Enhanced-radiation warhead
New Hampshire, 99, 125, 179
New Jersey, 114, 120
New York, 99, 179
New York City, 111–12, 113–21, 123, 133, 139, 158, 208

New York Times, 198
NMCC. *See* National Military Command Center
No first use doctrine, 2
NORAD. *See* North American Air Defense Command
Norfolk, Virginia, 111
North American Air Defense (NORAD), 88. *See also* Cheyenne mountain
North Dakota, 25, 93, 106
North Pole, 91
Northeast corridor, 111, 179
Norway, 179
NS-20 guidance system, 165
NSC. *See* National Security Council
Nuclear Bomb Effects Computer (Glasstone and Dolan), 197
Nuclear effects: 93, 115–18, 197–99. *See also* Biological effects; Blast; Climatic effects; Cratering; Ecological effects; Equivalent megatons; Fallout; Fireball; Firestorm; Genetic effects; Ground shock; Lethal radius; Nuclear winter; Overpressure; Thermal pulse
Nuclear freeze movement, 169
Nuclear policy, 1, 164; declared, 12, 172; ethical, 174; real, 173
Nuclear proliferation, 52
Nuclear strategists, 8
Nuclear strategy: 1–4, 7, 130, 172–74; Soviet, 115–18; U.S., 3–15
Nuclear theologians, 11, 126
Nuclear Weapons Databook (Arkin), 196
Nuclear winter, 106, 112

Offensive, 5, 21
Office of Technology Assessment, U.S., 123, 208
Offutt AFB, 188
Ogarkov, Nicholai, 4, 17, 69, 183
Ohio-class SSBN, 31, 104, 169
Omaha, Nebraska, 188
Omsk, 149
OMT. *See* Other military targets
On War (von Clausewitz), 7
OPK. *See* Optimum probability of kill
Optimum probability of kill (OPK), 25
Orsk, 39, 62–64

About the Authors

WILLIAM C. MARTEL is a Social Scientist for the Rand Corporation in Washington, D.C. Primarily a specialist on national security and foreign policy, he has worked on strategic and theatre nuclear issues. His earlier works include contributions to *Fighting Armies* (Greenwood Press, 1983).

PAUL L. SAVAGE is Professor and Chairman of the Politics Department of St. Anselm's College, Manchester, New Hampshire. His previous works include *Crisis in Command: Mismanagement in the Army* and *Managers and Gladiators: Directions of Change in the Army*, as well as articles in *Armed Forces and Society* and the *Catholic Law Journal*.

MICHAEL CARUSO is a writer living in New York City who has worked for a variety of magazines, including *The New Yorker, The Village Voice, The Nation,* and *Avenue*.